THE LEGEND OF
DRAGON QUEST

For Lina.

The Legend of Dragon Quest
by Daniel Andreyev
Published by Third Éditions
32, rue d'Alsace-Lorraine,
31000 Toulouse, France
contact@thirdeditions.com
www.thirdeditions.com

Follow us:
: @Third_Editions
: Facebook.com/ThirdEditions
: Third Éditions
: Third Éditions

All rights reserved. This work may not be reproduced or transmitted in any form, in whole or in part, without the written authorization of the copyright holder.

Copying or reproducing this work by any means constitutes an infringement subject to the penalties stipulated in copyright protection law n°. 57 298 of 11 March 1957.

The Third logo is a registered trademark of Third Éditions in France and in other countries.

Edition by: Nicolas Courcier and Mehdi El Kanafi
Editorial assistants: Damien Mecheri and Clovis Salvat
Texts by: Daniel Andreyev
Proofreading: Zoé Sofer and Jérémy Daguisé
Layout: Bruno Provezza
Cover Layout: Frédéric Tomé
Classic edition cover: Johann "Papayou" Blais
Collector's edition cover: Tony Valente
Cover assembly: Frédéric Tomé
Translated from French by: Mary Tissot (ITC Traductions)

This educational work is Third Éditions' tribute to the *Dragon Quest* game series.

The author presents an overview of the history of the *Dragon Quest* game in this one-of-a-kind volume that lays out the inspirations, the context and the content of these titles through original analysis and discussion.

Dragon Quest is a registered trademark of Square Enix. All rights reserved. The cover illustration is inspired by artwork from the *Dragon Quest* series.

English edition, copyright 2018, Third Éditions.
All rights reserved.
ISBN 978-2-37784-034-2

Daniel Andreyev

THE LEGEND OF DRAGON QUEST

TABLE OF CONTENTS

07 FOREWORD
09 PREFACE
017 INTRODUCTION

025 ⁍ CHAPTER I — YÛJI HORII, THE MANGA HERO

041 ⁍ CHAPTER II — ORIGINS

055 ⁍ CHAPTER III — THE ROTO TRILOGY

067 ⁍ CHAPTER IV — THE TENKÛ TRILOGY

079 ⁍ CHAPTER V — THE SONY ERA

097 ⁍ CHAPTER VI — DRAGON QUEST, TOGETHER

117 ⁍ CHAPTER VII — DRAGON QUEST XI: ECHOES OF AN ELUSIVE AGE

131 ⁍ CHAPTER VIII — DRAGON QUEST AND ITS SPIN-OFFS

149 ⁍ CHAPTER IX — MUSIC, CHORDS AND DISSONANCE

163 ⁍ CHAPTER X — DRAGON QUEST, HERITAGE

173 CONCLUSION
181 BIBLIOGRAPHY
189 AUTHOR'S ACKNOWLEDGMENTS

FOREWORD

HERE BE DRAGONS

I was a latecomer to *Dragon Quest*. In Japan this videogame series is now, after decades of success, a part of the culture—but for a European like me it has always felt much more exotic than that. Many of the early entries I played on Nintendo DS in the mid-2000s, decades after their original release. These were not just wonderful videogames but archaeological treasures, restored for new players and—thanks to the localizations—made new once again.

Dragon Quest as a whole I leave to this book's author, the heroic and hardy Daniel Andreyev. I first met Daniel in Japan and he regaled me with endless detail about all sorts of Japanese games, but even then, his passion for *Dragon Quest* stood out, and it is a series that rewards passion. These worlds are built to be poured-over, and luxuriated in, forever rewarding their most curious and dedicated players.

There are a few minor observations I would make about *Dragon Quest*. The first time these games struck me as special was around a decade ago, and the reason was a specific translation for English-speaking regions. *Dragon Quest IV* was re-released for Nintendo DS in 2007, and its localization used a total of 13 different English dialects to diversify the towns: you begin the game listening to Scottish accents, soon enough meet Bristolians, and even bump into English speakers with French accents. This was a new interpretation of the old game, replacing an earlier localization. It got some criticism.

But it really brought that world to life again, and made these places seem bustling and distinct. I live near Bristol so it was stunning to see that particular accent represented in this world, and the effort sometimes required to understand what characters were saying—you'd almost have to read the lines phonetically—felt to me like an accurate reflection of travelling to remote places within your own country, where your countrymen's accents can be hard to keep up with.

This is also a striking example of how the series has been changed over its history for new audiences. A few years later saw the release of *Dragon Quest IX: Sentinels of the Starry Skies*, designed for the ground-up for the Nintendo DS, and released swiftly afterwards in the west. Here was a completely modern *Dragon Quest* and to this day I've never had another experience like it: where the other games in the series are grand single player adventures, here you could play online with others and do almost everything together.

THE LEGEND OF DRAGON QUEST

Dragon Quest IX became a lunchtime game for myself and my workmates, played religiously every day for months and often with sessions stretching off into the evenings. We would go on quests together, take down huge monsters and bag great loot, but what kept it appealing for so long was the joy of adventuring with friends. Where *Dragon Quest* had always meant solo play, with this it became a group endeavor and, in the way it bridged single player and multiplayer, felt like the future. *Dragon Quest X* would take this concept to an extreme by being fully online, though sadly this means it is yet to see a western release and may never.

Such are the frustrations of a western *Dragon Quest* fan. Often, we play the games years later, and surely few of us have managed to play them in anything like the original order of release. It is sometimes frustrating. But it also leads to unexpected oases, a break from the 'normal' life of a videogame obsessive. I recently returned to *Dragon Quest VIII*, which was re-released on the 3DS. In the era of *Breath of the Wild*, this early attempt at an open world couldn't help but feel at first a little bare. But I remembered more, and I stuck with it.

Soon I had been taken away, and it was not nostalgia. It was the beautiful overworld score of Koichi Sugiyama, elevating these flat plains and blue skies into something faintly paradisal. The jaunty town themes and townspeople, who soon had me running every kind of errand. Toriyama's touching and hilarious character designs, from rough-and-tumble heroes to cackling rogues and everything in-between. The sometimes-pitiful enemies and jokey quests escalating into terrible foes and an epic journey, all stitched-together by Yuji Horii to feel like your own awfully big adventure.

Videogames are inseparable from technology, and as technology improves the classics of one age fade away. *Dragon Quest* continues to survive and thrive because of the quality of its craftsmanship. These are games made by masters. However and whenever we get them, they shine like jewels.

I can't think of a better companion for these adventures than Daniel. Enjoy the journey, and may the Goddess guide you.

Rich Stanton

RICHARD STANTON

One of the best writers in video game journalism, Richard Stanton is a true veteran who has done the rounds of the British press from *Edge* magazine to *The Guardian, Eurogamer, IGN* and *Rock Paper Shotgun*. He is the author of *A brief history of Video Games*, a book which traces the epic history of video games throughout the ages. Today he works for *Kotaku UK*.

THE LEGEND OF
DRAGON QUEST

PREFACE

PREFACE

SIMPLICITY has almost ceased to exist and attempting to explain soon becomes a nightmare. We lose ourselves in metaphors and synonyms when everything is there, before our eyes, even in video games. So let's begin with the fragrance of nostalgia, because that is what I like and that is the very heart of *Dragon Quest*.

It was a summer's day in 2000 in Japan. Regulars say that summer is not the best season for visiting because of the heat. And they are right. Everyone is trying to get out of the city, which has become a furnace. We are nothing more than pools of sweat, wandering from one air-conditioned shop to another. But back then, I had a very good reason for being in Tokyo. To be precise, it is August 26, in Akihabara, and the queues are growing longer in the video games district. Reservations are not commonplace in the *kombini*, Amazon is not the huge international distributor that we now know, so it is still worth waiting outside. Pre-3G and smartphone Japan was a totally different country.

Seikimatsu. A feeling often experienced by regular visitors to Japan. It describes the impression of the end of an era. A nation condemned to perpetual reconstruction by nature itself. And in this odd moment, there is a sense that this is also the last major release of a video game, an event capable of bringing so many people together. A few months previously, for PlayStation 2, helicopters were hovering over the district. The queues wind around buildings, into the park behind the department stores. Incidentally, the park with its basketball court no longer exists, because things always have to change. Soon, people won't even have to leave their homes. So this August 26, 2000 is a celebration: the arrival of *Dragon Quest VII* for PlayStation. On the sidewalk, a camera moves towards me, delighted to find a *gaijin*. *Dragon Quest* is still an all-Japanese phenomenon, enjoying only a tiny speck of success in the West, dating back to the NES era. When PlayStation 2 came out, foreigners flooded into Akihabara to buy their many consoles, but by August, they had vanished, as if they had melted in the sun. The huge camera turns its lens towards me and asks why I'm here and what I think of *Dragon Quest*. Totally alone and not yet used to TV, in a language I do not yet master, I mumble out some kind of vapid answer. I think I said something like "Because it's brilliant." Wow, well done.

That evening, in the little business hotel where I was staying that time, in a minute and not particularly comfortable room, I switched on the TV. Young tourists may not realize this but then, almost all hotels charged for use of the TV. Every set had a coin slot. A hundred yen for one hour. An evening in front of the TV for the price of ramen, roughly. That night, I came across the release of *Dragon Quest VII* in Akihabara.

THE LEGEND OF DRAGON QUEST

Much more interesting than me and my shy punchlines, the smiling, short-haired girl interviewed after me hesitated, thought for a moment, before saying: "*Dragon Quest* is actually very simple... fundamental even," as if she had drawn from her own memories, her own nostalgia, to answer the journalist. She was quite right, *Dragon Quest*, a simple video game, connects primarily with the eternal child that resides inside us.

While I was writing this book, a close friend sent me the new advert for the release of *Dragon Quest XI*. He added a cheeky: "The campaign for your book's not bad." The advert states: "And so we became heroes." There are *Dragon Quest* players of all ages, using all kinds of consoles. The ad starts with the same familiar fanfare found in all the episodes. All players, children, teens, adults, are represented from the salaryman rushing home to finish his session to the kid dreaming of teleportation, from the guy waiting in the rain for a new episode to be released to the girl studying, with a handwritten note pinned to the wall: "No *Dragon Quest* until exams are over," from school kids reading the guide-book during recess to mom demanding that the console be switched off for dinner. This advert is accurate in so many ways, even down to the accidental unplugging that we have probably all experienced! This series, more than any other, invites nostalgia. These two minutes remind us of who we are at a specific moment, where we come from and what brings us together.

This is where I come from. My first *Dragon Quest* was *V*. I still remember its crushed cardboard box. The logo caught my eye in the aisles of a second-hand game store in République, the video games district in Paris, especially in the 1990s. At the time, France was all about *Dragon Ball Z*. Fans everywhere were seeking out even the most trivial representation of Son Gokû and his family. The Internet as we know it did not exist. We were alert for news. We would try to piece together bits of the coming story with the first *shitajiki*[1] or a simple picture from a magazine, and let our imaginations run wild. The cover of the fifth volume represented so much: an invitation to travel, a long quest and a love story. The torn clothes and walking stick of the main character suggest a complicated journey. The cape recalls the post-apocalyptic costumes of *Fist of the Northstar*, while the hat, a kind of wound turban, is a direct reference to Son Gokû's clothes when he comes back as an adult from a long training session. The unique style of Toriyama is most obvious in the faces of the two heroes, gazing out towards the horizon, haircuts very reminiscent of Yamcha and Bulma. The sabretooth, which we assume to be both aggressive and loyal, reminds us of Cringer, the fighting companion of He-Man in *Masters of the Universe*. The little dragon makes me think of Lockheed, Kitty Pryde's pet in *X-Men* and, let's be honest here, who doesn't like baby dragon mascots? The range of colors reflects the good taste of Toriyama's beautiful

---

1. Literally "under-sheets," these document holders were made of plastic whose flexibility and transparency varied according to the versions. Rarely used in offices, they are generally sought out by collectors for their illustrations and the series from which they are taken.

PREFACE

drawings from those years. The balance between the sabretooth's black spots and the white of the hero's tunic is sublime, enhancing the other colors. The composition is also perfect. At the foot of the main character, Slime, the legendary monster of the series, adds a comical aspect to the illustration. I would realize only later that this was the first time that the "Pikachu of *Dragon Quest*" was depicted on the cover of a game of the series. Akira Toriyama took care to allow certain elements to extend slightly beyond his frame. The picture makes perfect use of the vertical format of Super Famicom cartridges, which were original at a time when most were horizontal. Even today, I still think that it is one of the most beautiful video game illustrations ever.

And so, I purchased a game for its cover. It was an impulse buy, a bit like choosing games for the screenshots on the back of the box. Of course, back then, with less information available and less experienced sales staff, that was what we often did. I could go on with the illustration of the instructions, which shows the same hero as on the cover, but younger, in the company of a mustached, square-built chap who, at first glance, appears to be his father.

As soon as I got home, I slid the cartridge into my console. And then, fantasy became reality. In 1992, *Dragon Quest V* was an RPG that was somewhat dull to watch. As was often said, "It arrived a generation too late." The graphics were not that different from those of the old NES. A lot of imagination was required to see the little splotches of pixels as the brave traveler depicted on the game cover. But in spite of the not-so-exciting first impression, I persisted. What made me persevere at first was the prospect of a story that covered several generations. *Phantasy Star III: Generations of Doom* was already available on Megadrive, proposing the exhilaration of an epic poem, relayed over several decades. The *Dragon Quest V* adventure relates a long family saga covering more than half a century. I did not know then that the *Dragon Quest* series was based on the traditional pattern of the "elected hero," like Avatar, the main character of *Ultima*.

I then bought the guide books from a Japanese bookshop in downtown Paris, partly for the same reason as I had bought the game: beautiful illustrations. These proved vital considering the laborious and complicated nature of certain passages. My Japanese was very rudimentary then, but I had faith: only a short time before, I had managed to finish *Breath of Fire* in Japanese. Even so, you had to be keen to get through *Dragon Quest V*. Paradoxically, with today's enthusiasm for retro-gaming, it would go down quite well.

Even with only limited knowledge of Japanese and somewhat difficult technical conditions, the story was very well told. This was perhaps what surprised players most. *Dragon Quest V* is a large family cycle of emotions, as transparent as an epic tale by Alexandre Dumas, the author of famous works such as *The Three Musketeers*. In the end, I was lucky that my first taste of the series was this excellent episode, since *VI* was far more extravagant, with its tales of parallel universes and heroes traveling on flying beds. A slightly puzzling game, but not without levity nor offbeat humor. One of the most emotional moments of *Dragon Quest V* is when we end up going back in time to change the past, thus saving the future. The time travel theme has been so often used in science fiction, particularly during the 1980s, that it should have left me impassive. It was not even the first time I had experienced it in a video game. But this adventure, with its simple graphics and persistent melodies, glanced lightly upon feelings that leave no one unmoved. "What would I have done differently if I could have changed things" is a very common concept used in fiction, from *A Distant Neighborhood* by Jirô Taniguchi to the *Quantum Leap* series. Well-told, it is so simple and so effective that it affects each and every one of us.

It was also around about then that my father would come into my room to see what I was up to. I was always playing *Dragon Quest*. He laughed at me, at my game and its characters who were following each other around. It even led to him coming up with a silly nickname for RPGs. As a true descendant of the Russian intelligentsia, he hated video games. Totally unyielding. I never managed to explain what I got from those hours spent glued to my screen. Since then, I have wanted to share the things I love. In my work, I try to understand why a work can create an emotion, convey something. And so, I will not fail you.

As I bring this preface to its conclusion, I am celebrating twenty years as a journalist and twice that in years. It just so happens that *Dragon Quest* is also celebrating its thirtieth anniversary. So many reasons to celebrate with a book.

If you are reading this today, I would like to thank you for your confidence. I am also counting on you, assuming that you know what an RPG is. And that you have heard of Akira Toriyama. The purpose of this book is not to review all the *Dragon Quest* games. I have no intention of summarizing the sometimes bizarre adventures that players can encounter, or of reviewing the characters of every episode. Do not expect a full alphabetical list of all the monsters either—that would bore the both of us. The same applies to details of sales and versions, listed line by line on *Wikipedia*. This book is not an almanac — there are plenty of perfectly good official Japanese publications for that. I cannot illustrate my ideas either, which makes the job somewhat tricky.

What has always interested me in video game journalism is not "How many levels," "How many weapons" or "How many characters can you play." The real question is why. This book looks at "Why *Dragon Quest*?" My goal is to describe the creation and development of a series, a legend, a commercial success, a sociological phenomenon, and my private passion. In short, I aim to get you interested and entertain you.

"Simplicity," as Bruce Lee said, "is the key to brilliance." In the simplest manner possible, I therefore invite you to join me in the imaginary world of *Dragon Quest*.

PREFACE

DANIEL ANDREYEV

Daniel Andreyev is an author and journalist of Russian origin. His career in video game journalism began twenty years ago, during the golden years of video gaming, with *Player One*, *Consoles +* and *Animeland*, with a particular interest in Japan. Having spent some time on translation, he is now part of the *New Games Journalism* movement, which places the player at the heart of the video game experience. He produces the *After Hate* and *Super Ciné Battle* podcasts. He also trades memories with his friends in *Gaijin Dash*, the *Gamekult* show on Japanese video games. He is a fan of far too many things to list them all here. But when he is not writing, not watching a movie, not reading comics and graphic novels, not climbing mountains or exploring ruined buildings, he might be cooking, exercising or dreaming of one day owning a dog.

THE LEGEND OF DRAGON QUEST

Introduction
What is Dragon Quest?

"Forget what you are escaping from. Reserve your anxiety for what you are escaping to."

Michael Chabon,
The Amazing Adventures of Kavalier & Clay.

INTRODUCTION

THIS is a story that begins, quite literally, with a fanfare. The opening of the very first *Dragon Quest* begins with synthetic horns. Precisely ten seconds of 8-bit instruments. A brief pause, then it begins. The main melody sets in, far more imposing and grandiloquent, accompanied by a screen that tirelessly invites you to begin the adventure: press "Start." These arrangements vary over time and with each episode, the horns become trumpets and synthesizers become orchestras, but the intention remains the same. For generations of Japanese players, these emblematic melodies are the signature of Japan's greatest ever role play series. Just a few notes let you know that you are setting out on a long journey. The theme reminds us that even the longest voyage begins with a single step, and that it is up to the player to face the dangers.

One thing that was very rare at the time is that not one, but three names are associated with the creation of this video game. It became customary to see their names displayed at the start of every session, in a deferential silence, before the sounds of the brass burst in. Yûji Horii, Akira Toriyama, Kôichi Sugiyama. In that order. This trio of artists represent the soul of *Dragon Quest*, the foundation stone of Japanese RPGs, the series that created the clichés of a style and even coined expressions that are now in popular use. Their work can be summed up by three modest concepts: adventure, simplicity, love.

Dragon Quest is not the oldest Japanese role-playing game, but it was almost certainly the spearhead and the first massive cultural phenomenon of its kind in Japan. Thirty years on, this name, which has since become a style and a trademark, is revered by players, for whom it means the promise of an epic adventure with a taste of nostalgia. It is, of course, also a label symbolizing a colossal commercial empire. Three decades have seen around ten canonical episodes and as many spin-offs on all generations of games consoles. In Japan alone, more than sixty million copies of *Dragon Quest* have been sold, all versions.

THE LEGEND OF DRAGON QUEST

DRAGON QUEST: A HARD-HITTING NAME

Yûji Horii came up with the sober but forceful title. He explains[1] that he chose this name because it combines the word "Dragon," which is meaningful to everyone, with "Quest," an enigmatic word with multiple meanings. When choosing the name, Yûji Horii recalled a lesson from his time at Gekigasonjuku school, founded by Kazuo Koike[2]. His mentor and friend told him one day that it was wise to associate one word that was easy to remember with another more complicated word. He also claimed that titles starting with the sounds "T" and "D" are much easier to remember for Japanese people. Young Horii remembered this advice when creating his major production.

A detail of importance is the choice of the western word "Dragon." He could have used the regular Japanese word, "Ryû." He had the choice. The word ryû has its own share of implications, and can be written with two different kanjis: 竜 and 龍. The first implies a degree of animality, like a large lizard[3], while the second, the traditional version, is more complex, incorporating a sacred, even divine dimension[4]. Paradoxically, dragons are not really the issue in *Dragon Quest*, at least, not to begin with. As we will see, the Japanese public would soon latch on. And, like everything that becomes popular, it was given a nickname. People started talking about "DraQue" (ドラクエ), following the tradition of taking the first two syllables of a compound name. A smart, effective and unique abbreviation. No risk of confusing DraQue with another game.

THE HERO FIGURE IN 1986

Dragon Quest, the first Japanese RPG for the general public, defined the codes of a whole genre and an entire industry, at least in terms of the hero. As in the first *Zelda no Densetsu*, released a few months before the first *Dragon Quest*, the protagonist does not speak. His contribution to conversation is limited to the choice between "yes" or "no." This could be considered, if not as a sign of laziness, at least as an economical solution. However, the approach remains the same: the hero is at the heart of the adventure. "Generally speaking, I think that a protagonist who speaks ends up distancing the player. He plays as if the character is an extension of himself. In this case, why would the avatar suddenly start speaking?" explains Yûji Horii, in a

---

1. In a special *Game Center CX* episode on "Yûji Horii, the man who created *Dragon Quest*."
2. Kazuo Koike, cult manga author, also worked under the direction of Takao Saitô on the *Golgo 13* series. He then wrote the screenplays for the famous manga *Lone Wolf & Cub* and contributed to its cinema adaptation in the 1970s, collaborating with artist Gôseki Kojima. He later worked with Ryôichi Ikegami on the creation of *Crying Freeman*. Kazuo Koike, born in 1936, still teaches today. Famous previous students include Rumiko Takahashi (*Ranma 1/2*, *Urusei Yatsura*, *Inuyasha*), Tetsuo Hara (*Hokuto no Ken*) and game designer Akira Sakuma, manager of the *Momotarô Dentetsu* game series. Along with Yûji Horii, he has held joint keynotes to promote his courses.
3. This distinction came from a 1994 issue of *Famitsû*, Japan's leading video game magazine, published weekly.
4. Also mentioned by Son Gokû and his friends in *Dragon Ball*, another manga that opted for a western-style "Dragon" title.

INTRODUCTION

joint interview with Shigeru Miyamoto, legendary creator of *Mario* and *Zelda*[5]. Horii develops his idea: "[The player] is playing as though the character is an extension of himself, so why is his avatar suddenly speaking of its own accord? He'll be struck with the realization that the character he's been thinking of as himself up until now is actually someone else entirely."

For the thirtieth anniversary of *Dragon Quest*, its publisher, Square Enix, organized a get-together for fans, with an exhibition on the series[6]. Ten life-sized portraits of the heroes of the saga were gathered together in a huge room at the entrance. Ironically, a single Roman numeral was marked above the heads of the protagonists, all lined up in the hall in decreasing order. On the publisher's official communication documents, the only indication is "*Shûjinkô*"[7], which simply means "hero." Yûji Horii's original idea was to place the player at the heart of the game, rather like those books in which the reader is the hero. In another room, dioramas showed major scenes of the various games. A fat tradesman being pursued by a wild waterfall, a traveler giving a ribbon to a killer sabretooth and, of course, some of the majestic fights against demons. The message is that the important thing is to experience the adventure.

A UNIQUE SUCCESS

On May 27, 1986, more than five hundred thousand copies of the first episode of the series were put on sale in Japan. By the end of the year, Enix had sold a million, reports Yukinobu Chida[8], producer of the series since it began. Although *Dragon Quest* caused a shock-wave in Japan, the western world had to wait to discover these fantastic adventures.

The first episodes were released in the US, but under the name *Dragon Warrior* due to legal issues[9]. In 1980, there was already a traditional Medieval fantasy role-playing game called *DragonQuest*, published by Simulation Publication. This situation lasted until 2003, when Square Enix finally succeeded in registering its name for the North American market.

Although France was much more open to mangas and *animes*, *Dragon Quest* was only really known because of the fame of its artist, Akira Toriyama. Fans saw it as the author's other success, marginal alongside *Dragon Ball*. The first work related to

---

5. 1989 interview, discovered by the "Game Staff List Association Japan," taking place shortly before the release of *Dragon Quest IV*, when Shigeru Miyamoto was working on *Zelda: A Link to the Past*.
6. Dragon Quest Museum was held in 2016 in Shibuya Hikarie, Tokyo, before being moved to Osaka.
7. However, in the screenshots sent to the press, the publisher and developer play around a little with the names of the heroes. Instead of the player's name, it was often marked "Enix," "Arus" or, more recently, "Eito" (*Eight*) and "Naïn" (*Nine*).
8. Interview taken from the documentary *Dragon Quest 30th Soshite Aratana Densetsu he*, 2016.
9. *Dragon Warrior* arrived in August 1989 on NES in the USA. The saga remained localized until the fourth episode in October 1992, before experiencing a long hiatus, which came to an end on January 25, 1999 with the release of *Dragon Warrior Monsters*. It should be noted that these western versions respect the tradition of always proposing ugly covers, with absolutely nothing in common with the original design and style of Akira Toriyama.

21

THE LEGEND OF DRAGON QUEST

DraQue to reach France was the cartoon *Fly*, or *Daino Daibôken*, its original title, based on a manga published by Shûeisha[10]. Ironically, in this modest initial contact with the French public, the manga never mentions the games series on which it was based, and its link with Toriyama is not cited once. It is not even a canonical episode that starts the ball rolling in Europe, but a spin-off on Game Boy Color, *Dragon Warrior Monsters*, released on January 25, 1999[11]. It was some time before the public made the logical connection between "Dragon," "Quest," "Toriyama" and "RPG."

PRINCIPLE

In time, what ultimately best defines *Dragon Quest* is the almost rustic simplicity of the games. A way of producing what I call the *"ligne claire"* of RPG, in reference to the graphic style of the Belgian school of comic drawings. This style describes a desire to get directly to the point, with limited resources and few special effects. What is essential here, marking an obvious similarity with these comics, is not only the simple line, but its legibility. Choices are precise and strict, even for details that could be considered as unimportant. *Dragon Quest*, as we will often see in this book, represents the incarnation of this *ligne claire* in the world of **RPG**.

The industry as a whole pushes the games towards sensationalism, with major productions becoming more like movies in their narrative approach. Yûji Horii, throughout his career, wanted to tell stories, making do with what he had, almost in opposition to the techniques of his era. It is not by chance that the sound effects have remained almost unchanged over the years either. From one episode to another, the same sounds are used for an opening door or for climbing stairs. When the characters accomplish a level of experience, a few high notes of a melody, generally the same one, ring out. It may be seen as old-fashioned to use always the same library of sounds, but it is also a very intelligent strategy. Even before retro-gaming gained popularity and became a trend, these sounds had become memory triggers to which the Japanese public responded.

To help understand the importance of *Dragon Quest* in the collective subconsciousness of Japan, we must go back to the beginning. Discussing this series implies

---

10. *Dai no Daibôken*, also known as *Dragon Quest: The Great Adventure of Dai*, is a manga by Riku Sanjô and Kôji Inada, supervised by Yûji Horii. The TV series was first broadcast in the West in Spain. In its European version, to avoid any similarity with the English word "die," the hero was renamed "Fly," which resulted in a noteworthy inconsistency: the hero is found by his adoptive father in a pram simply marked with the letter "D." D for Dai, not Fly.
11. Again, this first approach by *Dragon Quest* may seem somewhat absurd, but in 1999, releasing something similar to a *Pokémon* clone seemed quite logical. The publisher Eidos Interactive was in charge of this first incursion into Europe.

INTRODUCTION

describing its atypical creators, at the exact time when the industry was taking shape and getting organized. Understanding why *DraQue* is still a phenomenon thirty years later, why this ultra-basic and warm style is still successful are among the goals of this book.

At a time when all narratives were decompressed, when dialogs were overwritten to create atmosphere and present the outline of the game, Yûji Horii's saga stands out with natural simplicity, as if what best defines *Dragon Quest* today is its infinite modesty.

THE LEGEND OF DRAGON QUEST

Chapter I — Yûji Horii, the manga hero

"Our craft, Mrs. Weldon, is one of those in which it is necessary to begin very young. He who has not been a cabin-boy will never arrive at being a perfect seaman, at least in the merchant marine. Everything must be learned, and, consequently, everything must be at the same time instinctive and rational with the sailor—the resolution to grasp, as well as the skill to execute."

Jules Verne, *Dick Sand, A Captain at Fifteen.*

CHAPTER I — YÛJI HORII, THE MANGA HERO

WE RECOGNIZE stars from the aura that surrounds them. That is exactly what you feel in the presence of Yûji Horii. "The boss." And yet, he also gives off a sense of simplicity. The first time I interviewed him was in Japan, in truly exceptional circumstances. The pretext was the release of a *Dragon Quest Monsters*. No one was fooled: we were there to meet the star, not to discuss an nth spin-off episode, although we would obviously have to talk a little about it, for the sake of politeness. Because "that's why we're here." His aura is also apparent in the guard of honor formed by his team and all the various members of the organization staff. Horii hurried in with minimal politeness, sat in the center of the table facing the journalists, smiling a little but not too much, dressed in a relatively simple jacket and a checked shirt. There is no false modesty in his attitude; Yûji Horii knows exactly what he is worth. He knows exactly what his publisher owes him. He also wants to show that he is an "old-school" kind of guy. And he loves to talk about his work.

It is easy to imagine him, slightly balding, chain-smoking in front of his TV, thinking about his next move in a typically Nippon wargame[1], a vision influenced by the fact that, for years, in every photo published, he was smoking. Or behind his desk, leaning on a motorbike, answering journalists, bent over his game documents. He was something of a Japanese Easy Rider, but nicer and more polite. For many years, he defined himself as a "free writer," a freelance author, and his attitude probably stems from that. His glasses, however, remain his most important prop. Rectangular with smoked glass lenses, they complete the character. You imagine him behind them, scanning the people before him, but even so, they are far less intimidating than the black sunglasses he also tended to wear. Lots of the Japanese artists that I have been lucky enough to meet over the years have them: many of them suffer from extreme shyness. Sometimes, they simply refuse all photographs, even at public interviews.

But let's get back to the Yûji Horii interview. One of the many western press attachés turns to me: "You're lucky, you can ask him any question you like, questions we dream of asking." He is a little optimistic: in a room with three journalists, there are five POs[2] to look after the big boss. We certainly cannot ask him just anything; we are mindful of every word. This was 2006 and *Dragon Quest* had neither the fame nor the success that it enjoys in the West today. The balance of

---

1. Wargames on a console, and more particularly on a computer, are derivatives of table war games, strategic games simulating a conflict. It is often said that most of the cartridges of such games, notably developed by Koei in Japan, are now yellow, because they were originally purchased by forty-year-old smokers. Actually, I rarely imagine these games being played by anyone other than a forty-year-old Japanese man puffing away after work.
2. PO: press officer.

power between the press and the saga was a little different: the series needed journalists to boost its notoriety.

Yûji Horii always seemed more relaxed in later interviews. In Japan, there is a kind of protocol to be followed, so it always seemed as if the discussion could have been livelier if the meeting had been held elsewhere. That day, I asked him how he felt about *Pokémon* being broadly based on one of his games[3]. He replied that he was rather proud, before explaining that he saw the games as being quite different. When he left the room, trailing his escort, a sensation of emptiness lingered on behind him. "So that is the great guru of *Dragon Quest*", I thought to myself.

That was when I understood one thing about Yûji Horii: he is actually a manga hero. Since he was born until the creation of *Dragon Quest*, he has literally followed the same route as a typical protagonist in one of his video games or a manga hero. To explain this metaphor, and by way of introduction to *Dragon Quest*, I will start by describing the fascinating life of this *shônen* hero.

YÛJI HORII ORIGINS, "THE RESTLESS OF THE JAR"

Yûji Horii often reminds us that he comes from Hyôgo, Kansai. He has talked of the unique attitude that fuels him. In Japan, he is known as *Ichibiri Seishin*[4], which translates literally as "the restless of the jar," an expression for someone who is a little crazy, burlesque, with a certain tendency to fool around.

Yûji Horii was destined for originality. He was born on 6 January 1954 in the city of Sumoto. "Sumoto-shi" is on the natural island of Awaji, in Hyôgo Prefecture. The humid subtropical climate means cool winters and extremely hot summers, as is often the case in the Kansai region. If your own adventure takes you there, know that the place is famous for its onions and its oranges, known as "naruto," named after the strait, home of the well-known Naruto whirlpools, a natural feature caused by the opposing tides of Shikoku and Awaji Islands. Even with its view of the sea, this most beautiful haven reminds us that disaster is never far away, particularly in Japan. As well as the frequent typhoons, there are also earthquakes. The epicenter of the great Hanshin[5] earthquake that destroyed much of Kobe, was right here, on Awaji Island. Saying that nature and the melancholy of a devastated planet are fundamental concerns for a large number of Japanese creators is something of an understatement. For Yûji Horii, this concern is not only present in his work but also, years later, in a more material form, with his contribution to the "hometown tax donation[6]."

---

3. Notably the monster recruitment system in *Dragon Quest V*.
4. Mentioned in *Game Center CX* No. 106: "Yûji Horii, the man who created *Dragon Quest*."
5. The great Hanshin earthquake on January 17, 1995, caused 6,434 deaths, mainly in the city of Kobe.
6. Furusato Nozei, also known as Hometown Tax, offers a tax credit in exchange for financial donations made to a person's place of birth. This very popular measure was introduced to revitalize the country areas left deserted by the rural exodus and the aging of the population. Millions of yen are thus paid to the Japanese provinces every year.

CHAPTER I — YÛJI HORII, THE MANGA HERO

In spite of its natural hazards, the place is heavenly. As a boy among pine trees and daffodils by the sea, Horii developed a taste for dreaming and escapism. The fact that so many of his heroes begin their adventures on an island that they end up leaving is not coincidental. In fact, it is a real archetype. In *Dragon Quest VII*, he literally puts the player into the role of a fisherman's son, fascinated by epic tales, who later discovers that the world is far larger than it first appears. For example, in the manga he supervised, *Dragon Quest: Dai no Daibôken*, Dai lives alone on Dermline Island, inhabited by animals and monsters that live in peace until an old demon wakes up and destroys the reigning harmony. Horii's childhood memories were to become ingredients for his creations.

Horii also loved to play. Since elementary school, he has played smartball (a kind of simple version of pachinko), before discovering mah-jong, which he loves. He often alters the rules of card games to create a new form of fun. From a modest family—his father worked in glazing—, the young Yûji had dreams of success, imagining himself as a lawyer. However, this was not to last.

When he started middle school, he discovered an insatiable hunger for manga. Until then, his choices had been typical of a boy his age, joining a few intra-school clubs, but nothing in particular. Such clubs are very important to the social functioning of a school, because as well as making friends, it is often in such places that tastes are defined and passions served. He tried swimming, saxophone and learned the tea ceremony, before devoting all his time to the manga club. By the time he reached high school, Yûji was decided: he was going to be a mangaka.

Ultimately, Yûji Horii's dream has always been to tell stories, and he was lucky to realize this very early on in his life. Having decided to draw manga, he spent his nights working on the project, skimping on sleep, and getting punished on a regular basis for his repeated lateness. Although he lived just ten minutes from school by bike, which is a true luxury in Japan, he arrived late almost two hundred times during his second year of high school[7]. His enthusiasm was relentless.

On his brother's advice, he used the summer vacation of his third and final year of high school to try and realize his dream: he applied to be Gô Nagai's assistant. At the time, the future creator of *Mazinger Z*, *Devilman*, *Cutey Honey* and *Grendizer* was one of the most popular manga artists in Japan, along with Shôtarô Ishinomori and Osamu Tezuka. Animation was a huge success on Japanese TV and the young man began to dream of adding his name to the prestigious list of Gô Nagai's assistants, since so many of them later became famous. Yûji Horii finally met the master... but unfortunately, they did not get along and he was rejected. The early demise of his career as a mangaka is perceptible between the lines of the games that Horii later designed. *Dragon Quest* is not just the first classic Japanese RPG, it is also the archetype of a *shônen* tale, like *Dragon Ball*. It is not just intended for young boys; it is a genre that promotes positive values such as abnegation, friendship, courage, will power, and in which old

---

7. Equivalent to 11th grade in the USA.

enemies can become allies. Throughout his work, Horii has never stopped repeating "it is all about how you tell the story."

"OK, NOW WHAT DO I DO?"

That was the question facing Horii shortly after this rejection, when he only had a few months left to decide what he was going to do for a living. He said to himself: "In the meantime, I'll go to college," and set his sights on Waseda.

After high school, Japanese students have to take college entrance exams. This is a formidable ordeal, a drastic selection process that leaves behind so many young people. In other words, you have to work specifically for the institution to which you are applying. The better the college's reputation, the tougher the competition. It is actually the most difficult period in the whole educational process, and students often make themselves ill in their attempts to succeed.

His repeated absences and Gô Nagai's recent rejection could have put Yûji Horii off, condemning him to select a lesser establishment, but the boy lived his life in "difficult" mode. He opted for Waseda, one of the country's most prestigious universities. To give an idea of the level of competition, more than one hundred thousand people take the entrance exam for just five thousand places. And even once you get in, nothing is certain, because you still have to pay the enrollment fees for the private college, which can be up to a million yen[8]; these fees are redistributed as grants to those most in need. Yûji Horii succeeded in 1972! He passed the exam and naturally chose literature. Times were changing for this young man: he left the paradise of Awaji Island for Waseda, in the northern area of Shinjuku, in Tokyo.

Waseda prides itself on the success of its students. They include no fewer than seven of the country's Prime Ministers. As well as being a pool of political talent, plenty of "industrial captains" also spent time here. Tadashi Yanai, CEO of UNIQLO, Lee Kun-hee, CEO of Samsung, and even Hiroshi Yamauchi, ex-CEO of Nintendo, who brought a small family firm into the world entertainment market with his Nintendo consoles. Numerous athletes and artists also went to Waseda and even future video game creators went there to finish their studies in a totally different field. Tomonobu Itagaki, designer, developer and programmer of the *Ninja Gaiden* and *Dead or Alive* series did just that, graduating in law from Waseda in the 1980s. Waseda, along with its eternal rival, Keiô college, is also partly responsible for the development and growing popularity of baseball in Japan.

These were exciting times and Waseda was a bubbling cultural center that many yearned for; Horii, on the hand, was interested in neither sports nor politics, but in the manga club, of which he was an active member: "Manga Kenkyûkai." Everything

---

8. Approximately eight thousand, five hundred euros, or nine thousand dollars.

CHAPTER I — YÛJI HORII, THE MANGA HERO

went well for him that first year, memories of which he often shares with Waseda's young students[9]. He contributed to the college's manga magazine, *SoûdaiMan*, mostly sold at the annual Wasedasai celebration, a two-day festival that attracts thousands of people. He also wrote for Comikets, the Comic Market for mostly amateur manga. But most importantly, it was here that he met other students who shared his passion. He became friends with Yasuyuki Kunitomo, probably best known in the West for his manga *Junk Boy*, adapted as a cartoon in 1987[10]. Mitsuru Ebina was another fellow member of the club. Although now semi-retired, he has a modest reputation as an independent, keeping his distance from the major publishers. It was an ideal place for meeting people and Yûji Horii made some decisive contacts. During his college years, Yûji Horii drew a lot, to the extent that he became the manga club's most gifted member. His mentor, or *senpai*, the affectionate Japanese term, was Kenshi Hirokane, a mangaka who has had several award-winning successes (notably *Kachô Kôsaku Shima*). He specialized in manga with a social dimension, often set in the world of business. Horii also met Seisuke Ôkawa and, although he did not know it then, they would work together almost two decades later on a joint project, the *Itadaki Street* video game. He also met Akira Sakuma through the Waseda Manga Kenkyûkai; he was resitting a few years at Rikkyô college, where there was another very active manga club. So many crossed destinies surround Yûji Horii. Akira Sakuma and Takayuki Dôi (future artist of the *Dragon Quest* instructions), were to come up with *Momotarô Dentetsu*, another video game phenomenon, some ten years later. Sakuma came up with the concept, which was illustrated by Dôi. Sakuma became one of Horii's closest friends, and they supported each other in their respective projects. The future creator of *Dragon Quest* encouraged him to design a game, assuring him that it was also a particularly profitable activity. Even today, souvenirs of one of their last get-togethers can be found on the Internet; 2004, on Akira Sakuma's blog[11]. More than five hundred years between them all, jokes flying all afternoon, mostly about the fact that it is their children, not them, that know *Dragon Quest*.

Revolutionary Japan

Back to college in the 1970s. There were psychedelic times, with exultation everywhere. Japanese students sensed the spirit of revolt during these years. An ideological revolution, encouraged by what was known as the New Left[12]. In a context of rebellion against pro-American bureaucracy and support for the Vietnam War, the country

---

9. Even today, he is a willing participant in interviews with the young members of Waseda's manga club. https://www.waseda.jp/inst/weekly/features/specialissue-draque1/
10. *Junk Boy* was one of the first *animes* to be published in a format that was later to become very popular: OAV, i.e. produced directly for the video market.
11. December 11, 2004: http://sakumania.com/diary/nikki/041211.html
12. *Shin Sayoku* in Japanese

THE LEGEND OF DRAGON QUEST

was disconcerted by this protest movement inherited from the western New Left. Numerous student demonstrations took place and revolutionary communist leagues recruited large numbers of young people, turning them into radicals. Dozens of factions were created, spilling over into extremism. Among the most violent, *Nihon Kakumeiteki Kyôsanshugisha Dômei Kakumeiteki Marukusu Shugiha*[13], nicknamed *Kakumaru-ha*, made sorry headlines. The activists of all these small groups ended up doubting the devotion of their comrades, and those who were not radical enough had to be traitors. And traitors to the "Cause" must be got rid of... On November 8, 1972, Daisaburô Kawaguchi, a young man of barely twenty, was executed by fellow members of *Kakumaru-ha*. Ultimately, they killed each other off almost entirely, in a suicide action similar to that of a sect. This assassination rocked public opinion, still in shock after the events of the *Asama-Sanso* incident: that same year, a hostage crisis in a mountain chalet was instigated by revolutionary communist groups belonging to the Unified Red Army (URA)[14].

The connection with our story is not the revolutionary ardor of *Dragon Quest*, far from it. Daisaburô Kawaguchi was, in fact, a classmate of Yûji Horii, starting the same year in the literature section at Waseda college. The reaction of the authorities and faculty management was radical, although obviously not to the extent of the revolutionary communists: Waseda was locked-out. This lock-out situation lasted a full year, during which students were left to themselves. For Yûji Horii, it was an opportunity for having fun.

Photos from this era show a dashing chap with shoulder-length hair, a slightly rebellious expression on his face. It is easy to imagine the young man smoking his hours away, gazing at the ceiling. And this is exactly what he did during the college lock-out. He settled into a hall of residence in the Takadanoba district (with Waseda being nearby, it was just like his schooldays on Awaji) and spent his time playing mah-jong, to the extent that the other residents of the hall ended up complaining about the noise of his game sessions. It comes as no surprise that his game partners were none other than the members of his manga club, including Akira Sakuma. He and his friends went from one *nomikai* to another, drinking parties during which *yaminabe*, "mystery stews" were cooked up from ingredients contributed by those present. This popular dish was perfect for the students, with their erratic sense of humor. Yûji Horii even said of himself that "perhaps this lock-out turned him into a good-for-nothing."

SOTSUGYÔ, THE END OF A CYCLE

All this free time enabled Yûji Horii to read manga, particularly in the issues of *Garo*, a specialized, and rather underground publication. One of the stories that he

---

13. 日本革命的共産主義者同盟革命的マルクス主義派 in kanjis.
14. Most of these events are described in all their atrocity in *United Red Army*, a docufiction by Kôji Wakamatsu.

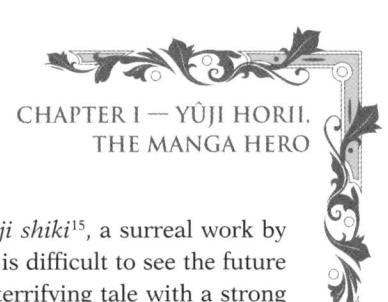

CHAPTER I — YÛJI HORII, THE MANGA HERO

discovered and preferred above all others was called *Neji shiki*[15], a surreal work by the famous author and essay-writer, Yoshiharu Tsuge. It is difficult to see the future creator of *Dragon Quest* appreciating a lugubrious and terrifying tale with a strong hint of psychoanalysis, in a country that is—ironically—not at all acquainted with analysis as it has been practiced in the Western world since Freud. The other cult work he discovered during this period was *Sekishoku Ereji*[16], a romantic manga for adults. Yûji Horii's tastes become more specific, quite different from what was found in the ultra-popular *shônen* magazines of the time.

In 1974, a publisher asked him to write something about his manga club in Waseda. He took up the challenge and, the following year, started to contribute to specialist journals and, most importantly, to books produced along with his fellow club members. The unusual *Onara Blues*, literally "fart blues," is worth a mention, but it was its successor that garnered the most interest. Assisted by Akira Sakuma and a few others, under the name Bôken Group[17], they published their first critical success. *Itazura Ma* or "The demon of pranks," a collection of ideas for practical jokers, was released at the ideal moment, at the same time as the first candid camera stunts. For a while, the team took turns writing tricks for the TV show, *Itazura Camera da!*[18]. This was his first experience of television.

All these occupations did not prevent him from completing his studies. At least not quite. In 1976, during his fourth year, he had a serious motorbike accident, and was unable to go to class for more than six months afterwards. Once again, like a *shônen* manga hero, Yûji Horii persevered and went back to complete his curriculum, but set aside his pens and pencils. "Yûji Horii was definitely the club's best artist, but the accident put a stop to all that," recalls Akira Sakuma[19]. Horii prefers to say that it was just "easier to write than to draw." His artist days were over, he would express himself in his texts, but without restriction. He became a freelance author.

TORISHIMA, EDITOR/GAMER

During his college years, Yûji Horii, along with his friends Akira Sakuma and Mitsuru Ebina, started to write regularly for *Gekkan Out*, a magazine mostly about *anime*. He initially picked the pseudonym "Yûbô," which could be translated as "the Yû kid," and wrote a column called *Yûbô no Detakoto Makase*[20]. This soon became one of the magazine's most popular columns, generating a large number of readers' letters.

---

15. Translated in the USA for *The Comics Journal* in 2003 and adapted for the movies in 1998.
16. "*Red Colored Elegy*," by Seiichi Hayashi, is published in the USA by Drawn and Quarterly.
17. "The adventure group"
18. Literally, "It's a hidden camera!"
19. http://news.denfaminicogamer.jp/projectbook/momotetsu/2
20. Literally "Let Yûbo do it."

THE LEGEND OF DRAGON QUEST

It was also at this time that Horii met someone who was to play a crucial role in the future *Dragon Quest*. Kazuhiko Torishima only became known to the western public recently, but he was actually connected to the global success of *Dragon Ball*, which he published. This man, reputed for his interference in the manga he supervised, was an active contributor to the overall story lines[21] and the development of the heroes and antagonists.

You may even recognize his face, which is probably a little familiar. Somewhat in spite of himself, it's true, he became a model for various Akira Toriyama characters. Firstly, Dr. Mashirito in *Dr. Slump*. He is also recognizable in the features of the even more famous Piccolo Daimaô in *Dragon Ball*. Kazuhiko Torishima was mostly a talent scout. Throughout his career, he discovered artists such as Masakazu Katsura (*Video Girl Ai*) and Akira Toriyama (*Dragon Ball*). Torishima joined the Shûeisha publishing company immediately after leaving college and although he was aiming for *Monthly Playboy*[22] for the quality of the magazine's novellas, he ended up at *Shûkan Shônen Jump*[23]. Unfortunately, manga was not his thing. Even so, in time he got to like it, although his main interest remained video games. In the early 1980s, Kazuhiko Torishima found a partner to share his favorite hobby. Almost every evening, he met up with a certain Yûji Horii to discuss their joint passion. The beginning of a "bromance."

Yûji Horii was still freelancing. He was not overly busy and so had time to attend Kazuo Koike's manga course at the Gekigasonjuku school. He became interested in computers, or "PasoCon" as they say in Japan[24]. Under Torishima's influence, he bought a PC-6001[25] which cost the tidy sum of eighty-nine thousand yen[26] when it came out, and started coding simple games in BASIC. Torishima, who always had an eye for success, spotted his friend's potential and told him about a competition organized by a young publishing firm called Enix. It was not about esport, but game creation. The first Game Hobby Program Contest was held in 1982. Torishima, who occasionally ordered articles from him, advised Yûji to attend. In fact, he encouraged him to enter. Yûji Horii put his heart and soul into the project, motivated as never before.

---

21. Today, he is chairman of the Hakusensha publishing house.
22. Published under license in Japan by Shûeisha, *Weekly* and *Monthly Playboy* were two separate magazines, differing from their western model, being less erotic. *Monthly Playboy* was withdrawn from publication at the end of 2008.
23. The legendary *Weekly Jump*, the most popular major manga pre-publication anthology, which saw the launch of *Dragon Ball*, *Saint Seiya*, *City Hunter*, *Naruto*, *One Piece* and *Hunter X Hunter*.
24. PasoCon is an abbreviation of *Pasonaru Conpyuta*, *Personal Computer* in Japanese.
25. The Nec PC-6001 was one of the most popular computers in Japan in 1982. 16KB RAM, 128x192 resolution with four colors or two in semi-graphic mode, technical capacities that show how developers took their machines to their limits.
26. Four hundred and fifty dollars in 1982, i.e. the equivalent of one thousand two hundred dollars in 2018.

CHAPTER I — YÛJI HORII, THE MANGA HERO

"THE GREAT MARTIAL ARTS TOURNAMENT"

Remember the famous destiny of the *shônen* manga hero mentioned at the beginning of this chapter? Let's see: Yûji Horii comes from a beautiful place, suffered a major rejection, took up new challenges, was knocked back by an accident that actually made him even stronger and more motivated. The only thing missing is a tournament for him to face his rivals, who will later become friends, and his life will be even more like a *Dragon Ball* cliché. And that is exactly what happened. Ironically, this Game Hobby Program Contest was the starting point, some years later, for the manga that related the origins of the *Dragon Quest* series, written, illustrated and supervised by the great Shotarô Ishinomori[27].

In 1982, Enix was eons away from being the publisher we know today. The name comes from the abbreviation "Eniac," i.e. *Electronic Numerical Integrator Analyzer and Computer*, to which the word "Phoenix" was added later. This strange acronym was a good name for the young service company. Having tried the real estate advertising industry before starting up a chain of shops, CEO Yasuhiro Fukushima, ex-architect turned entrepreneur, finally decided to concentrate on video games[28]. He used competitions to find the talents he needed for his publishing business. There is a difference in mentality here compared with the western world: in the USA, where games creators tended to be selected from among IT enthusiasts, Japan sought out both coding experts and manga fans.

The deadline was set for December 20 with a first prize of three million yen and one million for second place[29]. Three hundred games entered, only thirteen of which were ultimately published by Enix. A little known fact back then, the young company did not develop any games internally[30]. Enix did nothing more than publish and promote. The prizes of this contest were actually a sort of advance payment of royalties. A way for the company to cover its risks. The non-negligible advantage of this competition was that it identified the industry's future talents. The conditions were actually very similar to those of a literary contest and winners were decided by a very honorary "*Game sakka*[31]."

It took young Horii six months to code the game in BASIC, following the advice of an introductory guide to programming, giving him the impression that nothing was impossible. He decomposed a few programs of the era, such as *Star Trek* or

---

27. Shôtarô Ishinomori is one of the biggest mangaka of the 20th century; he wrote and illustrated the *Cyborg 009* manga, inventing the famous superhero, Kamen Rider, star of the live action series of the 1970s. As well as *Dragon Quest*, he also illustrated the adventures of *Zelda*, published in the USA in *Nintendo Power* then by Viz Media.
28. *Power-Up: How Japanese Video Games gave the World an extra life* by Chris Koehler.
29. Three million yen was worth thirteen thousand six hundred and fifty dollars in 1982 and thirty six thousand three hundred dollars in 2018 and one million yen four thousand five hundred and fifty dollars in 1982, or twelve thousand one hundred dollars in 2018.
30. The workings of Enix at the time are described in detail by Toru Hidaka in *The Untold History of Japanese Game Developers vol. 1* by John Szczepaniak.
31. Literally, "game author."

35

Nobunaga no Yabô, to understand how they worked. His game was called *Love Match Tennis* and, as its title suggests, it was a tennis game. With no music and just a few brash sound effects, *Love Match Tennis* was nothing if not rustic. The entire game fit onto an audio cassette, a medium with multiple faults, including loading time, extremely limited memory and reliability. The keyboard arrow keys were used to play the game with relative accuracy. It should probably be noted that a touch of color prevented *Love Match Tennis* from being totally monochromatic. At the time, however, it was impressive, particularly for a lone creation.

Yûji Horii's style is present in the tiny details. Even the cover of the game was totally different from what was available then: in the foreground, a profile view of a young female tennis player. Behind her, a man and woman playing. A rather sober scene compared with the market's usual offering: no close-ups under tennis skirts here. Another interesting detail of the game is the dialog. *Love Match Tennis* enabled three characters Maiko, Kumiko and JUN[32] to play against each other, proposing the partners in increasing order of difficulty. The characters expressed themselves after the game, each in their own manner. Yûji Horii always allowed himself a touch of humor and narration in his works, and even in what appears to be a simple tennis video game from the early 80s, he attempted to add atmosphere and personality.

Yûji Horii did not win this first Game Hobby Program Contest. The contest winner was Kazurô Morita with his humbly named *Morita no Battlefield*. A few years later, he created the long series of *Morita Shôgi*, simulators of the traditional Asian strategic game. Horii finished at the bottom of the podium, but with the promise of being among the thirteen published by Enix.

Yûji Horii attended the ceremony as a winner, but also as a journalist, which may be somewhat incongruous in terms of deontology. He cared little about mixed genres and conflicting interests and, even as he became a renowned developer, he never held his tongue in his regular magazine chronicles on video games. He also related the contest in his own column, *Gekkan Out*[33]. For his article, he interviewed the second prize winner, Kôichi Nakamura, with whom he became friends. At first, Nakamura did not even understand who this cool, sunglass-wearing guy was. The relaxed Horii told him, "I created that game," pointing at *Love Match Tennis*, although he was in his role as a journalist.

Horii's article on the contest and its winners was published[34] in *Jump* magazine, which had then began to cover more than just video games. He described six different games, allowing a well-placed box for his own creation. However, he wrote even more on Kôichi Nakamura's *Door Door*, a puzzle platform game demanding address and strategy. The player controls Chun, who is being chased by four aliens that must be trapped. The program is lively, incisive and addictive, exactly what video games needed at the time.

---

32. Written in Roman capital letters on the screen.
33. *Gekkan Out no Sekai*, April 1983.
34. Entitled "*Asonde Tsukute Maikon Game*" or "Having fun creating micro-computer games" was published over two pages in *Weekly Jump* no. 14 in 1983.

CHAPTER I — YÛJI HORII, THE MANGA HERO

Kôichi Nakamura was actually the total opposite of Yûji Horii. One dressed like a beatnik, with a mane of hair, often represented in caricatures, like that of a manga hero; the other, the very incarnation of a good boy. In a close-fitting suit, like all the other salarymen at the ceremony, Nakamura blended into the background, good as gold. Horii, on the other hand, donned his best sweatshirt and smoked glasses for the big day. Decorated with a pink flower like all the other winners, as if it were a Japanese graduation ceremony, Yûji Horii stood out among the other participants, decked out in their Sunday best.

It was the beginning of a true friendship between Horii and Nakamura, further supporting the parallel between Horii's life story and that of a *shônen* hero: having failed to win the tournament, Yûji Horii befriended his rival.

KÔICHI NAKAMURA, THE GENIUS

The word *genius* is often bandied about, but in this case, it is well-deserved. Kôichi Nakamura is a true genius of programming. His high school club did not make manga. His thing was coding and math. For example, he wrote the entire *Galaxy Wars* video game in BASIC on an old Tandy TRS-80. Nakamura is also a hard-worker; he delivered newspapers to earn the money for his first PC-8001. He also developed coding tools that he would send to the specialist *I/O* journal, which earned him twenty thousand yen[35], his first income from the industry. The vacations were an ideal opportunity for this genius to spend even more time programming. He set about porting the arcade game *Space Panic*, which was released as *ALIEN Part 2*, to the PC-8001, again for *I/O*. These games were generally provided free, in the form of code to be copied. All these amateur conversions were borderline in terms of legislation, since obviously the fans did not ask the copyright holders for permission. In fact, *Scramble*, which he programmed next, was renamed *Attacker* to avoid such problems. The workaholic went from one development to another! Next came *River Rescue*, an adaptation of *River Patrol*. By the time he was nineteen, Kôichi Nakamura had earned more than two million yen in royalties and fees! He was already a star in the tight circle of amateur coders. When he arrived in Tokyo, he signed up for college, but Nakamura did not want to wait. He was overflowing with ideas and concepts, and the contest came at exactly the right time.

Door Door[36], the game Nakamura submitted to the Game Hobby Program Contest, was Enix's first Famicom game. It was a huge success and two hundred thousand copies were sold. With his loot, Kôichi Nakamura, just twenty years old, founded Chunsoft. Chun is both the name of the hero of *Door Door* and the traditional reading of the "Naka" ideogram of his own name, as pronounced during mah-jong games.

---

35. Approximately ninety dollars at the time, or two hundred and forty dollars today.
36. Nakamura was still at high school when he sent his game for the contest.

THE LEGEND OF DRAGON QUEST

In addition to its later contribution to *Dragon Quest*, Chunsoft also created several quite different styles of games, including sound novels (graphic and textual adventure games) and *fushigi no dungeon*[37]. In spite of all the acquisitions, mergers and bankruptcies of our era, Nakamura is still CEO of the company he created in 1983, a rarity in the Japanese video game industry.[38]

YÛJI HORII MYSTERIES

Before finding the idea that would bring him and Nakamura together on the same project, Horii continued to work alone. Story, design, graphics, a total of six months' work. His current passion, whodunits, were something of an editorial social revolution in Japan, and he wanted to make one into a game. He drew inspiration from two American successes, the *Zork* series by Infocom and particularly *Mystery House* by Sierra On-Line, the first game designed by Roberta Williams[39], whose visual features he copied. When it was finished, Enix was delighted to publish it, since all the contest games had achieved success. This game was *Portopia Renzoku Satsujin Jiken*, literally "The Portopia serial killer"[40]. Unknown to the public in the western world, the adventure soon developed a cult following among large numbers of Japanese gamers. Particularly well-written and funny, it is often cited as a reference by the most famous Japanese game designers. It is no surprise that Hideo Kojima[41] loved *Portopia*, since he has always tried to reproduce the style (a combination of drama and bawdy humor) in his own productions.

In *Portopia*, the goal is to solve murders from a series of enigmas based on the environment visited and the objects collected. The astonishing modernity of this adventure is clear, even more than thirty-five years later. It is a first-person video game, with quite adequate rendering, in spite of the limitations of the old PC-6001. The keyboard commands were still quite basic: go, call, inspect, seek or telephone. The original version has no music and cannot be saved, but Horii was ambitious, even for his first adventure game. *Portopia* is not a totally linear game and can be finished without having to complete every part. He tried, in vain, to program an algorithm to respond

---

37. The Dungeon RPG style is inspired by *Rogue*, a 1980s game based solely on the exploration of a randomly generated dungeon, with turn-based combats. This style became popular again when Kôichi Nakamura decided to make the first spin-off game of *Dragon Quest*, *Torneko no Daibôken: Fushigi no Dungeon*, literally "The great adventures of Torneko: the mysterious dungeon."
38. Chunsoft first merged with Spike in 2012. It diversified, publishing both adventure games, like *Samurai Dô*, *Way of the Samurai* in the West, as well as the *Kenka Banchô* series, a kind of simplified *GTA* with Japanese goons. Spike was made up of ex-Human studio personnel, mainly specialized in sport simulations: car racing and wrestling. In November 2013, Dwango bought Spike Chunsoft.
39. Creator of the adventure game saga, *King's Quest*, by Sierra On-Line, which was then called On-Line Systems. It was the success of *Mystery House*, among other things, that encouraged Roberta and her husband, Ken Williams, to change the name of their company.
40. Never released in the West, by convention ポートピア is retranscribed as "Portpia," although "Port Pier" would be much more logical in context.
41. Revered creator of the *Metal Gear Solid* series and adventure game author.

CHAPTER I — YÛJI HORII, THE MANGA HERO

to the player's different commands, but this proved too complicated for the times[42]. The *Portopia* plot is mostly set in Sumoto, Kobe and Kyôto, i.e. his home town and two other Kansai cities that he knew well. He tried to reproduce the atmosphere of the streets and ports, to the point where keen fans would make a pilgrimage to visit the actual sites used in the game[43]. It is always much easier to represent places that you actually know and love, even with the limited technical capabilities of a PC-6001. What's more, Kansai has a unique charm that goes beyond good food, local dialect and cultural treasures. Setting one of his first works in the places where Horii spent his childhood is not without significance.

The code of *Portopia* was soon finished in his free time, between *Nobunaga no Yabô*[44] game sessions with his friend Akira Sakuma. The latter was his tester, expressing frustration at having to enter the various commands on the keyboard, which he did not find particularly user-friendly. This comment remained in Horii's mind, until he started to consider the Famicom version of his game. Nintendo's latest console had no keyboard, which was quite restrictive. However, in spite of this disadvantage, the cartridge version came out two years later[45].

Nakamura's desire finally became reality when *Portopia* was converted for Famicom. Nakamura developed an interface for use on the game controller, so the player could select an action without having to type in instructions. It was no easy task and the constraints were many. To begin with, the memory available was extremely limited, to the point where strategy and sacrifice were necessary for the adaptation to succeed, but there was also another problem: the cartridge had no save function. Luckily, this did not last. Neither did it prevent the Famicom version of *Portopia* from selling six hundred thousand copies, a number that still stirs the dreams of the Japanese market today. Then, it was a humble adventure that became a huge phenomenon. It became one of the cornerstones of a genre that later came to be known as visual novel. In one of his radio shows, Takeshi "Beat" Kitano[46] played live, resulting one of the first mass spoilers, revealing the name of the murderer to his listeners.

Emboldened by the success of *Portopia*, Yûji Horii started on two new investigations based on the same system. The first game, *Hokkaidô Rensasatsujin Okhotsk ni Kiyu*[47], was not published by Enix but by ASCII and developed by the Loginsoft teams, a branch of the most popular PC magazine. For the first time, Yûji Horii delegated his work, only taking charge of game design and the scenario. His friend Gôzô

---

42. Horii brought this up in a joint interview with Rika Suzuki published in *Beep* in 1987.
43. http://www.itmedia.co.jp/games/articles/0509/06/news029.html
44. *Nobunaga's Ambition*, its western title, is a strategy game by Koei, which has released multiple episodes since 1983.
45. The relatively long conversion time was partly due to an industry that was still, at the time, rather slow to respond, and also to the number of different conversions: PC-6001, PC 8001mkII, FM-7, X1, MSX and finally Famicom.
46. "Beat" Takeshi (real name Takeshi Kitano), comedian, author, director, painter and actor, is one of Japan's most fascinating artists. As well as films that have become classic movies, such as *Sonatine* or *Hana-bi* (published as *Fireworks* in the USA), he also designed a game based on his TV show, *Takeshi no Chôsenjô*.
47. Literally, "Hokkaidô serial killer, missing in Okhotsk".

THE LEGEND OF DRAGON QUEST

Shiozaki, chief editor of *Login*, dealt with production[48]. Surprisingly, Horii took his time preparing this new investigation. He took a year to develop it, setting the story in Hokkaidô, simply for the pleasure of going there to scout around with his friends. Of course, the whole team was keen on the idea of eating crab, a delicacy typical of the region!

He programmed his third police investigation by himself. *Karuizawa Yûkai Annai*[49] was published by Enix, but was not released for Famicom because its storyline was considered too serious for the console's players at the time. This time, the plot was set in the mountains, mainly in the city of Karuizawa, Nagano Prefecture. He added a number of references to RPG, a genre in which Horii was becoming increasingly interested. For example, the hero finds himself in a combat situation, with a menu from which he can select his fighting moves. Having remained unpublished since 1986, mobile phone versions gave it a second life in Japan[50]. *Portopia, Hokkaidô Rensasatsujin Okhotsk ni Kiyu* and *Karuizawa Yûkai Annai* were released together as a trilogy called Horii Mysteries.

THE FINAL JOKE BEFORE DRAGON QUEST

Our *shônen* tale made a shy entrance in 1986, release date of the very first *Dragon Quest*, our topic of interest today. The stage has now been set for the story to be told properly. However, one thing remains to be discovered: what did Yûji Horii mean when he described himself as *Ichibiri seishin*, a "restless of the jar." His love of schoolboy pranks and jokes can be illustrated by a scene from one of his first games.

In *Hokkaidô Rensasatsujin Okhotsk ni Kiyu*, with the investigation in full swing, we are brought face to face with Megumi Nakayama, a student, beside a traditional Japanese bath. This scene contains absolutely nothing of particular interest, other than a cute girl, wrapped in a towel by a pool. But, if you do nothing for two minutes but wait, without touching the controls, the beautiful Megumi will take pity on you. She will smile, remove her towel and allow you to enjoy the view.

"That's all," she'll say a few seconds later, covering her naked body again. It is this momentary madness, this "restless of the jar" side of himself that Yûji Horii totes from one game to the next.

---

48. An important friend who was later to head the *Famicom Tsûshin* magazine.
49. Literally "Information on the *Karuizawa* kidnapping."
50. Firstly for iMode, the ancestor of mobile Internet at the end of the 1990s, then for smartphones in 2002.

THE LEGEND OF DRAGON QUEST

Chapter II — Origins

"The rewards for being sane may not be very many, but knowing what's funny is one of them."

Kingsley Amis, *Stanley and the Women*.

CHAPTER II — ORIGINS

It all began on May 27, 1986, the day on which *Dragon Quest* came out in Japan. An initial five hundred thousand copies were produced, which today seems huge for a name that was totally unknown. The stakes were high. RPG was totally new to the general public, and no one was ready for it. Sales were not good initially, according to game producer Yukinobu Chida, but luckily, double the initial production were sold by the end of the year, thanks to Yûji Horii's zeal and a few stunts. But let's leave that for the end of our tale.

Revolutionizing video games

With the booming popularity of personal computers, making an RPG in the mid-1980s was no great risk. The main thing was to target the right population. The world of game consoles was still a little uncertain, but the market was active and the revolution still in progress. *Super Mario Bros.* was released in September 1985[1], *Zelda* a mere three months before *Dragon Quest*. A new population had to be persuaded, and the task at hand was almost educational in its nature.

RPGs existed, but only for computers. *The Black Onyx*, considered to be the first Japanese RPG, came out in 1984, but was mainly aimed at aficionados. *Druaga no Tô*[2] by Namco had a few subtle ingredients of RPG, well-hidden in an arcade game. Fans also discovered *Dragon Slayer* and *Hydlide*. The offer was limited to PC-8001, Sharp X1 and imports for Apple machines. This was certainly a paradox, considering that RPG was to become the all-powerful genre for Japanese consoles, the kind that could make or break the fate of a manufacturer[3].

In the meantime, Yûji Horii was working on an editorial project with his friend Kazuhiko Torishima. Until now, *Weekly Jump* proposed several pages on video games. Put to the test of popularity surveys, like manga, they only provoked modest enthusiasm. The success of the MSX, then Famicom, was like a breath of fresh air to attract a broader audience.

---

1. October 18, 1985 in the USA
2. *Tower of Druaga* in the West.
3. Many analysts highlight the absence of major RPGs, notably *Dragon Quest* and *Final Fantasy*, as being responsible for the decline and ultimate abandonment of SEGA's Dreamcast or the early withdrawal of Nintendo's GameCube.

THE LEGEND OF DRAGON QUEST

Torishima drew inspiration from a concept he had seen in *CoroCoro Comic*, a competitor magazine[4] for an even younger readership, whose issues had a number of pages sealed together so that they were impossible to read without being cut. This method not only aroused curiosity, but also helped to overcome the problem of *"tachi-yomi,"* the typically Japanese tradition of reading in bookshops[5]. The pages contained solutions, advice and techniques to complete the games. So *Weekly Jump* did the same. The magazine inserted its video game pages into a full-color booklet, between the cover and the contents page. A paper knife was required to access the little booklet stuck inside *Jump*. It was called *Famicom Shinken*, as a tribute to the manga *Hokuto no Ken*[6]. The games were rated, but by number of "Atatatata," Kenshirô's battle cry.

Famicom Tsûshin[7] was not far behind and the success of *Famicom Shinken* brought about the advent of video games journalism for the general public. The first author to write in this famous booklet was none other than Yûji Horii, under the pseudonym Yûtei, alias "Emperor Tei."

Torishima and the handful of editors who managed the booklet soon realized the limits of the concept. They wanted to do more, like describe the various phases of game creation. Describe each step, from the first ideas put down on paper to the final stages of production. They soon realized that this would be a unique, exciting and complicated task. Shûeisha recognized the benefits for itself: participating in the development of a game meant having exclusivity over all the information, pictures and testimonials related to the project. Shûeisha also imposed a counterpart: the right to publish a manga based on the license. Following this agreement, unique in the video game world, *Dragon Quest*: Dai no Daibôken[8] was born. Readers found themselves with a choice of several shônen comics at once. None of the protagonists were the same; the adventures were totally different, with nothing in common except for certain elements of their worlds and particularly the monsters[9]. Yûji Horii was eager to start creating an RPG, a genre that fascinated him.

---

4. *CoroCoro Comic*, a magazine published by Shôgakukan and featuring its stars, such as *Doraemon*. It published the very strange manga *Super Mario-kun* with its extremely schoolboy humor.
5. Today, almost all magazines and books are sold sealed in one way or another, which has practically eradicated this habit.
6. "Hokuto Shinken" is the martial arts school of Kenshirô, hero of the manga *Fist of the Northstar*.
7. The magazine then became *Famitsû* in 1995.
8. Manga often known in Europe as *Fly* (see chapter 1).
9. In 1991, Enix published its own magazine, *Shônen Gangan*, enabling the games publisher to keep control over its own licenses. The magazine did not only publish *Dragon Quest* and expanded its collection to competitor series, such as *Tales of* or *Fire Emblem*.

CHAPTER II — ORIGINS

AMERICAN CLASS

Dragon Quest was not built in a day. The game, whose theme is often based on travel, actually began with a journey. In 1983, Enix decided to reward the winners of the Game Hobby Program Contest with a trip to the USA. Yukinobu Chida from Enix thus accompanied Kôichi Nakamura and Yûji Horii to AppleFest '83 in San Francisco. The American market was then divided between PC and the luxury Apple niche, with its Apple II range. It was also the year in which Apple brought out Lisa, the first computer with a graphic interface for the general public. Imagine a huge convention, California-style: thousands of Apple products almost religiously gathered into a prefabricated construction, for a company already keen to maintain its cult image.

Wandering the aisles of the trade fair, they came across the third episode of *Wizardry*, which already had quite a reputation among hardcore Japanese players, those who could overcome the language barrier[10]. Some years later, the Sir-Tech series became so popular in Asia that a Japanese division was created. This Nippon section was ultimately the only remaining branch of *Wizardry*. The discovery of *Wizardry III: Legacy of Llylgamyn* was a revelation. Horii and Nakamura felt a shock, a bit like that experienced by players trying *Dragon Quest* for the first time.

Wizardry became the natural bridge between the world of micro-computing and traditional role-playing games. Yûji Horii was obsessed with the series and this demonstration of a new episode put him into turmoil. He was so affected that he decided to program a fake-3D dungeon in his own game that he was finishing, *Portopia Renzoku Satsujin Jiken*[11]. He went even further, adding some rather ambiguous graffiti. On one of the walls of his maze, the facetious Horii scrawled the strange words "*Monsutaa Sapuraizudo Yuu*" ("The Monster surprised you!"), a direct quotation of one the well-known gimmicks of the *Wizardry* series that appeared whenever a monster emerged.

Yûji Horii and Kôichi Nakamura were convinced that the future belonged to RPG and dreamed of creating such a game for the newly released Nintendo console. They knew that the task would be complicated and that sacrifices would be necessary, because the Nintendo-manufactured cartridges only proposed very little memory space. For an RPG, a genre rather demanding in this area, it was hell. Graphics, sounds and dialogs are all resource-hungry, but worst of all, there was still no cartridge with a

---

10. The success of *Wizardry* in Japan completely overwhelmed its authors, Andrew C. Greenberg and Robert Woodhead. Treated as celebrities at every *Wizardry* convention in Japan, Woodhead ended up falling for the country and, in 1991, *Wizardry* gave birth to a whole series of spin-offs, designed exclusively in Japan. By only proposing episodes produced in Japan after 2000, the license effectively became a Japanese series. As for Woodhead, he married a Japanese girl and made his home in the land of the rising sun. As well as creating several of the very first anti-virus products for Macintosh, he and his wife founded AnimEigo, a pioneer in the translation of *anime* for the USA.
11. See chapter 1.

# THE LEGEND OF DRAGON QUEST

battery to allow game saving, which was a huge handicap for a genre that involved a certain amount of investment from the player[12]. The biggest problem, according to the two designers, remained the lack of a keyboard. Without this tool, complex commands were impossible: they were limited to the Famicom controller with its four buttons and a cross for directions.

THE TWO SCHOOLS OF RPG

The two RPG fans were divided. Horii swore only by *Wizardry* and its dungeon combats. Nakamura discovered another great name in computer role play games in the US: *Ultima*, one of the most legendary of all video games. Created by Richard Garriott[13], *Ultima* became a model of its genre and a true RPG institution. Developed first for Apple II, each episode of the saga placed the player in the body of Avatar, embodying Virtue from our world, intended to restore balance to the world of Britannia.

The differences between *Ultima* and *Wizardry* are huge: they are more like two schools of thought, two separate philosophies. The first bases the whole experience on immersion in Britannia, with each screen sculpting the contours of a rich, hypnotic world. This environment and all its possibilities are what makes the adventure so attractive. The story, particularly in the first few episodes, follows the main archetypes of western-style heroic fantasy.

By nature, *Wizardry* is far more combat-based. Confrontations are in the "first-person," as if the player can see through the character's eyes. The protagonist thus challenges monsters while the rest of the screen displays data on the adventurers, viewpoints, magic and other statistics. This view is particularly immersive, especially for movement. *Eye of the Beholder* or *Shining in the Darkness* are games that have made abundant use of this style, reproduced years later by FPS[14] games.

To represent its world, *Ultima* opted for a sky view from the very first episode. Avatar is seen from above, so that the player's field of vision is not limited by the first obstacles. This is ideal for all aspects related to exploration, but rather clumsy when it comes to fighting, being neither exciting nor immersive. A long debate began between Nakamura and Horii: which RPG style was best? If you have already played *Dragon Quest*, you will know that they opted for the best of both worlds, i.e. an *Ultima*-style overview, but with *Wizardry*-type fighting.

---

12. *Zelda no Densetsu*, released on February 21, 1986, just a few months before *Dragon Quest*, was not concerned by this detail because it came out on the Famicom Disk System, which enabled game saving.
13. There is so much to be said about Richard Garriott that one book would not be enough. Creator of *Ultima*, in which he plays the role of Lord British, he became a private space traveler, like his father.
14. First Person Shooter, such as *Doom*, *Quake* or *Half-Life*.

CHAPTER II — ORIGINS

AN RPG ABOVE ALL

Back to Japan, where Enix was very pleased with the results of *Door Door* on Famicom. The company's producer, Yukinobu Chida, sensed the public's enthusiasm for the Famicom, so cheap and easily available. Sales of the first cartridges confirmed the trend and at a meeting, Kôichi Nakamura proposed a whole series of games for the Nintendo console. These included *Door Door 2*, a version of *Neutron*, and more generally lots of action and shooter games. Chida feared saturation and wanted to start on new projects. Why not RPG? This was what Nakamura, who had bought an Apple II the previous year for *Ultima*, had been waiting for. They both agreed that it was time to bring the genre, seen as being "too complicated and reserved only for expensive computers," out of its elitist niche.

RPG had a unique aura. Figures all over the screen, a crowded interface, what the Japanese called games for *"mania"* at a time when *otaku* was not yet a common word. Famicom's success came at precisely the right time. For a publisher, one of the best ways of assessing the popularity of a platform was to consult the user surveys conducted by means of postcard-type coupons inserted into the game boxes. These forms, filled in and returned by post, revealed the players' opinions. This was common practice in Japan in those days. It is also why "complete games," i.e. those containing exactly the same equipment as when brand new, are rare collectors' items, because Japanese consumers, like the highly disciplined users that they were, generally used their coupons.

Enix teams reviewed them regularly. One day, one of the coupons stood out. Chida was surprised, a certain "Sugiyama Kôichi" had written his name in hiragana, as a child would. One of the assistants realized who it was and informed the producer: this Sugiyama was none other than the composer of the same name, who was already very successful, mainly in the pop music sector.

In 1985, Kôichi Sugiyama was a true celebrity. For more than a decade, he had been the official composer for Fuji TV and his freelance career was booming since his departure from the TV channel. Sugiyama was particularly sought after, for both classical and variety, and his jingles, whether in pop songs or adverts, were recognized throughout the country. He was a celebrity in the world of animation thanks to a number of theme tune compositions that had become classics. His work can be heard in the *Wanpaku Omukashi Kum Kum* series, to a lesser extent in *Gatchaman*, and is also on the *Cyborg 009* soundtrack. He left his mark on a whole generation of children with his title song, *Kaettekita Ultraman*[15], one of the hymns of the famous giant in the *live* series. *Space Runaway Ideon*[16], a cartoon that is still revered today, was his biggest success.

---

15. *The Return of Ultraman* is a 1971 series that marked the start of the second era of the famous hero of the *tokusatsu* genre.
16. *Densetsu Kyojin Ideon*, called *Space Runaway Ideon* in its English version, is a 1980s robot series, directed by Yoshiyuki Tomino immediately after *Kidô Senshi Gundam*. Although Kôichi Sugiyama's composition was somewhat joyful, the public would always see *Ideon* as being mostly dramatic. It has to be said that Tomino held nothing back in killing off the characters of the series. *Ideon* is thus considered to be a precursor in sci-fi for its dark themes.

THE LEGEND OF DRAGON QUEST

When he met the producer of Enix, Kôichi Sugiyama was already fifty-five years old. However, he was getting ready to compose the music for a game, *Wingman 2*, the PC adaptation of the manga and *anime* of the same name. Sugiyama was a real video game fan, to the extent that he even took the time to send in his survey postcard. When not working on his music, he loved playing *Donkey Kong*, *Lode Runner* and, obviously, shôgi. Chida mentioned his dream project, the famous RPG, and asked if the composer would like to participate when the time came. Kôichi Sugiyama agreed and the producer made a mental note of this spoken promise.

Akira Toriyama, already a star with Dragon Ball

As well as the music, the Enix project had another crucial requirement: an artist was needed to invent its universe. Yûji Horii contacted his friend Torishima, who was still working at Shûeisha. At that moment, he was actually editing a manga, whose mass publication had just begun. It was *Dragon Ball*, written and illustrated by Akira Toriyama. If you are reading this, you almost certainly know his master work, perhaps one of the world's most famous manga. Back in 1985, however, the artist was not the discreet superstar that he is today. With a square, smiling face and bright eyes, he was still allowing himself to be photographed, as testified by the many pictures from those years. He even attended meetings. The years spent drawing *Dragon Ball* literally broke him, to the point that he found it difficult to finish his work.

In 1985, Toriyama was impatient and full of ideas. However, he was also under contract with Shûeisha and it was unthinkable to leave his job, subjected to the exacting rhythm of weekly publication, for any length of time. This crazy pace was what ultimately wore him out. Then came about a relatively unusual event in the world of video games, because no one in the industry had yet collaborated with a manga publisher. Under Torishima's control, Shûeisha loaned the artist Akira Toriyama for the Enix project. The latter subsidized the RPG entirely, without any form of intervention from Shûeisha. Torishima thus managed to avoid creating a "committee," which was how most cultural projects were organized in Japan. Enix took all the financial risks.

According to Torishima[17], this was a way of protecting *Dragon Quest* from any counter-productive involvement by Shûeisha. The publisher could have slowed down or even damaged the project, for example by adding the validation stages that Japanese bureaucracy is so keen on.

---

17. https://www.forbes.com/sites/olliebarder/2016/10/15/kazuhiko-torishima-on-shaping-the-success-of-dragon- ball-and-the-origins-of-dragon-quest/#11d40be25e55

CHAPTER II — ORIGINS

Toriyama became one of the first artists credited with creating game characters, at a time when the industry was still mainly using pseudonyms to avoid head-hunting by competitors. This also meant that Toriyama received a percentage of sales, which again was rare for an artist involved in a video game in those days.

RETURN FROM EXILE

While everyone else was getting started, Yûji Horii disappeared for a whole week, without telling anyone anything. Concerned, team awaited the author's return. During this crucial week, he was recharging his batteries on Ôshima Island, having settled into a small ryôkan, spending his days wandering the countryside. He was inspired by the plains, beaches, mountains, blue skies and particularly the sea. While he was there, he decided his game would be a heroic fantasy with a simple world in which the hero ends up saving a princess from the tyranny of an evil king. With one subtle, but important detail: he imagined an adventure whose hero became stronger as he progressed. This was a fundamental difference compared with the other games of the era, particularly console games. It went against current video game conventions with characters who did not get older and whose capabilities did not change over time. A phone call from a concerned Chida interrupted the dreams of the lonely wanderer.

Horii rushed back to Tokyo and announced the title of the game to his team. It would be called *Dragon Quest*. He liked the word *"Dragon"* because it reminded him of the fantasy world, which was also his theme. *"Quest"* was a complicated word that formed a kind of balance in the title, an essential key to being memorable[18].

As an echo to the title, the last boss of the game becomes the Ryûô, Dragonlord[19] in the English version. Yukinobu Chida tells how the big hit at the time was *We are the world* by Michael Jackson, a global success that embodied solidarity and enthusiasm. The team recognized itself in this song, motivated to prove to the world that such a game was possible.

In the meantime, Kôichi Nakamura was hard at work, compensating for the lack of a keyboard. He copied Horii's idea of a graphic menu which had already been developed for the Famicom version of *Portopia Renzoku Satsujin Jiken*[20]. Nakamura developed a system with a number of windows, inspired by the financial world. The display of both the menu and sub-menus was a technique rarely used for anything other than stock exchange computers. Players could thus continue the adventure while consulting their feature points.

---

18. See the introduction of this book for a more detailed explanation of this reasoning.
19. Previously named King Dragon and DracoLord.
20. See chapter one.

THE LEGEND OF DRAGON QUEST

In spite of his skills, Yûji Horii delegated all the programming to his friend Kôichi Nakamura, known to his friends as Nakamura-kun. Yûji spent all his time on the scenario, dialogs and the actual design. He sketched hundreds of pages of squared paper pads. Each unit on the sheet was a texture representing an environment. In the end he drew them one by one to form a kind of map with squared edges. He also came up with around thirty different patterns that he tried to keep simple in order to save resources. The memory available on the cartridge being limited, each pixel was precious. Finally, each zone was attributed monsters, which would appear at random. It was important to him that the game gradually became more difficult. The two friends agreed on one thing: the overall view of the game was to be in map form, like *Ultima*, but when a combat situation arose, a short, slightly scary sound warned the player of the switch to a subjective view in a small window, similar to *Wizardry*. For the two designers, it was the best of both worlds.

Creating a game back then was a grueling task with complex constraints, and Kôichi Nakamura had to overcome many difficulties. Programming a game that scrolled on the screen in four directions was no piece of cake with the limited capacities of the Famicom[21]. Furthermore, since *Dragon Quest* is an RPG with a sizable lifetime, the question of game saving was important. Saving a game was impossible, so *Dragon Quest* used a system of passwords. These long codes of twenty characters appeared to be issued randomly, and were used to save the player's progress, including all equipment, money, etc. When the code was decomposed and analyzed, it was exactly like a haiku[22]: 7/5/7/3. This system caused significant trauma among players at the time, particularly those whose handwriting was bad, who could not spell, and of course the fools who lost their loose bits of paper. A single inaccurate character was enough for the player to get a "wrong code!" message.

Interestingly, Yûji Horii nicknamed this save code "*Fukkatsu no Jumon*," i.e. "the resurrection spell." Mischievously, he even considered including it in the game's narrative. At the end of the adventure, when the hero comes face to face with the dragon king, the latter proposes a pact, the kiss of death to allow the player's avatar to join him reigning over the world he is supposed to be protecting. If the hero accepts, the adventure comes to a sudden stop. It was the first "bad ending" in the history of Japanese role play games. Ironically, *Dragon Quest* did still propose a code to bring the player back to the very start of the adventure, level 1. A real gibe for part-time heroes. *Fukkatsu no Jumon* has become a sort of cultural reference in common use[23]. Beyond the video game context, it is cited in TV shows, like a nod and a wink to a large proportion of the middle-aged population. The resurrection spell became a very early meme.

---

21. *The Legend of Zelda*, released a few months before *Dragon Quest*, opted for a world broken up into scenes limited by the screen.
22. A haiku is a Japanese poem comprising three lines.
23. In a way, the expression described the entire code, a bit like QTE (Quick Time Event) defines the act of hitting a series of buttons shown on the screen to continue an adventure, instigated by *Shenmue* on Dreamcast.

CHAPTER II — ORIGINS

Save codes also existed in the West, although they were not known as "Resurrection spells[24]." The *Dragon Quest* and *Dragon Quest II* codes made the headlines again in 2016. A few clever-clogs found out that some of these passwords could predict the future[25]. These functional codes actually referred to current news events, thirty years later! For example, the code "きょうわと うのきりふだみ ながえらぶ なまえ," "*kyôwatô no kirifuda mina ga erabu namae*" is somewhat threatening. Once you know that "*kirifuda*" means card play, or "trump" in English, the message becomes clear. This "spell" can be translated as: "Everyone chose Trump, the republican candidate." The same code also enables the player to become a level 23 hero equipped with an iron ax and a leather shield. Some passwords have quite different messages: the wedding announcement of singer Masaharu Fukuyama with actress Kazue Fukiishi, the eruption of the Mihara volcano or the classification in order of popularity of the idols of the J-Pop group AKB48 in 2013. An astonishing coincidence for a poor man's Nostradamus, compressed into a 512 kilobit cartridge.

Hardship and creativity

Creating in times of hardship is probably the best way of doing your utmost, including in video games. The first *Dragon Quest* was completed in spite of absolutely unbelievable constraints. The memory space available was so limited that Yûji Horii had to abandon more than half of the katakanas of the Japanese language. Of the forty-five existing syllabograms, Yûji Horii only used twenty. Katakanas are generally used to transcribe western words and are essential in everyday life. They are particularly important in a heroic fantasy context. Most expressions come from years of literature and traditional role-playing games, such as *Dungeons & Dragons*. As with *Portopia*, which suffered the same problem, Horii tried to find equivalences. Although less impressive than an Oulipian[26] feat, the young designer was shrewd. If he could not write "pendant" in katakanas because the symbols were not available, he sidestepped the problem and used "ring" instead. *DraQue I* is a mosaic, a motley patchwork of making-do and big ideas.

In 1986, RPG was a blank page, and Yûji Horii gave his all. HP, magic, arms to be equipped: he set up all the bases and clichés that the West already used. As soon as the hero gets out of the game's first castle, having been informed of his quest by the king, he can see his goal, the ultimate palace of evil, home of the Dragonlord. At a time when RPG was still unknown to the general public, he felt it was important that the player could see exactly where he had to be at the end. Similarly, western RPGs

---

24. One of the best known passwords in my school playground was ICARUS FIGHTS MEDUSA ANGELS, which made the angel Pit invincible in the *Kid Icarus* game.
25. http://rocketnews24.com/2016/11/10/824026/
26. Oulipo (short for Ouvroir de littérature potentielle, the "workshop of potential literature"), is an international group of intellectuals who described themselves as "rats who construct the labyrinth from which they plan to escape."

51

demanded more efforts to learn their mechanisms. Horii simplified everything into a single menu and one button to press. He made the game so that players completed the first levels of the adventure quite quickly, meaning that no one was put off. Death was punished only by resurrection in the castle, again, to make the game more accessible to the general public. All the experience accumulated was preserved, but at the price of half the player's money. Horii again added his touches of humor[27]. For example, I love the casual attitude of the king who welcomes back the recently dead-then-resuscitated hero: "What, dead again?![28]" All the gentle irony of *Dragon Quest* is right there.

Horii also thought to write a few additional quests, to enable players to improve their level as naturally as possible. However, what was most impressive of all at the time was that he designed an open world that never blocked the adventure physically, except by monsters that could not yet be vanquished. The hero, having left the first city, could thus explore the entire map, although he had to be cautious not to be killed in a fight. The bridges between the different regions were markers, indicating the presence of enemies of greater resistance. This was one of the very first approaches to a non-linear design in the history of video games.

TORIYAMA COMES INTO PLAY

Akira Toriyama's artistic direction of *Dragon Quest* was fundamental to the saga's identity. The role of the creator of *Dragon Ball* was to conceive all the protagonists. The player's avatar is conform to design tradition: a small boy who grits his teeth, like Son Gokû, a cape and blue armor that were to become his distinguishing features. His horned helmet is a bit like that of the robot Grendizer. This was his very personal combination of warm efficiency and *kawaii*. But the most important element of *Dragon Quest* is the monsters. They are what the player sees most during the adventure, and Yûji Horii sent Toriyama little sketches of the entire bestiary to help with their creation. Toriyama interpreted the sketches, often simplifying them, removing a few lines, keeping to the strict minimum. For the Slime, the creature that was to become the mascot of the series[29], Horii sent a kind of blob of decomposing mucus, largely inspired by the basic monster in every chapter of *Wizardry*. Toriyama shaped it into a droplet, added round eyes and a blissful smile. One of the unique and exceptional characteristics of the work of the *Dragon Ball* artist is that all the monsters fix their eyes on the player.

---

27. From the very first episode and in every chapter in the saga, the player can meet a totally subsidiary character who generally offers an exceptional experience. This is systematically followed by a slightly worrying fade to black, and the sound "Puff Puff." In manga, this sound corresponds to the action of rubbing your face between a woman's breasts, generally for sexual pleasure. This recurrent gag is directly inspired from one of the first chapters of Toriyama's *Dragon Ball*.
28. "おお！しんでしまうとはなにごとだ！" is a well-known punchline for Japanese gamers, to the extent that it was used as the title of a compendium of famous *Dragon Quest* quotes, published for the thirtieth anniversary of the series.
29. See chapter 1.

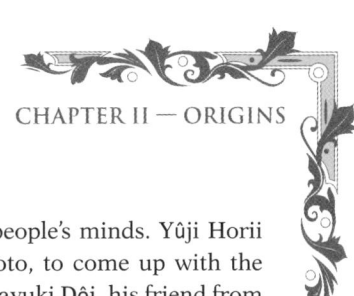

CHAPTER II — ORIGINS

The saga's logo, as well as the Slime, would remain in people's minds. Yûji Horii asked his friend and colleague from *Jump*, Kazuo Enomoto, to come up with the logo. To illustrate the instruction booklet, he thought of Takayuki Dôi, his friend from college. The actual development, which took place in a separate room not far from the Enix head office, lasted for a total of ten months and involved six or seven people at most. Everything went extremely quickly. Yûji Horii founded his own company, Armor Project. It was a structure dedicated solely to the production of *Dragon Quest*, providing a legal framework for the sacred pact he had signed with Enix. While the firm could not make *DraQue* without Yûji Horii, the opposite was equally impossible.

A WEEK FOR THE MUSIC

One important element was still lacking: the music. Remembering their previous meeting, Chida contacted Kôichi Sugiyama. This was when the *Dragon Quest* project suffered its greatest hitch: Kôichi Nakamura doubted the composer's ability to adapt to the circumstances of the game and its atmosphere. Voices were raised. Luckily, the young man set his doubts aside the next day, for the good of the company. Chida organized a meeting between the three creators. Horii and Nakamura were won over by this already old man; in spite of the large difference in their ages, he was obviously a keen and tenacious player.

And so, Kôichi Sugiyama composed the music, as well as a number of atmospheric jingles. Sugiyama used his experience from TV and his knowledge of jingles to produce catchy sounds for level increases, appearing monsters and so on. He likes to say that it only took him five minutes to write the famous *Dragon Quest* overture. After a week of tireless effort, he had eight themes for the game. What he did not yet know was just how legendary they would become: arrangements, orchestrations, nothing altered the essence of his compositions. The same tunes are used in every episode, or at least that is the players' impression. The music is an integral part of this almost nostalgic experience.

A HELPING HAND

After an epic last rush, during which all Yûji Horii's friends were all asked to participate in the tests to identify any last bugs and make sure that the adventure was perfectly balanced, *Dragon Quest* was finally finished. All that remained to be done was to sell it, which was no mean feat. A new genre, a system that was more complex than a simple action game, a recent platform. The success that they hoped for failed to arrive, falling far short of Enix's ambitions. Yûji Horii then drew out his secret weapon: he wrote a few good articles on *Dragon Quest* for *Famicom Shinken*, the video games column in *Weekly Jump*. What better than a positive review in one of Japan's most

THE LEGEND OF DRAGON QUEST

popular magazines, read by children, teens and adults alike? Toriyama's drawings helped to trigger interest on the same pages that published *Dragon Ball*. *Famicom Tsûshin*, a weekly publication on video games for consoles, was launched a week after the release of *Dragon Quest*. This was a happy coincidence, further promoting the project of Yûji Horii and his team. The rest is history.

THE LEGEND OF
DRAGON QUEST

Chapter III — The Roto trilogy

"It is the easiest thing in the world for a man to look
as if he had a great secret in him."

Herman Melville, *Moby Dick*.

CHAPTER III — THE ROTO TRILOGY

THE ATTRACTION of *Dragon Quest* has been its perpetual revival, without ever giving the impression of changing a thing. The first years of the saga, which covered a full decade, represent the period that I like to call the golden age of *Dragon Quest*. This golden age[1] refers to the origins, when all the rules and the entire universe were being created and taking form to become the well-known recipe of the series. It is full of memory triggers for a whole generation of Japanese players and has all the ingredients of its notoriety and personality: the Slime and the dragons, the epic and synthetic music, the famous three notes that indicate each "level up." The things that so affected the collective subconsciousness that Enix never changed them. This aspect is often derided by critics of the series, who are often those who started off on the wrong foot. However, I do not use the words golden age simply in reference to a nostalgic tenderness for a "time when everything was better." It was an actual period in the history of *DraQue*. The RPGs that came later are no less interesting or amusing. The idea that things were better then, that they are horrid today and that nothing will ever be the same, is an aberration and, incidentally, goes against the whole philosophy of the saga. The golden age of the series stretches over the generation of cartridge consoles that we used to blow on to get them to work better. We were a little crazy back then. This is a period that lasted ten years. And *DraQue* afforded itself the luxury of starting with a trilogy.

DRAGON QUEST II

There were only eight months between the releases of *Dragon Quest I* and *II*. Barely eight months, which gives some impression of the slightly crazy atmosphere of the second half of the 1980s, when everything happened quickly and, more importantly, went well. Subtitled *Akuryô no Kamigami*[2], this new adventure proposes a hotchpotch of ideas that Horii and his team had not been able to include in the first, due to a lack of time and memory space. The slogan used for all promotion actions was simple, almost radical in its efficiency: "The legendary hero wakes again."

---

1. "Golden, Silver, Bronze and Modern Age" are terms used in superhero comics to refer to the different eras of the genre. The Golden Age represents the creation of archetypes. The Silver Age refers to the period in which Marvel emerged to compete with DC and until the death of Gwen Stacy, a turning point in the life of Spider-Man, the hero who best represents the silver age of all superheroes.
2. Literally, "The pantheon of evil spirits," it was renamed *Dragon Warriors II: Luminaries of the Legendary Line* for its NES release in the USA.

THE LEGEND OF DRAGON QUEST

Rather than living the adventure alone, in this game, the player controls a team of three heroes. Pushing the limits even further and assisted by a cartridge with twice as much memory, *DraQue II* proposes combats with hordes of monsters. Instead of a single solitary antagonist, the enemies line up to attack. This development had a price: battle settings were abandoned in favor of black backgrounds that took up much less memory, which remained an obsession for the team. Other elements were also set aside, such as the movie images to develop the story line, which Horii ended up adding as background to the instruction manual. He also considered adding an alternative and much more dramatic ending, but there, the team stopped him: *Dragon Quest* had to remain, if not joyful, at least light-hearted.

In many respects, this second adventure was everything you expect of a sequel, being longer, more substantial and much harder. Yûji Horii actually spent a lot of time calibrating the game to ensure that the level of difficulty was perfectly adjusted. In the game's first master[3], he realized that the adventure was impossible to finish. Battle-stations in the premises provided by Enix! Assisted by the testers, some of whom were his friends, Horii went back over the statistics of each enemy to restore balance. After much effort, the development was finally complete at the end of December. It was now up to Nintendo to meet the challenge of producing enough cartridges for the big day, but this complicated rework delayed the project by a month, and it was not released until January 26, 1987. On that day, Shido became a legend among players. Ask anyone who finished the game back then if they remember the last boss whose energy was recharged at random. It was enough to double the sales of the original and make history.

DRAGON QUEST III: THE STAIRWAY TO SUCCESS

Designing a game is an adventure in itself and *Dragon Quest* was no exception. The creative challenge is to find a new way of telling a story, however simple it may be. This justifies spending some time here to describe a few of the creation stages, milestones of this golden age, starting with Yûji Horii's best memory: the moment he completed what later came to be known as the Roto Trilogy.

February 10, 1988, and the Japanese were lining up in Tokyo. In orderly lines, two by two, they will not move again until the kickoff at dawn. Lines of more than ten thousand people formed in front of every major store, such as Bic Camera. There was talk of miles of lines in the Shinjuku and Akihabara districts. From time to time, a member of staff would go down the street, encouraging people to stay in line. It was still early. At the other end, another employee held a sign: "This is the end of the line

---

3. The first version of the game before the test phase.

CHAPTER III — THE ROTO TRILOGY

for *Dragon Quest III*." The sign changed when the store opened: "*Dragon Quest III* sold out today. Next available—unknown." Small stores that picked up on the magnitude of the demand soon started proposing special offer packs to drain off their unsold stocks.

The event was covered on TV with the headline: "A first for a simple game." Reports showed the first ecstatic buyers, showing off their Famicom cartridge to the unlucky ones who turned up, hands in pockets, for the 9am opening of the stores. Yûji Horii went out to see the excitement for himself. He was delighted: his game had become more than a piece of work, it was a true social phenomenon that affected the entire population. It was a Wednesday.

THE SERIES THAT LEFT ITS MARK ON JAPANESE SOCIETY

A million *Dragon Quest III* cartridges were sold that first week. The first estimates predicted sales of two million copies for the game's entire life, but the actual figure was almost double that, reaching around 3.8 million. From then on, everyone in Japan was aware of the *Dragon Quest* phenomenon. The ritual of lining up in front of store entrances for the release of every new episode of the series gained momentum throughout Japan. Large stores set up a special organization, devoting all the cash desks on all the floors to the sale of the game, hoping to sell their first day's stocks in an organized, incident-free manner. The paroxysm of this culture of lining up on the street was reached for the release of PlayStation 2 and *Dragon Quest VII*. Thereafter, the lines became more moderate, partly due to the development of online sales and pre-orders, even in the *kombini*[4].

Horii was not the only one affected by the historic release of *Dragon Quest III*. Even today, the people who were in the street reminisce about that day. Many of the urban legends concerning the sale of *DraQue*, often relayed in the press, date back to this same period. No, the government never asked Enix to release *Dragon Quest* on a public holiday. However, the publisher did take one precaution: the major episodes of the saga were no longer released on a Saturday, or on a day when fewer people were at work and, most importantly, when there was no school. On Wednesday, February 10, 1988, two hundred and eighty-three children were stopped[5] by the police for skipping class to go and buy their cartridges.

There is no shortage of jokes to feed the collective imagination of that generation's players. Twenty-seven years later, SEGA parodied this moment of video game history in *Yakuza 0*, as part of a hilarious sidequest. Set in 1988, the extremely classy hero

---

4. "Kombini" is short for "convenience store," the name given to small local chain stores, often open 24/7.
5. Source: Fuji TV news broadcast.

THE LEGEND OF DRAGON QUEST

Kiryû has to get back a young boy's cartridge, stolen from him by a yakusa. As the story unfolds, he comes to realize that the boy's father had set the whole thing up. He wanted his son to have the cartridge on the day of its release, without realizing that the famous cartridge had in fact been stolen from his own son. It was ridiculous, particularly in view of the name of the game in question: *Arakure Quest III*.

Each release became a sort of big date, to the extent that Miyamoto admitted that the imminent arrival of a *Dragon Quest* sent the Nintendo cartridge resources and production lines into overdrive[6]. Even the manufacturer bowed down to the enthusiasm generated by the Enix series, and scheduled its releases accordingly. A rather pleasant problem to have to deal with.

Yûji Horii remained the first name displayed whenever *Dragon Quest* started on a Famicom, thus ensuring his fame from the first second of each of his games. This form of recognition for the author was completely new in this business. For example, even today, Shigeru Miyamoto, creator of sagas like *Mario*, *The Legend of Zelda* and other Nintendo mascots, all of which play a major role in video game history, has never had a game start with his name. He became known to the general public much later, towards the end of the 1990s. But let's not forget that Horii worked freelance. Unlike his game designer colleagues, he worked for himself and did not have the discipline of a *"kaishain"* or employee, an attitude that Miyamoto was keen to promote. And what Horii still wanted more than anything else was to be a manga author. He liked to imagine different worlds, and ways in which to explore them. He had a secret intention: to create a sort of harmony between the worlds he was writing, always using the same graphic, mechanical or language elements to form a coherent universe.

IMPACT ON SOCIETY

A tombstone in a village in *Zelda II: The Adventure of Link* is marked: "Here lies the hero Roto." Roto is the name of the legendary hero mentioned in the first *Dragon Quest*, a way for Yûji Horii to create his own mythology. As it was, it was a huge gesture from one creator to another, from one game to another. But this Easter egg is more than that, it is yet another pop culture reference that illustrates the range and impact of *Dragon Quest* on Japanese society[7].

Most of the elements of the first *Dragon Quest* became very popular in Japanese pop culture. The humor, as seen with the surprising personalities of the NPCs and the

---

6. http://www.glitterberri.com/developer-interviews/miyamoto-horii-discussion/
7. This was visible at least in the Japanese version of *Zelda II*. Even more amusing: Squaresoft did something similar in the first *Final Fantasy* with its tombstone engraved with the words "Here lies Link." In its American version, the Squaresoft translation team chose "Here lies Erdrick," in reference to the American name for Roto.

CHAPTER III — THE ROTO TRILOGY

"Puff puff"[8] moment, the charming little Slimes, Dragonlord, the precisely orchestrated combats and the musical contributions of Kôichi Sugiyama all define the *Dragon Quest* genre. This lore also includes the presence of a Golem guarding a village entrance, one of the game's rare bosses who became a true icon of the series. Metal Slimes, which give much more experience but are much rarer, were also present from the very first episode. There are dozens of versions of the mascot, including one with a *kawaii* rider on its back.

Dragon Quest thus made a real place for itself in Japanese culture. Even the game's vocabulary is commonly used outside the video game context. 会心の一撃, "*Kaishin no Ichigeki*," literally "critical hit," for example, has become a common expression known to everyone. A Google search brings up a whole series of surprising results, including a RADWIMPS[9] hit, which has absolutely nothing to do with *Dragon Quest*. *GanGan Ikôze* became a common word from *Dragon Quest* from version *IV*, referring to the automatic team fight: "*Let's go all-out*" is its most common English translation. Years later, Google Play based its advertising on this short and now iconic phrase[10]. In Japan, this simple command was subsequently reused over the years, ultimately becoming the name of Enix's publishing company, Gangan Comics. Paradoxically, it is not even the most popular strategic command. According to various surveys, that would be "*Meirei sasero*," literally "obey orders," which enables each character to be controlled individually.

Kôichi Sugiyama was unstoppable. *Kimikyoku Dragon Quest*, the orchestral version of his themes, was released in various formats: vinyl, cassette and later on CD. For the first time, a video game soundtrack was recorded by a symphony orchestra, the NHK, although a synthesizer version and an original medley from the series were also added to keep everyone happy. In the light of its success, from then on, Sugiyama always produced remix versions for his soundtracks. Every time, a theme in brass, in piano or vocal. He was also the first composer in the history of video games to perform a concert in public. He directed the orchestra himself and these Family Classic Concerts were held almost annually. He even used his fame to enable other artists to perform on stage. Such artists include Nobuo Uematsu of *Final Fantasy*, Nintendo's Kôji Kondô and the talented and versatile Yôko Kanno.

Aside from the record industry and the publication of its famous *guide books*, *Dragon Quest* was not a series that was easily suited to merchandising. There were

---

8. See the previous chapter.
9. RADWIMPS is a Japanese pop group that became famous in 2016 for the soundtrack of one of the biggest ever Japanese box office triumphs, *Kimi no na wa*, better known as *Your Name*.
10. In the ad, a Japanese guy who is trying to make friends in what looks like a shared house or university dormitory, recognizes the music from an episode of *Dragon Quest* on the smartphone of two young Americans. He waves his arms around to get their attention, crying out "*Gangan ikôzé*." The logic behind this ad is rather strange, but the basic idea is that you can make friends if you have a smartphone. "We are linked by *DraQue*."

no hero figurines. You might have expected to find plastic monsters in toy stores, like the slightly ridiculous baddies of *Ultraman*. However, this was not the case. It was only much later, after *Dragon Quest VIII*, that a multitude of everyday objects related to the series began to appear. However, Enix found a way to use its brand in various ways. From playing cards to school supplies, it was impossible to miss Slime, the saga's emblem. It was even said that anyone who lived in Japan during the 1980s knew how to draw this big-eyed blob. In this context, Enix launched one of the most unlikely goodies, *Battle Enpitsu*, literally "combat pencils." They were affectionately known as *"BatoEn,"* and each one carried the effigy of a monster and a number. The pencils could be rolled like dice and combats could be fought among classmates according to predefined rules. Most schools had very strict rules over games that could be brought to school and *Dragon Quest BatoEn* were an easy way to get around them. In pre-mobile phone and Game Boy Japan, their success was phenomenal. A true spark of genius!

Dragon Quest success stories were many and even more bizarre initiatives therefore followed. One example: a ballet. *Ballet Dragon Quest*[11] was one of the most extravagant examples, where tutus danced alongside video game horsemen. The troop performed more than twenty times from 1995 to 2007, even putting on a show in Shanghai. Even more eccentric, *Dragon Quest Fantasia Video* was a live action[12] film with the heroes of *Dragon Quest I*, *II* and *III* in the form of a musical, accompanied by an orchestra[13]. Craziest of all, it was produced by Toshio Okada, who went on to create Gainax[14].

FINALLY, A TRILOGY

Until now, I have purposefully left aside the background story or lore. What actually constitutes the identity of *Dragon Quest* is the traits of its creators: Horii's mischief, Sugiyama's vigor, Toriyama's clean lines. The thing is, in the shell of the first *DraQue*, Yûji Horii did not create iconic moments just because they were the first or the best known. He laid down the foundations of an edifice that players only discovered after the first three games had been released. Today, people often talk of a twist, others use the less polite (vulgar) term mind fuck. I prefer to see it as a feat of writing that I will now explain.

YÛJI HORII'S SECRET PLAN

Horii had a secret plan that is easier to understand when you look at the map of his world—which he drew himself, school-boy style, on squared paper. In the top left-hand

---

11. https://youtu.be/_naF5JwYFmI
12. A film with real actors.
13. https://youtu.be/NCfPaihOsvE
14. Gainax is the animation studio known for *Top o Nerae! Gunbuster* and *Evangelion*.

CHAPTER III — THE ROTO TRILOGY

corner of the map, there is a rather strange sector, much denser than all the rest. This part actually represents the entire game area of *Dragon Quest I*, reproduced almost in full. Going back to the initial episode was therefore all part of Horii's plan. The first *DraQue* tells the story of Lora, a full-blown damsel in distress cliché, and a hero, descendant of Roto[15], who restores peace to the world of Alefgard, threatened by Dragonlord. The adventure ends with a sudden message in English[16], even in the Japanese version:

```
        GREAT !!

     YOU REGAINED PEACE
       TO THE WORLD !

  BUT YOU DECIDED TO START
      ON A NEW JOURNEY .

    MAY GOD BE ALWAYS
         WITH YOU !
```

Set a hundred years later, the heroes of *Dragon Quest II* are the direct heirs of the characters of the first episode. The hero incarnated by the player is another descendant of the famous Roto, and his two companions also turn out to be heirs of others kingdoms from the first game[17]. The world of Alefgard, in which the two adventures take place, reveals only a few clues to any continuity. *Dragon Quest II* does not play on the connection with its predecessor. However, an overall narrative arc is revealed and everything falls into place with *Dragon Quest III: Soshite Densetsu he...*[18]. This new adventure takes the idea of an open world prototype one step further. Again, and this is a constant, what makes *DraQue* exceptional is not its very elaborate scenario, but the way in which the adventures are played out. If the story remains in players' memories, it is, among other things, because of the final twist. You think you have finished the game, but then... "Surprise, here comes the REAL last boss." Just when you think that you have done away with the demon Baramos and everyone is celebrating the return of the heroes, the party is interrupted by an earthquake. The real enemy, Zoma, lord of the dark world appears, opening a breach into the dark world, into which the hero throws himself wholeheartedly.

This has become such an overworn cliché in video gaming that it may now appear tedious having been reproduced in every conceivable manner by dozens of classics, starting with *Castlevania: Symphony of the Night*, which is perhaps the best known example. But the twist does not stop there. In this second part of the quest, the player has to find a familiar artifact, the "rainbow drop," which was already used in the first

---

15. Erdrick in English.
16. The punctuation is authentic.
17. The prince of Sumaltria and the princess of Moonburg.
18. Literally "*Dragon Quest III: A legend was born....*" In its NES version for the USA, it was first released as *Dragon Warriors III: The Seeds of Salvation*.

episode[19]. Having received the title of hero of Roto, he disappears from Alefgard, leaving his sword and shield to his descendants. *Dragon Quest III* ends with the message: "A legend begins." At the end of the title sequence, the phrase that punctuates the adventure: "To be continued to *Dragon Quest I*"[20].

DRAGON QUEST III, A CONCEPT TAKEN TO ITS LIMITS

Dragon Quest III effectively closes a circle, forming a trilogy that started barely two years previously on Famicom. Through the dialogs, Yûji Horii satisfied himself by leaving a few clues so that the player would understand that he was actually the hero Ortega, Roto's ancestor. *DraQue III* is therefore a prequel, relating the events that happened before parts *I* and *II*. With this narrative feat, he created a trilogy, the "Roto" trilogy.

Imagine the impact this experience had on players back in 1988, with no help from video games journalism and even less from the Internet. Alefgard, the original world of the first *Dragon Quest* became the underworld of this adventure, an underground kingdom, where the sun doesn't shine. The idea was that *Dragon Quest III* was a mirror, reflecting the first game, as if analyzing it and producing a mise en abîme. Visiting the same towns and villages, collecting similar objects and ending up in a dungeon that is slightly different but thematically identical: this is the route to the title of hero of Roto. The story has come full circle, and the descendant will take up the quest again in *Dragon Quest*, a flamboyant example of masterly writing, and well in advance of its time.

THE SEMINAL DRAGON QUEST

Yûji Horii introduced the notion of professions, because although the protagonist is always a "hero," the other characters choose from the typical jobs of a fantasy world. Wizard, cleric, merchant, thief, etc. These different categories have a huge influence on the capacities and feature points of the team, also affecting the spells and techniques that can be learned during the adventure. You probably already know all this, because similar systems are common, notably in *Final Fantasy*, which uses them regularly. At level twenty, a character can change class in the temple of Dharma, an element that is almost systematic throughout the series.

---

19. In *Dragon Quest III*, the "rainbow drop" creates a bridge that leads to Zoma's final castle. In episode *I*, it also creates a bridge, leading to the island of Dragonlord/Ryûô.
20. In the remake of *Dragon Quest III* for Super Famicom, the English mistake is repeated. However, this new version refers to *Dragon Quest I.II*, the latest remake on Super Famicom.

CHAPTER III — THE ROTO TRILOGY

This was also the first game in the series in which the player could chose the gender of the hero. This had few consequences, apart from certain pieces of specific equipment, but it enabled Akira Toriyama to draw two different avatars. He really went to town with the different jobs: they are both *kawaii* while remaining very typical. It was impossible to mistake a cleric for a fighter, merchant or jester. A few iconic enemies were also added to the bestiary, such as the trap-box or *"Bakudan Iwa,"* the stone-shaped head that explodes in the hero's face. The day and night cycle was another of the game's subtleties, particularly for 1988[21]. The tavern, an air-borne vehicle, Zoom, the teleportation spell and, most importantly, the save battery, also made *Dragon Quest III* a pivotal element of the series, in which the formula really took shape. After this episode, every *DraQue* bears some resemblance to it.

However, there is one other tiny, unique detail of importance. For attentive players, the entire world appears to be closely based on ours. Its different points of interest correspond roughly to those we know. Romaria is a mixture of "Roma" and "Italia," Champani[22] refers to the French Champagne region, while Assalam is an Arab land. You can guess Portoga. Even Japan is represented, with Jipang. This word actually recently became quite hip in Japanese pop culture as a metaphorical reference to an archaic but idealistic world[23]. Yûji Horii did not hold back on jokes either and, it must be said, these varied atmospheres enabled the various localization teams to have fun adding different sonorities to the dialogs[24].

Dragon Quest III, often listed as the favorite episode of the series in Japanese surveys, materializes this balance between the transparency of the quest, the different adventures and the rigorous aspect of its system. The final twist perpetuates the legend of this adventure. It is as if an entire era was summed up in a game. "That's what a 1980s Japanese RPG was."

---

21. The whole *Dragon Quest III* world follows a day/night cycle, except for Alefgard.
22. シャンパーニ in Japanese.
23. A few years later, the *Tengai Makyô* game series became a sort of Jipang reference.
24. For its American release, the language of *Dragon Warrior* was translated into imitation Shakespearian English, peppered with comical "thees" and "thous" in the manner of Marvel's Thor by Lee and Kirby. *II* and *III* continued this tradition of old English, but more common phrasing returned with *IV*. Most surprisingly, "old English" made a big come-back in the remake of *Dragon Quest IV* for DS, with a number of characters also having Scottish and Irish accents. Generally speaking, with *Dragon Quest*, as time passed, the translations became more precise and the first NES versions have little in common with the recent remakes.

THE LEGEND OF
DRAGON QUEST

Chapter IV — The Tenkû trilogy

"Without the hard little bits of marble which are called 'facts' or 'data' one cannot compose a mosaic; what matters, however, are not so much the individual bits, but the successive patterns into which you arrange them, then break them up and rearrange them."

Arthur Koestler, *The Act of Creation.*

CHAPTER IV — THE TENKÛ TRILOGY

TRAVELLING *without moving*. The title of Jamiroquai's album sums up the paradox of *Dragon Quest* in the early 1990s. The saga's evolution is difficult to pinpoint, and yet Enix and Chunsoft continued to recruit more and more people for its production. As if a monster of ambition was deploying all its strength to produce more or less the same thing: an elephant giving birth to a mouse... The Chunsoft team thus expanded, producing a number of future video game stars, such as Kan Naitô, a twenty-one-year-old genius spotted by Kôichi Nakamura and head programmer of *Dragon Quest III* and *IV*. It was all too slow for him, so he proposed an idea for a spin-off series to *Dragon Quest*, which was rejected. He left to join SEGA, founding the company Climax. He then produced two classics, *Shining in the Darkness* and *Shining Force*, a tactical-RPG[1], in quick succession. His third original creation was called *Landstalker*, and although it was a little like *Zelda* in its offer, it was actually the famous *DQ* spin-off series that had been rejected by Enix. When he left, he took with him two talented brothers, Hiroyuki and Shûgo Takahashi, who went on to perpetuate the heritage of the *Shining* brand for some years. They founded Camelot and worked for Sony, SEGA, and mainly Nintendo, creating the *Ôgon no Taiyô*[2] sagas. For Sony, they produced the original *Minna no Golf*[3]. Both were sports fans and came up with a simple approach to a game style that was previously considered complicated, developing their concept in the *Mario Golf* and *Mario Tennis* series.

I have taken the time to list the successes of these youngsters from Enix because each of their productions bears the marks and mannerisms of *Dragon Quest*, in their visual appearance or approach and particularly, the objective of being easy to control. The obvious icons of *Shining Force* and *Golden Sun* illustrate the link perfectly. The ultra-accessible *Everybody's Golf* revolutionized a genre that was previously held to be impermeable to the general public. There was also one habit that most productions found difficult to get away from: that of representing characters that walked on the spot, even when they were not moving. As if the gesticulation in its characters, even while stationary, was a meaningful feature of *Dragon Quest*, a sort of attachment to the past that was fun to watch.

In 1990, it was time for a change, or at least the pretense of change. Gone was the narrative arc lasting several games. Yûji Horii did not use the same process in the

---

1. In Japan, they were referred to by the very generic term simulation game. It was only in their ultra-simple approach that they differed from the more complex wargames.
2. Released as *Golden Sun* in the West.
3. Released as *Everybody's Golf* in the West.

subsequent *Dragon Quest*. The "Tenkû" trilogy, composed of *DraQue IV*, *V* and *VI*, is totally apocryphal. The obvious links between the various chapters of the Roto trilogy are shattered. The only affiliation between the next three games is purely emblematic. Tenkûjô, alias the Castle in the Sky for fans of Hayao Miyazaki movies, is mentioned in the fourth episode. Zénithia, in the Western version, returns in episodes *V* and *VI*, although their worlds are quite different. Horii's approach was to leave a few clues for players to use their own imagination. The Tenkû series adventures form an informal trilogy and Enix stopped communicating on this aspect[4].

Dragon Quest IV

For episode *IV*, Horii tried a new approach: he imposed a format called "Omnibus[5]" in Japan, bringing together a disparate group of adventurers with nothing in common, each one being the protagonist of his own chapter. At the end, they team up for an ultimate quest, used as a "bookend" to close the scenario[6]. This time, customization was not possible: the names, categories and aptitudes of the characters were all pre-defined. In many ways, this episode signals the return to a more linear structure[7]. Instead, there is a cart system to switch between the members of the team, which was much larger this time. This major change—which may seem insignificant—left a deep cultural footprint. Here, I am talking about the artificial intelligence of the characters. It may seem anecdotal, particularly for players like myself who prefer to control their team manually rather than involving AI, but today, if it remains in players' memories, it is probably due to the fact that most of the attitudes of these strategic commands became famous catchphrases. But we will come back to that later.

I have no wish to speak casually or with distance of this opus, however, *Dragon Quest IV* still remains one of the least popular episodes. This may seem strange: its characters and atmosphere comply with the codes set up by Yûji Horii and his team, but there is something that means that this adventure fails to trigger any enthusiasm, if only in truisms such as: "It's not the best *Dragon Quest* but still..." If it happens to be your favorite episode, I apologize, but the fact remains: this episode was always seen as a pleasant stage, but nothing more. Perhaps the strong point in the canonical series is that there is no subtext: it must be taken at face value.

A few examples illustrate this apparent disenchantment. Apple's App Store proposes most of the smartphone remakes of *Dragon Quest*, and it is generally mid-table in

---

4. It is interesting to note that the phrase "Tenkû series" was re-used several years later in official Square Enix press releases.
5. The term exists in the movie industry for anthology films, particularly in the field of animation. It refers to a compilation of several segments, generally produced by different teams. The first movie of this kind to gain fame was *Meikyû Monogatari*, called *Manie Manie* in the West. Katsuhiro Otomo, author of *Akira*, participated in four such feature films of this genre.
6. In 1994, this concept inspired Square for its own RPG Omnibus, *Live A Live*, which drew inspiration from several different worlds, such as the post-apocalyptic world of *Akira*, *2001: A Space Odyssey* and even westerns.
7. Remember the unlimited exploration of the first *Dragon Quest*.

CHAPTER IV — THE TENKÛ TRILOGY

terms of number of downloads[8]. Similarly, in the popularity charts for the series' episodes published regularly in the Famitsû magazine and based on its readers' opinions, it always ranks fairly low. A classification defined by players on the official site[9] places the Nintendo DS edition of *DQIV* in eighth position, between *DQVII* for PlayStation and *Dragon Quest Monsters Joker 2*, while the NES version is in twelfth place. As you can see, this episode is not particularly well-loved. However, if, like me, you appreciate adventures that take their time to tell a story, develop the characters and end up with the formation of a sacred union to fight a common enemy, *Dragon Quest IV* was written for you.

When *Dragon Quest IV* came out the popular series in Japan was *Lodoss tô senki*, a saga based on the books by Ryô Mizuno[10]. There was a general increase in the number of people wanting to relate to fictional characters and seeking out epic adventures. Yûji Horii's games, while developing their mechanisms in a subtle manner, continued to propose originality with each adventure. Thus, in this fourth opus, he did not settle for a simple narrative arc by the hero, but offered seven different destinies with a larger team of characters.

For once, Horii developed his characters around their quests and objectives. His talent as a writer was no longer expressed only in his wit and a certain taste for video game dialogs. For the first time, the heroes were more than just sound boxes for the player: they were not simply avatars but had a past, hopes and a "voice" of their own. They came together to overcome Psaro, the master of evil. The protagonists' intentions remained very simple, like the saga itself. For example, McRyan, the garrison captain, a mustached, armor-clad knight, attempts to solve a mystery involving children disappearing from his land.

Alena, a tomboy princess, dreams of traveling the world with her two subjects and tutors. My favorite is actually one of the latter, Clift, a cleric, who will always be remembered as a rather average lord[11]. In *DQIV*, there is a touching preference for quirkiness, such as these almost accidental secondary heroes. More generally, it was also the first time that the lesser characters were developed in a *Dragon Quest*.

Akira Toriyama reveled in all this extra characterization, drawing heroes with distinctive personalities and not just archetypical avatars. One of them, a plump merchant named Torneko, clumsy but determined, became extremely popular. This new style of antihero was sufficiently important and memorable to become the star of his own game. Remember?

---

8. The importance of this classification is only relative, since the number of downloads is affected by the various special offers and discount sales. All the same, it is priced at one thousand eight hundred yen, i.e. approximately eighteen dollars, which may seem expensive compared with market prices.
9. Dated 2010.
10. *Record of Lodoss War* was a huge success in Japan as well as in the West, with its anime adaptation in a format that was still relatively unknown in the West, OAV (Original Animated Video).
11. Kiryl in the West, remembered in Japan as a cleric with an instant death spell that almost never worked. The kind of magnificent loser that we all love.

THE LEGEND OF DRAGON QUEST

ON TO DRAGON QUEST V, THE QUIET MASTERPIECE

There is a natural transition from episode *IV* to *V*. For the first time, the series changed platforms, moving from Famicom to Super Famicom. At this point, in 1992, Yûji Horii's work became set in terms of technique. The formula had taken shape, a bit like a James Bond movie where you know exactly what will happen... Players knew that the same pattern would be repeated in each episode: Sugiyama's melodies, the colorful world of Toriyama and exploits that would take the team of adventurers around villages and castles. It was almost as if the stakes surrounding the series were tightening up as it grew in size. This routine was also due to the fact that the same three people were always in control, with the same director, Kôichi Nakamura, from the start of the saga.

What can you do when you are almost twenty-seven, you are rich and you made *Dragon Quest* immediately after leaving school. Change was required. In 1993, Kôichi Nakamura asked Enix if he could revive an old genre that he particularly liked, the roguelike genre. Based on his memories of the 1980s, Nakamura adapted this style of exploring a sequence of randomly generated dungeons to the *Dragon Quest* universe, structured around the character Torneko, the friendly merchant in *DQIV*, remember? In *Torneko no Daibôken: Fushigi no Dungeon*, the player explores a single underground system to find silver and objects to be sold upon return to the surface to extend his store and, above all, to feed his family. Random, implacable and demanding, its slogan was "a game you can play a thousand times." It was an incredible success, with the first *DraQue* spin-off selling more than eight hundred thousand copies. *Torneko no Daibôken*[12] became a style of its own and *Fushigi no Dungeon* a name that would return regularly over the next two decades. *Fuurai no Shiren*[13], *Chocobo no Fushigi na Dungeon*[14] and of course *Pokémon Fushigi no Dungeon*[15] are all shameless copies of the *DraQue* spin-off model.

In fact, Kôichi Nakamura had had enough. If he developed *Torneko* almost in parallel to *Dragon Quest V*, it was because he was seeking a way out. Over the previous years, he had earned a lot of money. An awful lot. After the contest that made his name, Enix published an advert showing Nakamura as a hideous caricature printed on a fake bank bill. From afar, it looks a bit like a dollar bill, complete with the pyramid and the eye of Providence. Its nominative value is four million sixty-seven thousand two hundred and twenty yen, and *"Paid Royalty"* is printed under the amount[16].

---

12. *The great adventures of Torneko*, an episode that has never been released in the West.
13. *Mystery Dungeon: Shiren the Wanderer* in the West.
14. *Final Fantasy Fables: Chocobo's Dungeon*. A product by Square, Enix's competitor at the time, depicting the large chick mascot of *Final Fantasy*. Easier than *Torneko*, it offered a *kawaii*-style adaptation of the design of the series' enemies.
15. *Pokémon Mystery Dungeon* in the West.
16. This is described in detail by Toru Hidaka, an Enix programmer, in the first volume of Szczepaniak's *Untold History of Japanese Game Developers*. The money from the contest that Yûji Horii and Kôichi Nakamura almost won was in fact a total of guaranteed royalties. In other words, there was no big prize, just a promise that bore a close resemblance to an advance payment on earnings. In Japan, it prolonged the myth that video games could make you rich quickly, which was actually true for little geniuses such as Kôichi Nakamura.

CHAPTER IV — THE TENKÛ TRILOGY

Much later, Kôichi Nakamura went through a tough period that many describe as depression; he was hugely rich and had run out of ideas. The situation overwhelmed him. His company, Chunsoft, was publishing the classics of a genre known as sound novel, mainly textual adventures, like photo-stories, but with a few fixed images and occasional animations. From *Otogirisô* to *Machi* and *428*[17], he tried to introduce players to another style, simply saying that reading was actually fun. He was only twenty-seven when the fifth *Dragon Quest* came out. It was to be his last. A rarity among the companies that merged to form large conglomerates, Kôichi Nakamura is still CEO of his firm, now Spike Chunsoft.

THE POWER OF NOSTALGIA

In the introduction to this book, I mentioned that *Dragon Quest V* was my favorite episode. Now you know what the cover looks like and, of course, when we look at it, nostalgia resurfaces. Whenever you try a *Dragon Quest*, you are always looking for that first impression again, the unique feeling, the enlightening sensation that you are falling in love. I cannot deny that I was lucky to start my relationship with the saga with this episode. It embodies the perfect combination of epic moments, infinite nostalgia and trivial stakes.

In this episode, all you have to do is help villages threatened by demons hiding in forests or caves. In *DraQue V*, there is a human dimension to the plot that passes at the speed of life, and that is its true strength.

September 27, 1992, *Dragon Quest V* became the first chapter of the series to be released for Super Famicom[18]. Technically, it was behind the times. This becomes all the more obvious when comparing it with what the competition was doing and the unused capacities of Nintendo's new console. This lag was not due to a lack of implication by the team—far from it. It was simply because the development time of an episode grew longer and longer with each release. And, conform to tradition, no-one started programming until Yûji Horii had finished the scenario. Rumor has it that the story and dialogs represented a total of two thousand eight hundred pages. This was actually exactly the kind of thing that Horii liked to show the TV crews that came to film in his office: huge boxes containing the preparation material, stacked up along the corridors of the offices.

---

17. *Otogirisô*, a sound novel classic on Super Famicom, later released again for PlayStation and Nintendo's Virtual Console. The ancestor of *Bio Hazard* (*Resident Evil* in the West) where the player ends up trapped in an apparently abandoned house. *Machi: Unmei no Kôsaten*, literally "the crossroads of destiny," was one of the biggest successes on SEGA's Saturn, with an adventure set in Tokyo. This time, actors played the characters of a game that was more like an interactive photo-story. *428* is one of the cult games on Wii. Another game with real actors, it is the spiritual sequel to *Machi*. One of the rare visual novels to have been honored with release in the West, due out in 2018.
18. It is interesting to note that the translations of *Dragon Quest* would experience a long hiatus from this point until the next generation on CD-Rom.

THE LEGEND OF DRAGON QUEST

Two types of Japanese were born from this adventure[19]: Biancas and Floras. These are the names of the two heroines, one of whom the protagonist must choose to marry during the course of the adventure. The story and twists of *Dragon Quest V* were the first to have such a large impact on pop culture, to the extent that they inspired a Japanese drama[20]. But let's discuss the multitude of details that marked the imaginations of Japanese players just as much as Mario, Ryu and Fist. For example, the pet sabretooth was one of the notable elements that survived from the beginning. "What did you call your sabretooth" was the question that everyone asked. The pre-defined names to choose from did not mean anything: Pukkuru, Borongo and Guéréguéré were both absurd and meaningless in equal measure. In fact, it was this type of idea, amusing and incongruous, from Horii, that players best remember. Yûji Horii did not simply want to make people smile though. He admits that he wanted to write a "game that would make players suffer." He therefore invented an entire saga that would last thirty years. It starts with the tears of a newborn baby that the player accompanies through a childhood full of challenges and suffering. If the golden rule of novel writing is to make life difficult for the hero, *DQV*'s story is a true masterpiece. The protagonist sees his father sacrifice himself and is imprisoned for years before finally getting married and having children of his own.

Obviously I'm not saying that marriage is yet another source of suffering in a difficult life, but the issue of note here is the pain of choosing. So many more things continue to happen over several generations. The subtitle of this adventure is *Tenkû no Hanayome*[21], for an important reason. The bride achieves "divine" status, and the sky is the limit.

DraQue V is also memorable for its battle system which enables the random recruitment of enemies. They can be lined up on the battlefield alongside or instead of the heroes. The team and monsters move around in a single parade all held together by magic. Yûji Horii always said he was flattered that this system was one of the major inspirations behind *Pokémon*. In truth, the first to come up with the idea of recruiting enemy monsters for the player's own team were the creators of *Shin Megami Tensei*[22].

In addition to all these qualities, *Dragon Quest V* was the first game in history in which the heroine could be pregnant. If there is one adventure whose nature and empathy can affect a player, it is this one. The advert for the DS version proclaims: "A game for you to try humanity." The quintessence of simplicity serving efficiency. It is still one of my favorite RPGs even now, and I cannot recommend it highly enough as a starting point for the saga.

---

19. In reference to an important choice to be made by the player.
20. See the last chapter.
21. *Hand of the Heavenly Bride*.
22. The *Megaten* series, created by Atlus, proposes RPGs generally set in a near future, with lots of contemporary anchors.

CHAPTER IV — THE TENKÛ TRILOGY

Episode VI, and the end of the golden age of Dragon Quest

To conclude this golden age, Yûji Horii came up with the idea of parallel worlds. *Dragon Quest VI: Maboroshi no Daichi*[23] was the perfect end for a generation: quiet, with neither tears nor regret, almost peaceful. A great game that would remain somewhat in the shadow of its predecessor, but whose story immerses those players who allow themselves to be drawn into a sort of melancholia. A strange feeling that is difficult to identify emanates from *DQVI*, a sense of gloom that was harder to understand than usual for a *DraQue*.

Again, the period between each major release was long, almost doubling each time[24]. This delta enabled Enix to work on a number of remakes[25]. *Dragon Quest VI* thus closed this era of glory, the golden age of the series. It was also the episode that took longest to release for the West. It therefore enjoys the amplified aura of all those pesky works that were never translated[26]. In a way, this sixth opus has every ingredient of a chapter to end an era: the last adventure on cartridge before moving to CD-Rom, the last adventure with Nintendo before switching to Sony for years... it has it all.

Nakamura was no longer in charge, it was the end for Chunsoft. This new adventure was developed by Heart Beat, a studio founded by Manabu Yamana[27] who learned his trade on the remake of *DraQue III*. Enix's decision to change subcontractors was a turning point for the publisher, which thereafter collaborated with more modest companies to produce its best-selling series. The design of a canonical episode thus continued externally, unlike with *Final Fantasy*, which chose to internalize its production from the start.

Once again, this "dream factory" had all the attributes of a "vintage" episode. Released on Super Famicom, even though PlayStation and SEGA Saturn sales were soaring in Japan, *Dragon Quest VI* was very avant-garde in its "old school" approach. It should also be pointed out that *Final Fantasy VII* had already been announced when this episode hit the shelves. This further accentuated the different directions taken by the two sagas[28]. In 1995, *DQVI*'s slogan was "only a *DraQue* can outdo a *DraQue*." The singularity of the series was clearly accepted.

---

23. Literally "*The land of illusion*," translated as *Realms of Revelation* in the USA, and *Realms of Reverie* for the European version. The mysteries of adaptation.
24. *DQIV*: 1990, *DQV*: 1992, *DQVI*: 1995.
25. *Dragon Quest I.II* in December 1993 on SFC and Super Famicom, *Dragon Quest III* on December 6, 1996. Note that the release dates were carefully picked to ensure huge sales for the end of year festivities.
26. Similarly, *Final Fantasy V* remained the "unpublished episode" in the West for years. A similar thing happened with *Seiken Densetsu 3*, the sequel to *Secret of Mana*.
27. Manabu Yamana was a veteran in the worlds of PC-8801 and MSX. After *Dragon Quest*, he devoted his time to various *Pokémon* spin-offs before starting his own RPG series, *Denpaningen no Rpg*, for Nintendo consoles.
28. This rivalry is discussed in more detail in the next chapter.

THE LEGEND OF DRAGON QUEST

At the time, I found this episode simpler. The monster capture system is extremely limited[29]. However, it is also the most beautiful episode so far produced in 2D. Even going back to it today, it is impossible not to appreciate the craftsmanship of the graphic artists of another generation, who had had time to master their tools completely[30]. To illustrate the progress margin of the series, it was the first time that the monsters were animated.

The narration spread across several generations thus disappeared, although the melancholy remained. It took me several years, as my Japanese improved, to realize this. During my various journeys through episode *VI*, I was captivated by its unique atmosphere. And yet the protagonist is the perfect cliché, fighting amnesia before realizing that there are two worlds, his world and another, that of "Dreams." At first, there is some confusion over these two separate but totally similar realities, a concept merely touched upon in *Dragon Quest III*, for example. At the time, Japanese players referred to the "upper" and "lower" worlds to distinguish between them.

"Stories usually include a new map that appears in the middle of the adventure. Perhaps we should try and make two maps from the start," Yûji Horii remembers in reference to this era. It is therefore not surprising that *DQVI* should be the episode that proposes the most means of transport, from ships to flying beds and carpets, winged horses and even a piece of an island. Dreams and imagination are the main themes of this adventure, a voluntary reference to Windsor McCay[31].

Dragon Quest VI was released in December 1995, a whole year after SEGA, Sony and NEC brought out their 32 bit consoles. In spite of this late arrival, the fact that more than three million copies were sold for Super Famicom speaks volumes about the popularity of this series. However, this adventure marks the end of a generation in many respects. Success that was all the more remarkable given that the product was unusually expensive compared with competitor games on CD. Eleven thousand four hundred yen[32] seems unbelievable in the context of the unprecedented fall in game prices induced by Sony's aggressive sales policy. Enix struggled to fit all the data onto a 32 Mbit cartridge with a battery for saving, equipment that was much more expensive than usual. However, this did not prevent the publisher from selling more than six million copies of just these two Super Famicom games.

For those who like an anecdote, Hitoshi Sakimoto[33] worked on this episode: he programmed Sugiyama's music in the game data. The very same composer who came

---

29. It was actually eliminated from the DS remake in 2010, although Slimes could still be recruited.
30. This observation is often also made in reference to *Final Fantasy VI*, the last episode released on Super Famicom, considered by the vast majority of fans to be the best episode of its generation.
31. Winsor McCay, creator of *Little Nemo in Slumberland*, American author of graphic novels and director of animation movies during the first half of the 20th century. He is cited as a major inspiration by masters such as Hayao Miyazaki, Jean Giraud aka "Moebius," Disney and Osamu Tezuka.
32. Approximately one hundred and fourteen dollars after inflation.
33. Hitoshi Sakimoto was one of several composers for *Tactics: Ogre*, *Final Fantasy Tactics* and *Final Fantasy XII*. He was also responsible for a number pieces of music for shoot-em up games, including for the famous *Radiant Silvergun*, which I highly recommend.

CHAPTER IV — THE TENKÛ TRILOGY

up with the melodies for *Final Fantasy XII*. He was one of the few artists who worked on Japan's two biggest and most famous sagas. I choose to finish on this musical note because *Dragon Quest VI* was also the last chapter for which Kôichi Sugiyama had to worry about the space required for his jingles or the sound quality of melodies. With the end of Nintendo's hegemonic position and uncertainties over the cartridge media of the N64, the future of *Dragon Quest* would be written on CD. This was a huge advantage for the soundtrack and in terms of production in general. It also meant that Enix could lower its prices a little.

Yûji Horii had to choose between refusing to grow up and the desire to take naturalism even further. The next generation was marked by the exciting rivalry with Squaresoft. "Only one will remain."

THE LEGEND OF DRAGON QUEST

Chapter V — The Sony era

"Doom has asked you to live on your knees. Every day of this life, he's beaten you as you lie there. What do you do? You stand up."

Thanos, *Secret Wars*.

CHAPTER V — THE SONY ERA

A YOUNG boy and his father are preparing for their prayers before a *saisen*, the box inside which an offering is placed before imploring the gods. They appear to be making their ritual visit to the temple, like so many Japanese. As is customary, they join their hands in prayer. *"Hayaku demasu yô ni,"* begs the child, bowing his head at the same time as his father. "Come out, quickly." The prayer is taken up by a whole gallery of people: a couple, a middle-aged man, even a young man whose dyed hair suggests rebellion. It is finally repeated again by a pretty young girl, who opens her eyes and raises her head: *"Demasu yô ni."* A crowd gathered in front of the temple takes up the prayer in unison, like members of a sect. *"Demasu yô ni!"* The advert's message is finally revealed. *Dragon Quest VII* will at last be released for PlayStation in 1999. But this is not the end, as a couple of Buddhist monks add: *"Demasu yô ni."* That new year, Enix produced a milestone advert to remind everyone that a new *Dragon Quest* was indeed coming out. One day.

It was the start of 1999 and never had a *Dragon Quest* been so eagerly awaited. In fact, episode *VII*, or *"Sebun"* as it appeared in the press, made fans wait another eighteen months after the advert I just described was first broadcast. From January 14, 1997[1] to August 26, 2000, the path of Enix and Yûji Horii was slowed by many an obstacle. This was the beginning of a new period, the "silver age," during which the saga would be modernized.

FILLING THE SPACE

As with the Super Famicom generation, Enix tried to fill the gap with remakes and spin-offs. *Dragon Quest III* was converted for Super Famicom; an update of the classic of all classics, the episode preferred by both the public and Yûji Horii himself[2]. Even more surprisingly, to take advantage of the *Tamagochi*[3] craze, Enix launched *Arukun desu*[4] in 1998, an electronic game in the shape of a Slime, for players to take

---

1. "Two years and eight months after *DQVI*" *V Jump*, the series' eternal magazine partner announced proudly when it published the first pictures of *DraQue VII*.
2. See chapter 3.
3. The little pet animal/egg developed by Bandai, well-known to all school children at the end of the 1990s. This little gadget had a liquid crystal screen and three buttons (in its original form) for handlers to feed and wash their pet. The goal was for the pet to survive as long as possible. More than eighty million little electronic eggs were sold.
4. "It's the little Aru!" The *"kun"* suffix, a familiar term for little, was actually a pun on the Japanese verb *aruku* (to run) in the original title.

THE LEGEND OF DRAGON QUEST

care of one of these gooey creatures. The game, which was obviously pocket-sized, had a special feature: a built-in pedometer. Its success was such that *Arukun desu 2*, subtitled *Soshite, Shiawase ni*[5], was released one year later.

The most interesting project during the period before *DQVII* was *Dragon Quest Monsters: Terry no Wonderland*[6]. A spin-off game featuring Terry, one of the most popular characters from *DraQue VI*[7], is an RPG in which you spend most of your time breeding monsters. It was only fair: having served as inspiration for *Pokémon*, *Dragon Quest* used the same recipe again, with a few added extras. For example, the creatures of *Dragon Quest Monsters* were all asexual and could reproduce with one another. Another original concept for the Nintendo series, which was only copied in *Pokémon Gold & Silver*, i.e. two years later. Furthermore, a very rare occurrence in the video game world, *Dragon Quest Monsters: Terry no Wonderland* came out on September 25, 1998, only a month before the console, which was released on October 21 of the same year. *DQM*, as it was known, was compatible with both Game Boy and Game Boy Color[8].

As a seasoned strategist, Enix had waited long enough to move into the 32 bit era. More specifically, they had waited until the PlayStation market achieved five million machines before announcing their move to Sony. Of course, Horii and the others first considered staying with Nintendo, their natural ally since the outset. And for good reason: the manufacturer had a project for an optical reader, the 64DD, to be connected to the Nintendo 64. However, faced with the lack of enthusiasm for the platform, its high price and likely failure, Enix finally chose to jump ship[9]. Yasuhiro Fukushima, then CEO, took it upon himself to make sure that Hiroshi Yamauchi, the feared boss of Nintendo, did not blow a gasket upon learning the news in the papers[10]. Fukushima went to Kyoto in person to announce his decision. Legend has it that old Yamauchi merely replied "Oh, really?" Even so, Nintendo's trust in Enix was put under great strain when the company went with PlayStation. Unlike Squaresoft, Enix maintained a cordial relationship with the manufacturer[11]. It is probably thanks to this goodwill that Square was ultimately able to patch things up with Nintendo.

---

5. "*Soshite, Shiawase ni*," which can be translated as "And there was joy," is an obvious nod to the japanese subtitle of *Dragon Quest III: Soshite densetsu he*, "A legend was born."
6. *Terry's Wonderland* for its US release. I recommend checking out the cover, which is a true work of ugliness.
7. Terry's popularity can be explained by his strong resemblance to Trunks, son of Vegeta, a visitor from the future in *Dragon Ball*. Blue hair, piercing eyes and an enigmatic smile, he had all the assets of the hero of a *Dragon Quest* spin-off game.
8. *Pokémon* literally saved the portable Game Boy console, which was gradually being forgotten. To attract the new generation of players, Nintendo launched several remakes of its Game Boy, including the Pocket and Light versions. The Game Boy Color generation games found themselves in a sort of aesthetic no man's land, a kind of very basic wash drawing, almost as if the black and white pictures had been coated with colored soup.
9. With good ideas and a few innovations, notably the possibility of writing on the optical medium, the 64DD remains one of Nintendo's biggest failures. In spite of a few announcements, hardly any publishers wanted to develop games for the platform.
10. The industry had already experienced Hiroshi Yamauchi's fury when he learned that *Final Fantasy VII* was going to be released for PlayStation.
11. Enix was one of the few third-party publishers to support the N64 with *Wonder Project J2* and *Yuke Yuke Trouble Makers* (*Mischief Makers* in the West).

CHAPTER V — THE SONY ERA

THE SQUARE STORY, AS SEEN BY ENIX

I bring up Square at this point because this long-standing rival's attitude was decisive for *Dragon Quest VII* and even for the future of the company. I have been restraining myself from talking too much about this much-loved company until now. But it is time to consider the career of the eternal competitor: *Final Fantasy*.

The *Final Fantasy* story begins like that of its august predecessor: released immediately after *Dragon Quest* Famicom, its popularity finally took off with Super Famicom. Like Enix, Squaresoft[12] found the resources and time to produce three episodes for Nintendo's 16 bit console. But something happened to divide the series into two different schools: Squaresoft managed to stay aboard the technical train, while *DraQue* fell by the wayside. In fact, as we have already seen, the Chunsoft teams found it unnecessary to push the machine to its limits when the goal was to produce the simplest adventure possible. With *Final Fantasy IV, V* and particularly *VI*, Hironobu Sakaguchi and his graphic artists made huge progress in baroque imagery, pushing the resources of the Super Famicom to their very limits to showcase the wildest bosses and most bewitching landscapes... It was a matter of aesthetics and artistic choice. In three episodes, there was a real style revolution. Switching from the legacy of pixel-art with *FFIV*, this style became more somber, more evanescent with the next chapter, and certainly more affected. *FFVI* arrived, having assimilated the graphic codes of the 16 bit generation and venturing towards a more abstract, even more lyrical, representation. Whether you like *Final Fantasy VI* or not, it is difficult not to consider it as a technical triumph, and a certain form of climax.

At this precise point in their existence, what set the two sagas apart was that *Final Fantasy* had already begun its transformation. While Horii still personally supervised the development, wrote the story and read every single window of dialog for his games, Hironobu Sakaguchi remained the producer, but gradually delegated the various other tasks. Although he supervised the scenario of *FFIV* alongside Takashi Tokita, who was also responsible for the game design, he let Yoshinori Kitase take over for *Final Fantasy VII*. Although Yoshitaka Amano's paintings were important to trigger the imagination and add atmosphere to each project, his role was nowhere near as decisive as that of Akira Toriyama, who designed the characters and all the enemies for *Dragon Quest*. The much more conventional style of the latter, with simple lines that were easy to transform into pixels, was a delight for developers: it could be easily adapted, offering graphic harmony to all the games for which he was game designer. Always finding the same species of monsters confined within by a little battle window ultimately forges ties between players and their games. To a great extent, this also explains why all the adventures have a family feeling to them, each with their own aura[13].

---

12. Square subtly altered its brand over the course of its existence, opting for Squaresoft in the 1990s.
13. In Japanese, the *Dragon Quest* dialogs often seem to have been written by Yūji Horii himself.

THE LEGEND OF DRAGON QUEST

Final Fantasy systematically invents a new world[14], making a clean break from the previous episodes. Unlike *DraQue*, *FF* never remains in its comfort zone, nor that of its players. One person transposed the soul of one adventure to another: composer Nobuo Uematsu. An additional difficulty was that the artistic direction for each adventure was different each time. Make or break. The music also changed just as much as the characters and combats. Each *Final Fantasy* is completely different, with new mythologies to be discovered. It's all or nothing, since the next time around will be different again regardless. As if each story is as its name suggests, "final." *Dragon Quest* never went to such ends. Until now, its technical improvements gave the impression of having been prised into place, almost forced in. In a way, it had become impossible to make a *Dragon Quest* without its three founding talents, even from a legal standpoint. The almost fundamental difference was that, unlike the *Final Fantasy* teams, who had always been treated as employees[15], Horii, Sugiyama and Toriyama were artists, who held the intellectual property rights over their work.

The harmony of the little world of RPG came to a climax in a joint project. One fine day in 1992, Yûji Horii and Akira Toriyama were on the same flight as Hironobu Sakaguchi. They spent their trip chatting: the three of them wanted to work together on an RPG, something that had never been done before. *Chrono Trigger* was born from this conversation, a fantasy project and a gigantic enterprise involving more than twice as many people as a *Dragon Quest*. The writing was managed by Yûji Horii, who had just finished *DraQue V* and wanted to tell new adventures based on time paradoxes, which was his favorite genre at that time[16].

Along with scenarist Masato Kato, they spent many a long hour concocting the story. Akira Toriyama, in the meantime, drew the characters and *mechas*. *Chrono Trigger* is a flamboyant illustration of this period, when Square artists were studying the style of the master to be able to reproduce it properly in 2D. One of the best known photos of the team was published in *Famitsû* with one of the many stories written about the event. It shows Sakaguchi, Horii and Toriyama smiling broadly as they walk down the street. The first has his glasses tucked into his shirt, as if he had just left the set of *Miami Vice*, while the others are smoking and laughing. This is probably one of the last photos of Toriyama in public before he disappeared from the media scene.

The release of *Final Fantasy VII*, and the global passion that then followed, changed the balance of power. All the stars were aligned to crown this seventh episode with success. Another of Squaresoft's masters was called Tetsuya Nomura, a young character designer who had been in the shadow of artist Yoshitaka Amano, and came

---

14. At least, it did at the time. *Final Fantasy* broke from this tradition when Square decided to produce a sequel to *Final Fantasy X*, i.e. *FFX-2*.
15. Hironobu Sakaguchi and his team were only duly credited with *Final Fantasy V* and subsequent episodes.
16. Yûji Horii also admits to being a big fan of *The Time Tunnel* series, broadcast on NHK in 1967.

CHAPTER V — THE SONY ERA

into the spotlight with this edition. Voluntarily more commercial[17] and more suitable for 3D, his style breaks away from the voluptuous and metaphorical lyricism of his predecessor. The artist also had the presence of mind to make sure he was identified as an author, like Akira Toriyama. Like him, he then earned royalties on every product sold involving his creations. Like his characters, he became a video game star. Cloud, the hero conceived by Nomura for *FFVII*, is an ex-soldier from the elite forces with a dodgy past, but his appearance was what counted most. This character has a huge sword for churning up his enemies, obviously appropriated from *Berserk*, one of the most popular 1990s mangas. His spiky hair also recalls the Super Saiyans of *Dragon Ball Z* and he became an instant icon. Cloud thus literally embodied the era of his creation in terms of design, becoming a true symbol for Squaresoft. Adverts for *FFVII* flooded TV screens, showing the costly cinema sequences that filled three whole CD-ROMs. The Japanese publisher wanted to renew and modernize RPG, and wanted the world to know it[18]. The Japanese video game industry was booming and the resounding success of *Final Fantasy VII* placed tremendous pressure on Enix. The release of *Dragon Quest VII* was decisive for the industry as a whole.

When Enix once again postponed *DraQue VII*, due to come out in 1999, a wave of panic rippled through the industry. No other publisher wanted to release a game at the same time as this all-powerful blockbuster. Yû Suzuki made the most of this umpteenth delay to bring forward the project he had been preparing for years: *Shenmue*, the biggest SEGA production of all time, came out on December 29, 1999, just after Enix announced its postponement. "Of course," the premature release had nothing to do with that, claimed a smiling Yû Suzuki, when interviewed by *Famitsû*. At the Square Millennium Event, Squaresoft also made the most of the situation, announcing not one but three *Final Fantasy* editions, *IX*, *X* and *XI*, the last being the company's first massively multiplayer online role-playing game. Nintendo also seized the opportunity to release *Zelda: Majora's Mask*, Nintendo 64's swan song, in April 2000. Almost serene and proud of the excitement caused, Enix finally announced *DraQue VII* for August 26, 2000. Squaresoft could breathe again... there would be no confrontation. *Final Fantasy IX* arrived in stores a month before its competitor, on July 7 that same year. This may seem unimportant today, particularly in the West, but the Japanese publishers had been in a true state of panic. It was the first, and probably the only, time in the history of the two sagas that they were in almost direct competition, being released within a month of each other. And who won the duel? *Final Fantasy IX* finished with the second highest sales figures of the year in Japan. Squaresoft was disappointed by this performance, which failed to equal that of *FFVII* and *VIII*. *FFIX* sold 2.65 million copies, far fewer than the 3.8 million for *Dragon Quest VII*[19].

---

17. Part of the success of a style described as "commercial" was its reproducibility. Nomura's characters became icons copied by children and teens in their schoolbooks, probably leaving more of an imprint than Yoshitaka Amano's abstract illustrations.
18. After *Chrono Trigger*, Square worked with Akira Toriyama and DreamFactory again for a combat game, *Tobal n° 1*. An unprecedented marketing feat: a free demo CD for *Final Fantasy VII* was included in the box.
19. *DQVII* ended its career having sold 4.14 million copies, the best performance on PlayStation in Japan, even ahead of *Final Fantasy VII*.

THE LEGEND OF DRAGON QUEST

DRAGON QUEST VII

This is the first time that I have begun presenting an episode of the *Dragon Quest* saga with its commercial success. A one-off to help understand what came next and the difference in philosophy between Square and Enix. The multiple announcements and publications of the *Final Fantasy* series were actually designed by Square to cover the heavy losses due to the production, and future crushing failure, of the film *Final Fantasy: The Spirits Within*. The impact was such that the company almost went bankrupt. The feature film was in preparation for years at Square Pictures, a studio created in Honolulu by Hironobu Sakaguchi, with a budget of more than one hundred and thirty seven million dollars, and made the *Guinness Book of Records* as one of the biggest ever box-office failures. This disaster pushed Square into a storm of unprecedented magnitude in the video game industry.

Dragon Quest VII proposed very little in terms of image synthesis and movies, and certainly did not promote them[20]. And with good reason, because such sequences account for a total of less than five minutes in an adventure that lasts dozens of hours. What's more, I have to admit, they were particularly ugly. Indeed, Yûji Horii was not very happy with these scenes, which drew the player out of the immersive experience; he preferred to concentrate on the story and, in the case of *VII*, on the puzzle theme. The hero of *DQVII* is the young son of a fisherman, who lives on a little island, lost in the middle of the ocean, and who, as usual, dreams of adventure. He and his companions discover that the world in which they live is actually far larger than it appears to be. The player must then assemble all the pieces of the puzzle representing the other islands to open a magic passageway. If *DraQue VII* took so long to make, it is because Yûji Horii and his team worked their fingers to the bone to perfect this aspect of the game. The resulting episode is the longest in the entire series! In its original version[21], the first combat only comes about after three hours' play. Similarly, it takes twenty hours to get to the job system. The adventure's flow is voluntarily different, a real mosaic of little parts tenuously linked together.

A PATCHWORK OF ISLANDS

Instead of having a single planet spread over a large map, the team leaves a tiny island to explore other continents. Before the journey begins, however, you have to collect up the different bits of the map and place them on the right stand, a bit like putting together the pieces of a jigsaw puzzle. The heroes are then transported to their new destination, but in the past. There is obviously always a problem or a curse over a castle or a demon threatening the poor peasants. Having overcome the obstacle,

---

20. To promote its hit, Enix chose the most famous J-POP group at the time: SMAP.
21. The disjointed rhythm imposed at the start of the adventure was modified for the 3DS version. However, it remains equally surprising for a present-day RPG.

CHAPTER V — THE SONY ERA

the team can go back to their home port, but with the possibility of visiting this new place, now free of any threat, in the hero's own time and not just in the past. *Dragon Quest VII* is a journey that keeps going round in circles.

Although *Dragon Quest VII* brought the saga into a new era, along with the advent of the CD-ROM, this long adventure remains the true classic of the series. Villagers turned to stone or into animals, miracle cures to be found, lakes poisoned by a demon and even an oriental princess to be saved from a temple in the desert... this is a true *"commedia dell'arte"* of Japanese role-playing game. A small team of stereotyped heroes traveling from one world to another to ultimately slay the demon responsible for the abounding chaos. Each island visit reinforces the saga's clichés. Had the game not come out in 2000[22], *DraQue VII* would have been, in many ways, the seminal episode of a new generation, an adventure that would count. Without the constraints of a trilogy, the overall plot takes time to develop[23]. Obsessed with both the power of God and the afterlife, while remaining firmly down-to-earth, the story is woven gently and delicately, almost in dotted lines, as if each place visited was as important as the final boss. If it had been a film, *Dragon Quest VII* would have been directed by Terrence Malick. Surprisingly, it is quite complicated to finish. Not so much because of the difficulty, which is never the case with *Dragon Quest*—a game in which your characters can reach level 99—, but the real problem is the pesky bits of map that are sometimes hidden in totally trivial places, where you would never imagine finding an artifact so important for the rest of the adventure[24].

RPGs and large games in general often try to include twists which, as well as making them memorable, accentuate the thrill. *Chrono Cross*[25], *Baten Kaitos* and most of the episodes of *Metal Gear Solid* are examples that come to mind immediately. The end of *Dragon Quest III*, when the player thinks he has finished while in fact a whole world remains to be explored, is *DraQue*'s best attempt at a twist in the traditional sense of the term. Yûji Horii's style is transparent, and even the inevitable events experienced by the protagonist of *Dragon Quest V* seem to be logical. With *Dragon Quest VII*, he tried something else that was new to him: the anti-climax.

One of the most surprising moments remains the way in which Kiefer leaves the adventure. This young blond noble, heir to the throne of Estard, is impetuous, with plenty of personality, almost like a Rabelais character. Eighteen years old, he hates the protocols and customs of his rank and joins the heroes in their quest to head the expedition, sometimes taking his companions for his servants. We, however, know that it is not Kiefer in the middle of the game cover, but he has not yet realized that he is not the center of the world. This character alone represents a turning point in the conventions of fantasy. In *DraQue VII*, it is the fisherman's son, i.e. the hero, not the noble, who realizes as the adventure goes on that "real life is elsewhere" when he

---

22. As usual, there was a timing problem in *Dragon Quest*. In 2000, PlayStation 2 was already available.
23. You almost wonder if the last boss was not added at the very end to fill a possible gap.
24. In the 3DS remake, Yûji Horii and his team purposely simplified this by adding a sort of magic radar in the corner of the screen to indicate the presence of a piece of map. It is a bit like finding the crystal balls in *Dragon Ball*.
25. The "sequel" to *Chrono Trigger*.

makes friends with a tribe of nomads. After many hours of play, vanquished enemies and more or less unexpected developments, Kiefer finally falls in love with Lala, a dancer. He then starts to wonder about the meaning of his life. After all, if the hero has a destiny, why shouldn't he? He then considers his inheritance. Should he run away from it? Can he throw it all away? Should he ascend the throne, as his father's successor? Is he not allowed to have love and happiness?

Kiefer's reaction may seem insignificant, but his action will be meaningful, and in total opposition to what could be expected of a Japanese RPG: he leaves the hero's team. Kiefer choses his loved one and his clan instead of continuing the player's main quest. This departure can be viewed in different ways, but the symbolism is surprisingly strong. Here is a character who actually gives up and takes another path. I have always seen this as a sort of message for the player, almost a note of irony because he, on the other hand, continues the quest with the fisherman's son and his friends. Back when Internet was not so essential, you can imagine the obvious frustration of spending thirty, forty, even fifty hours on building up a character and then seeing one of your best elements leave the team. Whenever I play *Dragon Quest VII*, I know full well what will happen and yet I still find it hard to assimilate. Kiefer is always my strongest fighter when the separation comes and I suffer every time I see him go[26].

When the goodbyes get too emotional, Kiefer pushes his friends into one of the space-time portals. Later in the adventure, the player discovers a message directly addressed to the hero, engraved on a stone tablet by Kiefer himself. He asks that his father be reassured as to his fate: he has married and is still with the same tribe. This tablet is like a message in a bottle, a letter from another era, adding a surprising element to the quest, that of the inevitable passage of time. In the end, we even wonder if Yûji Horii was not directly speaking to the player, reminding him that there was more to life than video games.

Dragon Quest VII is an adventure that ends in a confrontation with a demon claiming to be God. It is the game of extreme-center. Everything is longer and harder, but also excruciatingly normal. However, this is the episode of the return to the West. Enix had not translated its star game for almost a decade. Production costs were higher and, as we have seen, there was always the question of the right time. When *Dragon Quest V* came out in Japan, it was too harsh, too old-fashioned and, let's be honest here, a little too ugly for the owners of American SNes. *VI* could have crossed the Pacific, but unfortunately the public had already moved on to PlayStation. The very late arrival of episode *VII* in the USA, on November 1, 2001, was certainly an obstacle but, luckily, a lot of PS2s were backwards-compatible.

When it finally came out in the USA, it was called *Dragon Warrior VII*. There was no European version. The non-Japanese public had been hoping for the saga to return for exactly eleven years. The industry had also changed a lot since 1989 and publication

---

26. For a long time, up to the end of the first CD, I believed that Kiefer would come back.

CHAPTER V — THE SONY ERA

of the first episode in the USA; console roleplay had become, particularly in the early 2000s, a major genre, studied and eagerly awaited by fans. Major distributors no longer hesitated about placing these games, previously considered as niche products, in their front displays. The American version of *Dragon Quest VII* sold two hundred thousand copies, a decent figure for an increasingly competitive market. However, Enix was satisfied, knowing that it had scored one over its rival at a key moment in the lives of the two companies.

Echoing *DQVII* and its characteristic ambivalence, let's finish with a detail that may appear insignificant at first glance, but which, after greater examination, proves to be of importance: the cover. The illustration on the game box, produced as usual by Akira Toriyama, had never been so trivial, comprising just three characters and a simple background. Since *Dragon Quest VI*, the heroes on the covers had all been smiling, but on *VII*, they looked absolutely carefree. More careful study revealed that something had changed, because although the clear lines of Toriyama were recognizable, the coloring was different. Indeed, from this episode onwards, the master used a computer to apply the color[27]. Not only was the texture different, being more uniform, but the shading possibilities were also improved. The sense of urgency, accident and expertise that only a hand-held brush can achieve were gone. With this new processing technique, the *Dragon Quest* saga once again showed that it was entering a new, more modern phase.

THE MERGER

In the early morning of April 1, 2003, *Final Fantasy XI* players witnessed a mandatory update. I switched on my PlayStation 2 and its hard disk. The modification was microscopic, barely a few megabytes, taking only a few seconds to download and the program rebooted as usual. There had been a minor but quite important cosmetic modification: the legal details were different. *FFXI* had become the first game marked Square Enix, the new entity born of the merger of two giants. As you can imagine, such an event did not happen overnight: the companies had been discreetly negotiating an agreement for three years. The two companies were in quite different situations. Squaresoft had been in financial difficulty since the fiasco of the film *Final Fantasy: The Spirits Within* and Enix did not want to sit down at the table with a partner that was losing money. However, Square had been partly recapitalized by Sony, which then held 18.6%, and the recent success of *Final Fantasy X* and *Kingdom Hearts* was helping to restore the company's image.

Enix had never aimed to become a movie studio. The only time the publisher had used real actors was to film adverts for its games in Spain and the Czech Republic,

---

27. Akira Toriyama or someone in his studio, but it is quite possibly that Akira himself continued to do everything.

because that was where the best value for money was to be found[28]. These ads were actually wonderfully kitsch, a bit like a *kawaii* version of *Game of Thrones*. Enix showed initial interest in a partnership with Square as well as with Namco[29]. The goal, of course, was to reduce development costs and to build a joint strategy for online games. Enix was already dreaming of running an online *Dragon Quest* to equal the success of *Final Fantasy XI*. In 2001, talk was officially of a "partnership" to avoid getting in too deep too quickly with a publisher in difficulty, as was the case of Square. In terms of finance, Enix was doing well, but the multiple delays of *Dragon Quest VII* were having an impact. The stock market value of the company was roller-coastering, falling by 40% in 1999, when episode *VII* was postponed again. It was perhaps logical that they were paying for ads in which Japanese people were praying in temples for their favorite game to come out.

Although Square was going through a difficult patch, its PlayStation period was flourishing, alternating commercial successes with audacious gambles. Behind *Final Fantasy*, there was the success of *Parasite Eve*, which tried to close the gap between survival horrors like *Bio Hazard/Resident Evil* and traditional RPGs. During this five-year period of video games, major sagas were developed, like *Front Mission*[30]. "Just under a million" copies sold for *Xenogears*, but this was a unique work, perhaps never equaled in its genre[31]. Remember Kôichi Nakamura, the genius director of episodes *I* to *V* of *Dragon Quest*? He was hired as a consultant for the first *Chocobo no Fushigi na Dungeon*[32]. Yes, a clone of the game he designed with Torneko, the debonair anti-hero of *Dragon Quest IV*. It was the first time a publisher pushed copying so far as to hire its inventor. Similarly, Square hired Yasumi Matsuno, Hiroshi Minagawa and Akihiko Yoshida, the three creators and artists of the *Ogre Battle* series, to produce a clone of their hit, *Tactics Ogre*[33], one of the most esteemed games of all time in Japan. This project became *Final Fantasy Tactics*, a tactical-RPG at least as popular in the West. A few years later, Square actually bought the entire company Quest to develop sequels to *Final Fantasy Tactics*[34]. This enabled Yasumi Matsuno to work on *Vagrant Story*,

---

28. I will discuss the different animated adaptations later in this book.
29. A few years later, Namco merged with Bandai on April 1, 2008, after the latter narrowly missed the chance of being bought out by SEGA. It was a time of mergers and acquisitions throughout the Japanese video game industry.
30. *Front Mission*, developed by the small, independent studio, G-Craft, became a kind of system laboratory for *Final Fantasy* because its producer, Toshirô Tsuchida, went on to produce the battles of *Final Fantasy X, XIII* and add his touch to various other projects.
31. Originally proposed as an outline for an episode of *Final Fantasy*, *Xenogears* is a mixture of RPG and robots, which was quite unique at the time. Its movie sequences were animated by the studio I.G, which also made the *Ghost in the Shell* films. In spite of its esteemed status, Square never agreed to produce a sequel, which resulted in its creator, Tetsuya Takahashi, leaving the company. He founded Monolith Soft. Today, he continues to make his "Xeno" games as the *Xenoblade* series for Nintendo.
32. *Chocobo no Fushigi na Dungeon*, alias *Chocobo's Mystery Dungeon* in the West, is a clone of the roguelike game invented by Kôichi Nakamura. To distinguish them, the latter insisted on the difference between the *Fushigi "No"* of *Dragon Quest* and Torneko and the *Fushigi "Na"* of the Chocobos, the little mascot of *Final Fantasy*.
33. Released on Super Famicom, for many years *Tactics Ogre* remained at the top of the chart tables published weekly by the magazine *Famitsû*. It is impossible to say whether this classification was infiltrated by a small group of fans of Yasumi Matsuno's work, but it gives an idea of the impact of this tactical-RPG on Japanese gamers.
34. *Final Fantasy Tactics Advance* and *A2*, sequels that were nowhere near as good as the original opus.

CHAPTER V — THE SONY ERA

his most ambitious PlayStation game, released just in time for the launch of the PS2. There were also the "treats," not exactly monuments but a few pleasant surprises. *Bushido Blade*, a samurai simulator, in which you could slay someone with a single swing of a sword, *Eïnhander*, an enigmatic shoot-em up, and the series of *SaGa* are all good examples that represent this highly versatile company perfectly[35].

A comparison with Enix's PlayStation era is required. Their greatest critical success of this period was definitely *Valkyrie Profile*[36], made by tri-Ace, a studio also responsible for the *Star Ocean* series, Enix's "sci-fi"-type RPG. Yôsuke Saitô, future producer of *Dragon Quest X* and *XI*, started out on full motion video games, placing actors in unusual situations, such as in *Eurasia Express Satsujinjiken*[37]. With the exception of *Dragon Quest*, these projects were generally small compared with those of Square. You might remember *Bust-a-Move*, a musical game released when this genre was booming in 1998. I know that Enix's commentators have sung their praises, but it is difficult to consider *Astrônoka*, *Planet Laika* and *Rakugaki Showtime* as anything other than anecdotal. At best, they find favor with the niche tastes of Japanese gamers. My favorite among them is the bizarre *Segare Ijiri*. In the self-proclaimed "*KusoGué*", literally "shitty game", the player controls an arrow-headed character. A multitude of coprophilic and unpleasant jokes have turned this "thing" into something of a value for collectors of games so stupid that they become delectable[38].

Enix became a *Dragon Quest*-dependent publisher and, to avoid being caught up in the same difficulties as Square, the firm began a hegemonic phase to diversify its activity. In 2001, it invested ninety nine million two hundred thousand yen in Game Arts[39]. Enix was attracted to this emblematic company because the studio, specialized in RPG with the series *Lunar* and *Grandia*, was working on an MMORPG[40] project.

The merger of the two big names was therefore logical but nonetheless, news of their agreement came as a shock to the industry. Many analysts were left perplexed by this new mammoth entity, because Square and Enix had quite different game design philosophies. Until then, the first did most of the work internally while the second subcontracted to a number of different studios.

The order of the names of the new company was "Square Enix" and not the reverse. This could be interpreted as Square having the upper hand. Furthermore, in Japan,

---

35. In spite of the enthusiasm sparked by Square releases, many games did not make it to the USA, and even fewer to Europe.
36. The tri-Ace studio was composed of the former masterminds of Wolf Team at Telenet Japan, a publisher that had made the glory of NEC and Megadrive with series such as *Valis*, *Arcus Odyssey* and *Cosmic Fantasy*. They were the only ones to defend the Mega-CD with strange, hybrid series, like *El Viento*. The team eventually split up: some of them founded tri-Ace, which mainly developed for Enix and others left to join Namco, where they created *Tales of Phantasia*, which became a reference in "Japanime" RPG.
37. In "Murder on the Eurasia Express," the actors, all *idols*, are preyed upon by an assassin on a train traveling across Asia.
38. The slogan of *Segare Ijiri* was "the worst present you could ever give." Sounds great, doesn't it?
39. Game Arts is now a subsidiary of the major GungHo Online group.
40. This MMORPG, delayed for a long time, was *Grandia Online*.

THE LEGEND OF DRAGON QUEST

this kind of detail is always important[41]. Yoichi Wada, from Square, headed the conglomerate and Keiji Honda, from Enix, was vice-president. The founder of Enix, Yasuhiro Fukushima, was named honorary president. Square once again appeared to be in a position of power. Everyone thought that the name of this new entity was only going to be temporary, but fifteen years on, it is still the same. Amateurs simply say "SQEX," conform to the Japanese tradition of compressing syllables. Three quarters of the firm's employees came from Square, which was easy to see as being a victory for the company, but behind the scenes of this merger, things were less obvious. The big bosses of Enix remained in the company's essential positions, and the cost of shares in the two companies favored Enix too. One Square action was worth 0.85 of an Enix share.

While this merger enabled Square to survive its difficult patch and perhaps to adapt to new markets, like that of the smartphone, the future revealed that the links between *Final Fantasy* and *Dragon Quest* had actually never been so overstretched. While the worlds could easily have been brought together with a few scenarists' tricks, this almost never happened. They only ever met on rare occasions, two to be precise. The Wii version of *Itadaki Street*[42], Yûji Horii's famous *Monopoly*, was one of the first neutral grounds on which the two trademarks came together in a kindly face-to-face. It was a summit meeting, a "race for fortune," tinted with humor and fun, a bit like *Mario and Sonic at the Olympic Games*. More surprisingly, they also met for *Mario Sports Mix*, also on Wii. In this game, Slimes, Metal Slimes, white mage, Moogle[43] and Sabotender[44] meet up to play dodge ball, basketball and hockey. The characters of *Final Fantasy* and *Dragon Quest* as they were, were like cousins meeting up for a family wedding, having fun together, but then not speaking to one another again. Although this changed nothing for *Final Fantasy*, for *DraQue*, the plan was to use Square's international structures and expertise to conquer the West. In general, all public relations were dealt with by ex-Square employees.

NEW HOPE FOR VIDEO GAMES

It is also likely that the new alliance made the *Dragon Quest VIII* project progress more quickly than expected. Released at the end of PlayStation's life, the seventh chapter was technically weak compared with other RPGs from the same period. Almost on principle, Enix had to rise to the challenge of making RPGs of a quality similar to what was available on the market, and in this, Akihiro Hino was a godsend

---

41. When giants Namco and Bandai merged, the group became Namco Bandai Holdings, before changing to Bandai Namco Games in 2014. This change, among other things, helped to unify the brand on the international market.
42. The English language version, *Fortune Street*, released on Wii, was the first game in the series to be translated and released in the West.
43. Moogle, or Moguri in Japanese, is one of the oldest mascots of *Final Fantasy*.
44. The recurrent cactus from *Final Fantasy*, translated as Cactuar in the US.

CHAPTER V — THE SONY ERA

to Enix. Hino, the golden boy of video games that everyone wanted back then, already had an excellent résumé. At the head of the Level-5 studio, made up of ex-Riverhillsoft[45] employees, he had proved his value by developing *Dark Cloud* and *Dark Chronicle* for Sony, two PS2 roleplay games that were well-received by the critics. The latter became one of the first RPGs to sell more copies abroad than in Japan[46].

In 2001, at the request of Yûji Horii, Akihiro Hino came to present a technical demo for a probable future RPG. The young team meeting the old. Hino was ambitious, but his company still had nothing like the reputation that it would later gain with *Professor Layton*, *Inazuma Eleven* and *Yo-kai Watch*.

The technology he presented was the same as that of *Dark Chronicle*, i.e. cel-shading, which involved lightening the polygons in an unrealistic manner to obtain a cartoon-style appearance. The process was introduced by the *Jet Set Radio*[47] game and was immediately a huge success. Bandai was also very interested in the technology, before using it in *Dragon Ball Z*. Yûji Horii saw cel-shading as a way of modernizing his saga, making it less outdated. *DQVIII* underwent a full technical revolution and, for the first time, the world was recreated realistically, on a 1/1 scale. In spite of his attachment to the stories, designing a world in this manner was something he had had in mind since the very first *Dragon Quest*. The fact that the series was now oriented by technique rather than by the scenario or its game systems was a major change.

The demo that charmed Yûji Horii was actually intended for Microsoft. Level-5 had been working on it for a long time, for a legendary unseen game, the *True Fantasy Live Online* MMORPG, a project whose pictures and videos had been haunting the dreams of Xbox owners. The rare excerpts released at the time showed absolutely sublime cel-shaded characters; I am no longer ashamed to admit it, I bought an expensive, heavy[48], Japanese Xbox solely for this game.

One day in 2004, barely five months before the release of *Dragon Quest VIII*, Akihiro Hino announced that *True Fantasy Live Online* had been abandoned. The failure of the ambitious project that pinpointed the complexity of working with Microsoft for the Japanese[49]. However, it was impossible to imagine that all these years of hard labor were not used to develop a game of great consequence for our story: *Dragon Quest VIII*.

---

45. Prolific publisher, known for its baroque games, *anime* adaptations and a few conversions, such as *Tactics Ogre* for SEGA Saturn. During its final years, Riverhillsoft made the memorable *OverBlood*, one of the first PlayStation games initially intended for the obsolete 3DO console.
46. In the five months that separated the two releases, Level-5 made a lot of changes, based on feedback from Japanese players.
47. Published by SEGA, *Jet Set Radio* first presented this technology under the name of "manga dimension" for licensing reasons.
48. The console weighed almost nine pounds.
49. Years later, *Scalebound*, by PlatinumGames, was also canceled in similar circumstances.

THE LEGEND OF DRAGON QUEST

JOURNEY OF THE CURSED KING

Early in December 2002, the first photo of *DraQue VIII* entered the meanders of the web. The textures used cel-shading, enhancing Toriyama's style to the point that it looked like an *anime*; a visual evolution that truly broke away from the previous episodes. The photo showed a character, with a bandanna on his head and a sword on his back, who we take to be the hero, running through a village. As for the decor, the change to a human-scaled avatar was immediately noticeable—the SD format[50] had been abandoned. With the release of this screenshot, the public went into shock: had Yûji Horii decided to create his whole adventure to scale? However, there was one element to reassure fans: one of the photos in circulation showed the legendary menu of the saga, cult but clumsy, still there at the top left of the picture. Yet there was absolutely no link with what was happening on the screen, as if it had simply been added to reassure the fans of the series, who might be shocked by all this modernity. If only they knew! The overall *Dragon Quest* frame was not that different in this eighth episode: the menus were still just as basic and the sound effect for climbing stairs was the same somewhat dated scratching sound well-known to early fans.

It is no insult to *DraQue VIII* to say that its main innovation was its undeniable beauty. Making the most of the best technology available, used at the right time on the right machine, PlayStation 2. I still remember my first games: I would spend hours just wandering around the same castle or simply walking alongside the walls to admire the details of their textures. This was the perfect adventure to show off Akira Toriyama's drawings, at long last. Between the first episode in 1986 and 2005, there had been two decades of *anime* imports bringing a ceaseless flood of mangas, a trend that accustomed the public to this visual style. This time, *DraQue*'s timing was perfect.

Saying that the synopses of *Dragon Quest* are trivial is an understatement! They are laughably simple, binary almost to the point of caricature. This eighth episode is no exception to the rule; it tells of a band of heroes chasing the mean Dhoulmagus, a magician who transforms people into animals. Although the content was still basic, the form was much more interesting. It is basically a chase, following a demon who is always one step ahead. It is difficult not to see the concept of the story of *Final Fantasy VII*, Square's star game, and Enix's previous competitor-turned-office-neighbor in this simple summary. Yûji Horii reused the outline of *FFVII*, adding his own comical touches. For example, Dhoulmagus' power lies within his staff and the curse is spread by contact with it. The most exciting moment of the game is when a dog catches the staff in its mouth. The dog becomes bewitched. Yes, we really are talking about a dog with a stick between its teeth. Anti-climax at its highest.

---

50. Super Deformed, or *chibi* in Japanese, is the simplified representation of manga, *anime* or video game characters, drawn with large heads on small bodies. This style was widely used by RPGs of the Famicom and Super Famicom generations.

CHAPTER V — THE SONY ERA

VIII, THE REASSURING EPISODE

The eighth, like the seventh episode, was an opportunity for the West to discover this legendary series. Over all these years, its reputation had grown from one game to the next, to the point where people would praise the saga without ever having played it. The friendly simplicity of *VIII* certainly did not put off the Europeans who were seeing the series for the first time. In spite of its technical progress, you do not get much more transparent than *Dragon Quest VIII*; it is the perfect illustration of the *ligne claire* of RPG advocated by Yûji Horii. "I am grateful for the merger [of Square and Enix], which enabled the release of *Dragon Quest* in more countries than Enix could have managed alone," he proclaimed[51] to the European journalists, delighted to present his game to a brand new audience. He had an ideal ambassador to conquer Europe because *DQVIII* was the first canonical episode to be released on the Old Continent. It did however, lose its number "VIII," becoming *Dragon Quest: Journey of the Cursed King* to avoid any confusion and questions like "will I understand even if I haven't played the other seven?" In the USA, it was published for the first time under its real name, Square Enix having obtained the copyright for the West[52]. *Dragon Warrior* ceased to exist and, with this localization, the whole world benefited from an improved version: actors lent their voices to the most important dialogs with a slight British accent to keep in line with this cloak and dagger world. The menus were also greatly improved. As a final touch, Kôichi Sugiyama's music was recorded in its orchestral version, which was precisely the type of addition to stoke the jealousy of Japanese fans[53]. Conversely, rather than making any additional effort, some of the sound effects were quite simply deleted. Unthinkable for the game's early fans.

In hindsight, what is most striking is that *Dragon Quest VIII* is the perfect echo of *Final Fantasy VII*. The latter basically relates the story of a group of heroes out to get Sephiroth, their sworn enemy. *DraQue VIII* follows more or less the same path, since the little posse formed by the protagonist and a few other colorful characters chase the demoniacal Dhoulmagus through a land already terrorized by the latter. This similarity is not coincidental as *FFVII* and *DQVIII*—to use only their initials—were the two RPGs to have launched their series on the international scene, raising them to the ranks of what are known as "AAA games." *Mutatis mutandis, Dragon Quest* is now a name that resonates throughout the world, a style recognized by a much larger population than its original Japanese audience.

With hindsight, I am not sure that *Dragon Quest VIII* deserves all this praise, but without it, the series would probably never have obtained this additional wave of popularity. Six hundred thousand copies were sold in Europe alone, in comparison

---

51. At *Eurogamer*, in January 2006. http://www.eurogamer.net/articles/i_dragonquestviii_ps2
52. See chapter 1.
53. The menus were entirely revised for the Western version, being considered, and with good reason, too obtuse and gloomy. Square Enix also added icons to make the whole experience more attractive.

THE LEGEND OF DRAGON QUEST

with the figures of episode *VII*, three times lower in the US. All the ingredients were present and, assisted by the sharp drawings of Toriyama and an irresistible and huge 360° world to explore, Horii finally had a world-famous *Dragon Quest*. This silver age, synonymous with experience and technical evolution, ended with PlayStation 2, before the unthinkable happened: Japan and its consoles lost their footing.

THE LEGEND OF
DRAGON QUEST

Chapter VI — Dragon Quest, together

"Everything communicates with something"

Roberto Juarroz

CHAPTER VI — DRAGON QUEST, TOGETHER

For more than twenty years, playing *Dragon Quest* was one of the most Japanese things you could do. Lining up in the street, waiting to buy it, then wishing the day away at work or at school so you get could home and play as soon as possible. Square Enix's advert to prepare for the release of *DraQue XI* summarizes this moment perfectly[1]. A moment full of dreams, nostalgia and, above all, the illustration of a moment of solitude. Even in Japan in the 1980s and 90s, video games were associated with the image of *otaku*, players alone in their rooms, locking themselves away in peace to be able to raise their characters up a level or two. The 2000s brought about a revolution, outmaneuvering this concept, upsetting all preconceived ideas. Yûji Horii anticipated the slump in the Japanese video games industry, bringing new life to his work: the concept of sharing.

It is often said that the Japanese games market was in disarray during the last decade. This is not quite true: it had simply taken to the hills. The previous generation of fans, and I count myself among them, preferred to lock themselves away to play video games. Having fun with a few friends meant each person bringing a controller and ordering pizza. Very few RPGs really tried to reproduce this atmosphere of friendly sharing and the best we could do was watch a friend completing his adventure. We spent many long hours taking turns watching one another progress.

Seiken Densetsu 2, known as *Secret of Mana* in the West, was one of the games that got closest to what could be described as a "friendly" RPG[2], involving cooperation. *Phantasy Star Online*[3] also revolutionized the console world, laying the foundations of a genre whose effects are still being felt today with Activision's *Destiny*. The whole concept of playing RPG with others changed radically with the arrival of mobile phones and their connectivity. I use the word radical because, in this new paradigm, we could visit other worlds without being tied to the TV screen in the living room, and most importantly, we could play anywhere.

---

1. As mentioned in the preface, this two-minute advert, only broadcast on the web, shows children, teens and adults in moments of pure nostalgia, with a single point in common each time: *Dragon Quest*.
2. It is no coincidence that the *Seiken Densetsu* games were re-released as a compilation within the first few months of the release of Nintendo's Switch in 2017. *Seiken Densetsu 2* is one of the friendliest action-oriented RPGs there is.
3. *Phantasy Star Online* is considered to be the first online console RPG experience. Created by Yûji Naka, one of the inventors of Sonic, it is similar to what is known as a "hack and slash," actually very like *Diablo*. In spite of the premature demise of the Dreamcast, *Phantasy Star Online* was a critical and commercial success that enabled the series to last long after SEGA's console disappeared.

THE LEGEND OF DRAGON QUEST

StreetPass in Tokyo

We are in front of Yodoba Akiba, one of the largest electronics stores in Japan, perhaps even in the world. When you go in, you may even feel slightly overwhelmed by the hugeness of the place, and its almost industrial treatment of customers, although the legendary standard of Japanese service quality is still guaranteed. The place very quickly became Tokyo's temple of high-tech, where people would get together and the media would come to do their street interviews[4]. However, we are concerned with what is happening outside, not inside the shop. Benches marked *Dragon Quest IX* have been set up beside the entrance, where nearby trees offer welcome shade, making it all the more pleasant. People are sat down, glued to the screens of their Nintendo DSs; they are all playing the latest episode of Horii's saga, which has become part of the urban landscape.

The StreetPass Era

July 2009 was particularly hot. It was also a time when society learned a new way of playing, thanks to *Dragon Quest IX*, because this episode enabled "group" participation: *Surechigai* was the word on everyone's lips. This function enabled the DS to exchange data automatically in the presence of other users. Furthermore, this exchange mode was always active, even when the portable console was closed and in sleep mode[5]. Thus, if you were near someone with a DS whose *Surechigai* was activated, an LED light came on to tell you that information had been exchanged between the consoles, and different bonuses granted to each player. From then on, and during the golden years of the 3DS, gamers developed the habit of checking whether they had come across another gamer, without knowing it. It was also a good reason for spontaneous little get-togethers outside, which helped you progress with your game[6].

The phenomenon was a huge success in Japan and became global when *DraQue IX* was released in the West. This was the *StreetPass* craze. People's paths crossed, they met, arranged to meet up and exchanged parts of their games tacitly, while also giving a few clues as to their identities. There was no danger for users, because the communication was indirect, remaining anonymous and perfectly controlled, but thousands of characters roamed around from one machine to another. Most incredibly of all, players were not really aware of this function, which was available in the very first DS

---

4. Akihabara station was partly refurbished in 2005, offering direct access to the store. This followed an extensive restructuring project in the district and its inevitable modernization. Akihabara can even be said to have been gentrified, and the main street there is now reserved for pedestrians on Sundays.
5. The DS design was inspired by the old *Game & Watch* produced by the same firm which was put into sleep mode simply by closing it, like a wallet.
6. When the 3DS came out, Nintendo proposed a series of games using this spontaneous exchange of data, including *Find Mii*, a sort of mini-RPG based on other users you met in the street. The players explored a dungeon and their levels were based on the number of other players encountered.

CHAPTER VI — DRAGON QUEST, TOGETHER

models. However, within a few months, the tactile possibilities of the portable console were relegated to gadget status, in favor of a new form of communication, controlled and risk-free for its youngest users. It should be noted that the excitement surrounding the *StreetPass* was a particularly urban phenomenon, particularly outside Japan[7]. Beyond the major cities, it was something of a myth. Like all fads, *Surechigai* eventually tailed off a few years later, returning sporadically at events and conventions[8][9].

Surechigai offered the possibility of a dungeon map exchange in *DraQue IX*. Whenever you completed this optional maze, you received a random new map that you could visit and distribute in turn. I spent hours exploring the various caves opened by each encounter until I finally found a map that gave me access to exceptional enemies, and fabulous treasures. I also made multiple return trips along the same corridor, to kill countless Metal King Slimes, a monster that was unusually generous with experience points. In turn, I also shared this miracle map, which ultimately transformed my four characters into demi-gods.

THE LEGENDARY MAP

One of these incredible maps was the subject of much conversation: the Masayuki map. So popular among adventurers that it became an urban legend. It was discovered by a player, supposedly of the same name, after 170 hours' exploration and spread very soon after the release of *Dragon Quest IX*, at the end of July 2009. The monsters hidden within were hugely popular and, one must say, somewhat upset the balance of the adventure.

At a Japanese developers' conference at the Tokyo Game Show 2009, Yûji Horii claimed to be stunned by the success of *StreetPass*, the function that no-one really used: "I thought it would be fun if the person discovering the map became famous," he explained, while continuing to play his DS to show off the intricacies of his design. As for the reasons for the phenomenal success of these map exchanges, he smiled at the crowd, replying in an almost magnanimous tone: "I thought that it would be interesting if reality eroded the virtual. We did it. I think, deep down, people love one another." He ends his explanation with a laugh: "It just goes to show that everyone gets all excited if there is something to be gained." And so, Masayuki and his map became part of the *Dragon Quest*[10] legend.

---

7. During the greatest peak in 3DS activity, the *StreetPass* worked in even the most remote rural areas.
8. Whenever a new episode of *Pokémon* is released, lots of gamers get their 3DS back out again.
9. The end of the *StreetPass* phenomenon is probably due to the fact that it was not included in the Nintendo Switch.
10. Masayuki became such a star that he was interviewed by *Famitsû* magazine in November 2009. He told the journalist that he had done nothing but sleep, eat and play *Dragon Quest* for two weeks, which explained why the map became available so early on.

THE LEGEND OF DRAGON QUEST

Within a few years, Japan became the promised land for these "participative" games. Since *Monster Hunter*, players had been going into McDonald's and poaching beasts on their PSPs along with other hunters met by chance, without actually talking to one another. Although not based on direct communication, *Surechigai* ended up becoming one of the most emblematic actions of its time, to the extent that it was considered one of the major marketing arguments of the 3DS some years later[11].

DraQue theme bars

Communication stunts in Japan were not limited to *Dragon Quest*: associative radios organized *DraQue IX*-themed get-togethers and theme bars created events for their patrons, offering them the possibility of recharging their consoles and logging on to free Wi-Fi. Sensing a real tourism potential, Square Enix teamed up with the Karaoke Pasera channel to launch an official *Dragon Quest* bar. The pretext was obvious: *Dragon Quest III* had made "Luida no Sakaba" an important location in the series, a place where the adventurer can create, perfect and delete his characters. Luida then reappeared in episodes *V* and *VI*. It was also where *DraQue IX* players went to organize their teams. In the West, it was generally called Patty's Pub, since Luida was called Patty in the English versions of the games. In January 2010, a real Luida's bar was inaugurated. The decor, staff costumes and even meals were based on elements of the series, either monsters or recurrent motifs from the various episodes. A risotto in the shape of a smiling Slime, a chicken leg stamped with the emblem of Roto, not to mention various ice creams and bentos. There were even cocktails named after spells[12]. Yûji Horii gave a few ideas for the menu and Kôichi Sugiyama paid a few surprise visits. In fact, if you are ever in the Roppongi area of Tokyo, the bar's chicken *kara-age*[13] is worth the detour.

Aware of the importance of the saga for the general public, Square Enix's marketing team worked wonders. For *Dragon Quest*, still not as effective as *Final Fantasy* in terms of merchandising potential, it was the start of the "collabo" era. This was what the Japanese called the partnerships and visibility exchanges between companies. The powerful Fuji TV was involved, broadcasting specific ads, while *Jump*, long-standing ally of the *Dragon Quest* saga, proposed new maps to be downloaded using a code via Wi-Fi. But the craziest stunt of all was McDonald's *no tabibitotachi*. The literal, and quite absurd, translation is: "travelers of McDonald's," two ideas that have no business being associated. A little software program could be downloaded onto the DS via the Wi-Fi network of any McDonald's restaurant. The program used precisely the

---

11. The paradox of Nintendo's 3DS was that its main sales argument was the 3D display, but the innovation that the majority of players appreciated most was the increased potential of the *StreetPass* function.
12. In 2015, for just about a month, Square Enix collaborated with HP for a special bar, serving no alcohol this time, but with PCs to be able to play *Dragon Quest X*.
13. A kind of Japanese chicken nugget.

CHAPTER VI — DRAGON QUEST, TOGETHER

same visuals as *Dragon Quest IX*, adding a large "M" logo here and there. The principle was extremely simple: a succession of battles. The only limit was that players could only play one game per day. And for fans of fast food, you could also win coupons for free hamburgers and desserts. Depending on the different operations, fans could download rare items and new quests that were only available in the franchise's restaurants.

THE CHANGE OF DIRECTION

Dragon Quest IX had a colossal influence on the Japanese industry, right from the day it was announced. This impact was not only due to good sales figures, although the *Nine* (as it came to be known) remains the best-selling episode to date in Japan as well as in the rest of the world. To understand the full scope of the phenomenon, we must go back to the day of the formal ceremony for the twentieth anniversary of the saga, attended by the members of the J-pop group SMAP[14], associated with the series since *DQVII*. When the logo of the new episode was revealed, the public and the entire web went wild. One of the reasons for this exuberance was the *Dragon Quest IX* platform. The game developed by Level-5 was for the Nintendo DS. For Square Enix, this was a strategic return to the most popular console in Japan, and no-one had seen it coming.

Logic and habit meant that the publishers moved on to the most powerful machine. Opting for the DS made perfect sense. Previously, Yûji Horii had always opted for the market's leading console. PlayStation 3 certainly ended up[15] making a place for itself, with no real conviction, mainly thanks the almost total lack of any direct competition[16]. Game development costs, which soared with the arrival of HD, further weakened an industry that was undergoing a serious transformation—at the same time, smartphones were taking over the country. In Japan, it is not uncommon to have to spend two hours on the underground to get to work, so almost everyone has a portable console. Western populations viewed the release of the new *DQ* on the DS as a backward step; the technical quality would necessarily be diminished. Never before had a major series decided to do a U-turn and propose a canonical episode on a portable console.

The announcement ceremony for *DQIX* was in full swing. SMAP members fought for the demonstration DSs provided for the occasion and started out on an adventure together. *Dragon Quest IX* was designed for a portable console and it was a multi-player

---

14. Yes, the boyband involved in *Dragon Quest VII*, SMAP, was still around. They officially split up on December 31, 2016, so there is no chance of seeing them again for *DQXI*.
15. PlayStation 3 finally overtook Wii in its last years on the market. However, global competition from Microsoft and a rather wobbly start certainly reduced its appeal. The relative modesty of Japanese publishers during this period contributed to this impression of a Pyrrhic victory.
16. So that this comment does not appear too unfair, please remember that the Xbox 360 was the most successful Microsoft console in Japan.

product. Their game was displayed on a wide screen. Characters were exploring a huge area, fighting battles in real time, not taking turns. The demo looked more like a game of *Zelda* than a traditional *DraQue*. The members of SMAP commented the adventure, watched by Yûji Horii: "Wow, we can go wherever we want" cried one of the pop icons: "Argh, a golem," enthused another. The third then made a remark that was quite astonishing given the positive reactions generally relayed by the Japanese media: "Oh, the game isn't finished yet?" The surprise and spontaneity of a banal question, but one that spoke volumes about *DQIX*. Yes, my dear Tsuyoshi Kusanagi, you are quite right. The game you are playing is far from finished. The entire development was reviewed mid-project. And even more astonishingly, the *DQIX* presented that day in Japan was nothing like the final product that was released. The action sequences with the characters wandering around swinging swords and axes at monsters simply disappeared.

Three years later, the *DQIX* demo presented by Horii and the SMAP group was nothing but a distant memory. *Dragon Quest* went back to being a traditional, turn-based RPG. However, as promised, you could still invite friends to join your quest, but the game's overall ambitions were scaled down. The project became more like a traditional role-playing game, with a gamemaster welcoming comrades into the game under his direction. This might be seen as a lazy option, but the truth about this radical change is that Level-5, restored to its technical tasks, had to review its copybook. The backstage conditions of this modification were painful. Square Enix fought bitterly with Level-5, whose name was later relegated to a less than prominent position among the legal information. Ironically, the studio was also doing its best to become the new dream machine in video games, taking over from Square Enix. For Fukuoka, "nothing is lost, nothing is created, all is transformation" and, some years later, Level-5 published the jolly *Fantasy Life*, a cross between the aborted *DraQue IX* and *True Fantasy Life Online*, the other incomplete project[17] of Hino's company. Relations between Level-5 and Square Enix finally deteriorated to the point that the little craftsman that had become great was not even invited to the *DraQue IX* launch party.

A PHENOMENON, AGAIN

To understand Yûji Horii's daring decision to return to a traditional J-RPG style, you have to remember that the *Dragon Quest* audience was actually quite traditionalistic. In episode *VIII*, fans had been shocked not to see the little black menu outlined in white which had become something of a comforter for several generations of gamers. With pressure like this, the saga was unlikely to change much, being more stagnant than the *Final Fantasy* formula which differed with each episode. The *DQ* players' reluctance to change and their taste for tradition was one of the reasons for this backward step.

17. See the previous chapter. Double irony: *TFLO*'s cel-shading technology was partly used in *Dragon Quest VIII*.

CHAPTER VI — DRAGON QUEST, TOGETHER

Short-term speculation regarded the episode's delay as causing a fall in the share price of Square Enix, which was as logical as the fact that its announcement had resulted in a rise in the share price of Nintendo. All these unusual circumstances did not prevent *Nine* from selling more than four million copies in Japan[18].

Even having been transformed, with battles in their initial form and everything else as normal as possible, *Dragon Quest IX* still deserves its status as a phenomenon. For the first time, people were talking about their adventures, inviting one another into their worlds and discussing strategies on how to overcome dangers and slay the bosses. Every week, Square Enix supplied the cartridge with quests to be downloaded and transformed the experience into a sort of epic adventure that players discovered in chapter form. No traditional RPG had previously succeeded in reproducing this serial nature, somewhere between a Dumas classic and the type of *anime* that is frequently seen on TV[19].

When Yûji Horii met Satoru Iwata, the legendary boss of Nintendo[20], he admitted that the trigger for the *Dragon Quest IX* project had been *Oide Dôbutsu no Mori*[21], the DS version of *Animal Crossing*. The simplicity of connection and the completely natural way of meeting up in a single playground made the next step obvious. The *Zeitgeist* of a mutating era is well and truly captured by this episode of the saga. I remember each session with my *Gaijin Dash* friends, helping one, being saved by another, all standing united, sharing a rather unique moment. With summer well underway, I roamed the remote areas of the isolated villages of Madeira, where I was hiking, in search of Wi-Fi in a desperate attempt to get hold of the week's latest mission. It is highly probable that *Dragon Quest IX* will escape the Square Enix remake cycle as long as it is associated with the console for which it was made. It represents a whole way of playing at a certain era[22].

SOLITARY MMORPG

DQIX was even more theoretical and more customizable that its predecessors, aiming to create the hero of *Dragon Quest III*, probably the most important one

---

18. The world-wide figure was more than five million. To illustrate the vivacity of the DS market in Japan, *Dragon Quest IX* was only the sixth best performing game on this console, behind *New Mario Bros.*, two editions of *Pokémon*, *Animal Crossing* and the second *Dr Kawashima's brain training program*.
19. There were other attempts at producing an "RPG series." The most notable is probably Capcom's collaboration with the famous Yoshitaka Amano, illustrator of *Final Fantasy: Eldorado Gate*, an adventure on Dreamcast in seven volumes.
20. Before the release of the biggest games on Nintendo consoles, Satoru Iwata granted interviews to his producers and designers, called "Iwata asks." Nintendo's CEO got on particularly well with Yûji Horii due to the fact that they were both visionary programmers and game designers.
21. Released in Japan in November 2005.
22. This is nothing more than pure supposition on my part: *Dragon Quest IX* could easily be released one day for a console such as Switch, leaving behind its *StreetPass* features. The most logical adaptation would be for mobile phones, for which the saga's most classic episodes are already available (see subsequent chapters).

THE LEGEND OF DRAGON QUEST

in the eyes of the Japanese public. The hero, or heroine, which was once again an option, was literally an empty shell to be brought to life. The character design step is a fascinating demonstration of the versatility and adaptability of Toriyama's style. We all remember the outline of the *"Dragon Ball verse,"* the hair of a Super Saiyan, the Piccolo-type extraterrestrial, the Trunks-type accessories. We all recognized something familiar in these protagonists that were invented *ex nihilo*. However, Yûji Horii still put a lot of effort into writing a coherent story that still appears to be based on the identity of this avatar, a bit like in *VIII*. This may seem to contradict the *Dragon Quest* spirit, but the player is thus returned to the heart of the story, like in *DraQue III*, which is quite obviously the point of reference for this new episode.

The characters accompanying the hero, which are also original creations, become the sidekicks necessary to make progress if the player cannot get together with real friends. In this process, there is an astonishing **MMORPG**-prototype aspect that was reworked in *Dragon Quest X*. Although Yûji Horii may have liked people in general, he preferred to keep them distant when he was having fun. As he said many times when his own **MMORPG** came out, he prefers to play all by himself.

In *Dragon Quest IX*, the player is a Celestrian, an apprentice protector of humans whose mission is to gather benevolessence until his defeat. Without wings or a halo, the Celestrian becomes visible to mortals. His goal is then to restart the celestial train that has crashed on the planet. *Dragon Quest VI* went a little vehicle mad with its flying bed, but *DQIX* deploys a whole new theme, with what is called *Hakobune*, literally "arks." In this game, it is a train called the "Starlight Express" in English. Proposing this means of locomotion in a work whose ambitions were popular to say the least is a stroke of pure genius, because the rail network is fundamental in Japanese society. It was the country's first social link, bringing together both the wealthy and the less well-off, on weekdays and weekends alike, workers as well as holidaymakers[23].

---

23. The train is so fundamental in Japan that it has become an icon to be collected and recognized: a pop culture entity, a bit like France's Eiffel Tower. It is impossible to summarize its preponderance in Japanese society herein, as the topic is vast. The train is one of the most important social vectors, like the language, traditional recipes and probably even more so, if at all possible, than baseball, the country's national sport, or even martial arts. Similarly, the train has been an atypical figure in various tales. For example, *Densha Otoko*, a romantic comedy that started as a forum chat, becoming a novel, a manga, a series then a film. In Leiji Matsumoto's work, which often features space transport whenever normal travel is impossible, the train symbolizes the melancholy of an eternal journey. The anonymous but present figure of the inspector is another fascinating concept, embodying the devotion and service that are so important in Japanese culture. One of the most memorable scenes of Hayao Miyazaki's work in *Spirited Away* is that of the young girl traveling silently in a wagon inhabited by spirits, a journey that can be interpreted in many ways, notably the heroine becoming an adult. More recently, one of the Japanese "sentai" type live series based the whole of its last season on the train culture. It has everything: the entrance ticket and turnstile, railroad switches and even the heroes' robot, which is an assembly of trains. In video games, the best known example is Taito's *Densha de Go!*, literally "Let's go on the train." (Taito is now a subsidiary of Square Enix.) Released at the end of the 1990s with the trend for realistic simulators, players drive trains according to the rules of the Japanese railway network, which means arriving precisely, to within a second, keeping to speed limits, and, of course, making the trip as comfortable as possible for passengers. Depending on the version (generally sold with a large joystick to reproduce the train dashboard), you even have to announce the destination to your passengers upon entering a station. It is no surprise that *Zelda* also explored this phenomenon with *Daichi no Kiteki/Spirit Tracks*.

CHAPTER VI — DRAGON QUEST, TOGETHER

Mangas had accustomed the public to the idea of a train flying through the skies or space, like the *Galaxy Express 999* imagined by Leiji Matsumoto[24]. There is no more explicit metaphor for an infinite journey. This message was treated brilliantly in *Dragon Quest IX* and later used again in *Dragon Quest X*, in which the train also plays a prominent role.

TEN ONLINE

While *Dragon Quest IX* uses most of the ideas defined by *Dragon Quest III*, it is, in concept, an RPG that makes perfect use of the system on which it was released. To the extent that a remake would appear to be a complex task. What would episode *IX* be like without its multiple player adventure and *Street Pass*? Square Enix's ability to make money with its previous *DraQue* editions was limited by one major factor. The new version had to become a potentially better experience so that Yûji Horii would put his efforts into it and improve his work[25]. As it was, *DraQue IX* could only exist on a portable console, more specifically the Nintendo DS. The long explorations in groups, train rides and endless sessions collecting experience points by wrist power alone would become a pleasant summer memory. Horii now had another goal: getting more people to play. He was dreaming of an MMORPG. Once more, he selected the world's most popular platform at the time and used the technical constraints to stoke his creativity. *DraQue X*, "Ten," as it became known online, was to be an MMORPG for Wii. It was the only one to come out on this console.

Summer 2012, three years after the release of *IX*[26]. It was as if *Dragon Quest* had become a date for holidaymakers[27]. I couldn't wait to take my copy of *Dragon Quest X* from its packaging and insert it into the Wii. Although I was delighted to be playing an episode of a new genre, it was not easy to watch the low-resolution graphics. HD had spread like wildfire over the past few years, with PS3 and Xbox 360, and episode *X* looked like a project created under pressure. Square Enix once again gave the impression it had taken a step backwards, by choosing an older, somewhat time-worn platform. In 2012, most players had gotten over "motion gaming," the Wiimote, and the initial enthusiasm for waving a remote control around in front of a TV screen. Wii was the best-selling machine at the time, but the project was also a test: Nintendo

---

24. Also the creator of *Captain Harlock*.
25. In a later chapter, we will return to the perpetual memory aspect of *Dragon Quest* in terms of remakes or simply porting the games to smartphones.
26. *Dragon Quest IX* came out quite quickly in the West, barely a year after its Japanese release. As for most Japanese video games, the period between releases tended to get shorter as the localization departments in the major companies grew larger. In 2017, *Final Fantasy XV* was the first episode of one of Square Enix's major sagas to come out at the same time throughout the world. Pokémon Company started doing the same back in 2013. However, delays in release dates still existed for *Dragon Quest*, which was more specifically intended for Japanese players. *X* was a special case, which we will look at in more detail later in this chapter.
27. The entire trilogy *IX*, *X* and *XI* came out in the months of July and August.

THE LEGEND OF DRAGON QUEST

had already announced its replacement product, the Wii U, and it was expected that *Dragon Quest* would continue along the same path. In ten years, the series' route had been completely erratic, almost anachronic. Nintendo's console was enjoying its last few months, but Square Enix was not put off.

X starts with a character creation phase, as was expected by *Dragon Quest* regulars. Akira Toriyama's character simulator in all its glory. My hero was, obviously, a blond-haired ersatz of Son Gokû, the most ordinary of avatars. He and his sister were living an austere life in an RPG village until a demon named Nelgel attacked their peaceful home. As always. Then along came a couple hours of introduction to the game, during which a completely new *DraQue* was presented. For the first time, the battles were in real time and all I had to do was validate the "attack" command and Kamuirobot (yep, that's the name of my hero) would strike out at the enemy until the bitter end. This introduction, surprisingly hollow, was barely long enough to cross a wide plain and reach the famous Nelgel for a merciless duel, which ended in the death of my hero. Already?

After an impossible battle, the avatar's soul was transported to a mystical place, where another Toriyamic character could be created. With this new body, freshly delivered to the world of Astoltia, the hero must find the emblems to enable him to slay Nelgel[28]. Being fed up with the "Super Saiyan" look this time, I opted for a sort of red demon, a way of expressing my affection for Piccolo[29].

OFFLINE GAME OVER

Suddenly the screen went black, displaying a laconic message. Square Enix informed me that I was not permitted to play *Dragon Quest X* outside Japan. This voluntary blockage by the publisher is the main reason for the Western population's lack of knowledge about this episode, even among its greatest fans. This had never been the case of *Final Fantasy XI*, for example, released back when the "gold merchants" trying to make money by creating a trade for the parallel objects and currency invading MMORPGs were not quite so well organized. To continue my adventure, I had to buy a router and subscribed to a VPN website[30]. The purpose of this operation was

---

28. But that was just the story of *Dragon Quest X 1.0*.
29. Piccolo is an extraterrestrial from planet Namek in *Dragon Ball* and I am only explaining this obvious fact to underline my undying love for this character, with whom I had identified when I was younger. Unlike Son Gokû, whose arrival on earth was like that of Superman, Piccolo was born on our planet, making him a true "son of a space immigrant". Strangely, none of the *Dragon Quest* characters copied his distinctive green-skinned look. It cannot even be achieved with the various character publishers of *DraQue IX* and *X*. There is a single Akira Toriyama creation that is specific to *Dragon Ball*: Piccolo and the Namek population.
30. Virtual Private Network, an inter-network connection that creates a tunnel, and enables the formation of a virtual local network. Among other things, this overcomes the network's geo-localized restrictions. If it works... the disadvantage of the system is that, in my case, I had to leave the computer switched on throughout my entire adventure.

CHAPTER VI — DRAGON QUEST, TOGETHER

to make the *Dragon Quest X* servers think that the player was actually in Japan. This may seem like a minor inconvenience to many of you, but I was no good at fiddling with my computers, being more likely to ask an expert for help with an operation that may appear elementary to some. My friend Michel, who has my eternal gratitude, came over to set it all up, and that very evening, I could finally teleport myself to Astoltia where I spent several happy weeks.

As with any MMORPG, you had to accept that it all took an incredible amount of time; hours and days that I would never get back. MMORPG is a concept that always scared me a little for that very reason and I am not alone, because I remember various disgusted comments from fans who did not want to get into an online game. For some players, it meant skipping a canonical episode, as was the case with the announcement of *Final Fantasy XI*. This attitude illustrates a rejection similar to the syndrome of a collector, disappointed that the covers of the books on his shelf are no longer perfectly aligned. But mentalities had also changed. The long term success of *Final Fantasy XI* made it one of the most profitable episodes of the saga[31]. It was time for Horii's series to take that step. The public had been somewhat taken by surprise with the Wii release, because it is hard to imagine a console less suitable for starting an online structure as complex as that of an MMORPG. USB keyboards are now recognized by all machines but Nintendo's system remains the only one of its generation to have no hard disk. To install it, this version required a flash drive of at least 16GB to fit the contents of both DVDs[32]. As I have already said, the Wii did not have high definition at a time when it was considered standard. It had Wiimotes, controllers that recognized movement. There is no system that makes you think less of an MMORPG than the Wii.

IX AND X, THE NEW GENERATION OF RPG

Although the Horii/Sugiyama/Toriyama trinity was still in control of this specific project, *Dragon Quest X* was a major upheaval for everyone because it was the first time that Square Enix did the development internally, without delegating the entire production process. The company had been working on this decisive change for a long time and a small team was working on the subject even before the end of *Dragon Quest IX*. Yûji Horii had thought long and hard about what he wanted to make this MMORPG unique and he wanted Yôsuke Saitô to be part of it. This new arrival, nicknamed "Yôsupi" by *DraQue* fans, was a big shot from Enix who had worked on *Star Ocean* and *Valkyrie Profile* as executive producer. Adventures based

---
31. In June 2012, at perhaps the pinnacle of *Final Fantasy XI*'s success, Yôichi Wada, CEO of Square Enix, announced that it was the most profitable episode of the series. This statement does not take into account *Final Fantasy XIV: A Realm Reborn*.
32. The DVDs were therefore returned to their boxes, there was no access to the disk for the whole adventure.

on actual sctors were his thing, like *Eurasia Express Satsujinjiken*[33] or *øSTORY*[34]. His masterstroke *NieR*, developed by Cavia, was considered a flop when it was first released but over time it gained its stripes, ultimately gathering a cult following, in the true sense of the word, revered by a small community of devoted activists[35]. Ironically, it was also the last game to be released by Cavia before the latter was taken over by its parent company, AQ Interactive[36]. Saitô then founded his own company, Orca, to complete the last few years' development of *Dragon Quest X*, which also meant he had to give up the idea of a *NieR* on PS Vita[37]. Fueled with confidence by the success of episode *IX*, Jin Fujisawa produced episode *X*[38], in which he was so involved that he also co-wrote the scenario, having the most experience of all the young talents involved in this adventure. He had been Yûji Horii's assistant since 1998, helping the creator of the series to write the titanic scenario for *Dragon Quest VII*. Rumor has it that Nelgel, the last boss of *DraQue X 1.0*, was based on Fujisawa's appearance, resulting in his moniker "Fujigeru," although this was never confirmed by Akira Toriyama. The common goal of this new team was not only to follow in the wake of its glorious cousin *Final Fantasy XI* and attract a younger population of players, but also to erase the bad memories of the industrial accident of *Final Fantasy XIV*[39].

Although my first explorations were made on Wii, the idea of playing flat out in bed led on my stomach, with the Wii U placed on the floor, was certainly an attractive, and possibly interesting idea[40]. The "high-quality" edition came out on March 30, 2013, just a few months after the release of the new Nintendo[41]. The fact that this improved and, most importantly, HD version, of *DraQue X* came out so early in the life of the MMORPG speaks volumes about how Square Enix planned the evolution of its product. The multiple future versions brought innovation each time, for a full multi-platform experience.

---

33. *Murder on the Eurasia Express*, mentioned previously.
34. *Love Story*, released on PS2.
35. Its sequel, *NieR: Automata*, came out in 2017. It is an incredible game, an essential for any self-respecting gamer.
36. To fully understand these companies at the start of the decade, it is important to recall the fate of each of them, although I will try to avoid any Wikipedia-type repetition. AQ Interactive (AQ for Artistic Quality) was the parent company of Cavia, as well as of Artoon (which produced *Blue Dragon*, designed by Akira Toriyama and based on a project by Hironobu Sakaguchi) and feelplus (*Lost Odyssey*, again by Sakaguchi). AQ has since merged with Marvelous Entertainment, becoming MarvelousAQL Inc.
37. Sony's portable console, which has had barely a mention in this work, since *Dragon Quest* did little to support it.
38. Only version *1.0*.
39. The first edition of *Final Fantasy XIV* was an incredible failure, to the extent that, three months after its release, the producer Hiromichi Tanaka resigned and was replaced by Naoki Yoshida. The project has since been entirely re-written and the MMORPG was re-released as *Final Fantasy XIV: A Realm Reborn*. This was a very tense period for the other leading franchise of Square Enix. It is not difficult to imagine conflicts over the *Dragon Quest X* project in this situation. In fact, the publisher was relatively candid, particularly for a Japanese company, with respect to this dry period, even including it in their communication plan.
40. In fact, it was almost impossible, considering the ridiculously short range of the Wii U tablet.
41. Released on December 8 in Japan, sales soon tailed off before the console was considered a failure by analysts and consumers. However, the idea of a tactile tablet was extremely attractive, but whether it was in the design, the concept or the finish, something, for once, did not work.

CHAPTER VI — DRAGON QUEST, TOGETHER

But that's enough technical babble; let's get back to Astoltia, where my red-skinned 'Ogre' awaits. In Japanese, *DQX* is called *"Mezameshii itsutsu no shuzoku,"* literally "The waking of five species," because, for the first time, you could play as something other than a human. As well as Ogres and Humans, you could choose the body of an Elf, a Dwarf, a Weddie (a sea species) or a Puklipo, which, as its name suggests, is a cute little character, like a slightly exasperating gnome[42]. Each land had its dominant species, which is another similarity with *Final Fantasy XI*. Although there was much debate within the team on this subject, Yûji Horii and Jin Fujisawa were adamant: there was something contradictory about a human saving the lives of all these different species scattered around the fantasy world[43]. Creating an MMORPG was an ideal opportunity to break away from convention and particularly that of embodying only humans.

From the first hours of the introduction, almost stripped of any system[44], *Dragon Quest X* became complete, like a traditional MMORPG using reincarnation, with jobs, guilds and quests—which bore a certain resemblance to *DQIX*—it had everything. Some players complained about the shallowness of all the little trials, designed to fill the time. In episode *X*, for example, they unblock special functions, an advanced job or even mini scenarios: Story Quests. These were all written by Jin Fujisawa, supervised by Horii, recalling the typical and warm simplicity of the series. The stories developed in *DraQue X 2.0* were the most touching tales that *Dragon Quest* had produced in at least a decade[45].

If the saga had evolved, it was because Yûji Horii wanted it to, but deep down, you cannot change your true character. He remained very shy and if he could avoid talking to strangers, he preferred it that way. This mentality may initially seem at odds with an MMORPG philosophy. However, he managed to make it work. Horii proposed a twelve, twenty-four and forty-eight hour character "rental" system. This had been intimated already in Capcom's *Dragon Dogma*, with "pawns" enabling players to make their hero available to others when they stopped playing.

The offline and therefore rental periods thus generated small amounts of money, and mostly very useful experience points. This avoided wasting time seeking out players of the same level—a necessary prerequisite in an MMORPG. The possibility of playing with other adventurers is not excluded and I sometimes met heroes who offered precious help, but ninety percent of my game time was still spent playing solo. It is strange to say, but *Dragon Quest X* is an MMORPG that can be played entirely alone.

---

42. Another species was added in version *3.0* of *DQX*: Dragons.
43. However, you could always go back to your original body, at the end of *DQX 1.0*.
44. Which is actually, and confusingly, called "Offline": it is of course impossible to play this MMORPG if you are not connected.
45. At least the little that I have managed to play it. I'll come back to this later in this chapter. Editions *2.0* and *3.0* are the work of Atsushi Narita, another rising star of the series.

Some of the concepts of *DraQue* were tinkered with a little to adapt to the current context. "Zoom," the teleportation spell, was limited to the mystical stones placed in the churches of various cities. Transport modes were considerably altered, offering the use of ships, trains and magic doors. Updates then brought the "Tornado," a little platform floating above the ground, which is a surprising cross between a Segway and a spinning top. Even classier, today's *DQX* players now travel on the backs of dragons.

When *Final Fantasy XI* came out, one of the biggest problems was the difficulty of going up a level. The game designers therefore came up with a system to collect offline hours to earn Genkidamas[46], the famous "balls" that doubled the experience gained over a given period of time. I particularly appreciated the idea of a salary paid regularly by the guild.

From the beginning, *FFXI* was intended for the general public, while *DQX*'s destiny was to open up the market even more. A monthly subscription was still mandatory, since this was obviously how profit was generated. However, Square Enix did not forget its younger players, allowing a free period every day, which inevitably ended up being very busy. This was known as Kids Time. For two hours a day, from 4 to 6pm and from 1 to 3pm at weekends, children, or at least those who declared themselves as such, could play for free. Japanese-style honesty: Square Enix trusted its users and even suggested they got together on servers dedicated to "kids." For the developer, the investment itself was relatively insignificant, and had no real impact on the game's profitability. The first subscription was priced at one thousand yen[47] for one month[48], and offers were available up to two thousand nine hundred yen for a quarter. Over the years, the publisher adapted its prices according to constraints and innovations, such as a day deal for the 3DS version[49]. Prices varied depending on the platform and the number of characters. Many functions still remained free, as illustrated by the 3DS application using the same *StreetPass* technology as *Dragon Quest IX* and enabling the exchange of character information. I spent many long hours, if not days, on the Wii U version, until an even shorter message than the previous ones put an end to my fun. Basically, it said: "Sorry *gaijin*, but we know you're hiding behind a VPN. So get out."

THE CURSED EPISODE IN THE WEST

Today, the absence of *Dragon Quest X* in the West seems even more illogical. There was obviously a question of cost: translating an MMORPG required a full-time team for each language, not to mention the need to moderate and monitor the game at all

---

46. These objects are well-known to readers of *Dragon Ball*: the energy ball that Son Gokû creates by accumulating the energy from various other characters.
47. Obviously exchange rates vary but this was well below the psychological barrier of eleven dollars.
48. For a three character deal.
49. Surprisingly enough, this 3DS version did not offer *Kids Time*.

CHAPTER VI — DRAGON QUEST, TOGETHER

times. Only a Chinese version exists so far to avoid neglect of the neighboring market and there has been no announcement of a possible English edition. Generally, the company's top brass merely respond "we will do it if there is enough demand," but it is probably more complicated than that. In view of the rather particular circumstances of the release of the original game on Wii, there is also a question of timing. However, the main reason, in my opinion, is a matter of choice, i.e. the initial choice of making an MMORPG for the Japanese population above all. Jin Fujisawa explained this in a keynote on *DraQue X* at CEDEC 2013[50], a conference for Japanese developers[51]. The challenge of the project was for him to convince the more reluctant parties. Although well-known at the time, the massively multiplayer game is astonishingly far more popular in China and Korea. Thus, the three fundamentals of the *Dragon Quest X* concept are, in his view: "To offer the same thing as a *DraQue*," "to be able to play alone," and finally "to have a game design that does not result in dependency," i.e. whose concept is not based on addiction, which was the main fear within his national population.

It is difficult to evaluate the success of *Dragon Quest X* in figures, but we do know that by the end of 2013, the game had sold more than a million copies. During his many interviews, Yôsuke Saitô declared that his objective was to exceed the one and a half million mark, between PC, Wii and Wii U. Special offers came out along with update launches and there were also versions distributed free with the purchase of a PC. In 2014, "Producer Yôsupi" declared that three hundred thousand players logged on every day in Japan alone[52]. It is particularly difficult to obtain and compare actual data concerning the Japanese MMORPG. A few amusing statistics have been published: more women play than men, representing fifty-four percent, there are twelve percent female elves, four percent dwarfs, seven percent ogresses, and ten percent of players have exceeded level ninety-three in all the available jobs. All these anecdotal statistics have been announced[53], but nothing to tell us more about the game's success. We only know that it is "doing well": minimal information, but customary with regard to online gaming figures.

Planned evolution

Dragon Quest X was designed to run for a total of ten years. After the PC version in 2013, came the "cloud gaming"[54] era. NTT Docomo opened a "dGame" service

---

50. Computer Entertainment Developers Conference.
51. Jin Fujisawa spoke in 2009, accompanied by Yûji Horii and producer Ryûtarô Ichigawa, to explain to the industry's professionals what had made *Dragon Quest IX* so successful.
52. In a conversation between the producers of *FFXI*, *FFXIV* and *DQX* on the *4Gamer.net* website. http://www.4gamer.net/games/139/G013991/20140307079/
53. http://hiroba.dqx.jp/sc/topics/detail/1ee3dfcd8a0645a25a35977997223d22/
54. Cloud gaming is an on-demand game service with most of the product running on remote servers which stream videos of the game being played.

THE LEGEND OF DRAGON QUEST

for use on tablets[55]. In September 2014, a rather meager 3DS conversion came out, with no keyboard, limited by the number of buttons on the console. It was not really a very successful gadget and it proved impossible to play without a very high-speed connection. I have never been able to explore it properly in spite of all the trials I have conducted. Even on a machine with a larger screen[56], you cannot always make out the characters and if there are more than twenty players in Patty's Pub, which is where most of the important actions take place, such as changing jobs or recruiting companions, all you get is a series of still shots, or GIFs of pitiful quality. When it was released, the game box[57] was severely criticized by users on *Amazon*, *Yahoo* and social networks, which led to Square Enix removing the product from stores temporarily. Ironically, this box has become a collectable, now worth more than four times its original price. The service has since improved, but it is obviously a backup offer. PS4 has the promise of technical quality, with a Full HD[58] version in 60 fps and the possibility of Remote Play on the PS Vita. This is clearly the best edition of *DraQue X*. To conclude, this overview would not be complete without the Switch, the latest platform to host Yûji Horii's MMORPG[59].

One day, shortly before I reached the end of my adventure, *Dragon Quest X* suddenly stopped working. The error message informed me that my VPN had been detected. Within the past weeks, Square Enix had set up a system to detect foreigners and kick them out. I was particularly gutted having gone to great pains to buy and install all the equipment, not to mention the game itself, on Wii and Wii U. I saw hundreds of hours of play go up in smoke. I always have the same impression with RPGs: the illusion of doing great unnecessary things, minor acts of heroism that will be forgotten on a tiny speck of a server somewhere, ultimately disappearing completely. More than any other game genre, MMORPGs involve a certain concept of wasted time.

From train to airport

For a series that everyone believed to be rooted in nostalgia, *DraQue* dealt with progress better than *Final Fantasy*, which suffered a few tricky moments[60].

---

55. But not the Apple brand.
56. 3DS XL models.
57. The *DQX* 3DS box sold only contained a download code, as did the Switch version.
58. 1920x1080 for the technically-minded.
59. The Wii version was stopped in 2017 because it had become too expensive for Square Enix to update such an old and inferior version. However, a passageway was created to persuade *DQX* Wii fans to move to Switch, with a totally free download of this latest version.
60. We have already mentioned *Final Fantasy XIV*, and although an entire book would be necessary to describe the problems encountered by *Final Fantasy* over ten years, I will recall a few details for you here. After *FFXII*, an episode whose completion was an ordeal and a director who officially "fell ill," came the *FFXIII* saga. Having gotten off to a good start, it ultimately fell into oblivion due to its perilous and truly disastrous sequels, although its heroine did become a fashion icon for Vuitton and Nissan. The saga was a commercial success, but its image was not good for the series as a whole. Finally came *Final Fantasy XV*, whose development was a series of industrial complications, dead-ends, mistakes and the sidelining of its director/designer/star, who had been in command for five years. In short, it was not an easy decade for *Final Fantasy*.

CHAPTER VI — DRAGON QUEST, TOGETHER

In one of its recent extensions, *DraQue X* explored a new dimension, introducing another "Hakobune," the famous magic train that first appeared in *DQIX*. Clues suggested that the two worlds were connected. Another theory was that *Nine* was in fact the sequel to *Ten*. There was nothing definite but fans started talking about a "Hakobune" series, like the Roto and Tenkû trilogies.

Horii and Sugiyama implied that there was a certain logic in the two adventures, which could well be continued in episode *XI*. *Dragon Quest IX* and *X* were the start of the bronze age of the series, based on communication and connectivity. I still feel nostalgic when I think of all the time I spent on it.

There is a certain solidarity in the world of Astoltia. It may not have been possible to step in and join another team temporarily but the *DQX* environment was still very positive, perfect for the younger players[61]. For example, if another player was in a difficult battle, although you could not help directly, it was possible to offer encouragement with the specific "*Ôen*"[62] command, which triggered a clattering sound and your character raised a small fist towards the sky. The power of the heroic colleague receiving the encouragement was momentarily increased with this salutary support. It was so cute.

THE FINAL BELL FOR A GAIJIN

Periodically, once a year in fact, I still take a few minutes to log on and see if my Kamuirobot character still exists. One solution would be to wait until I went back to Japan but, let's be honest, who wants to shut themselves away to play an MMORPG when visiting the archipelago? Another option was that when nostalgia finally became too much, I would take a few minutes to log on on the 3DS, which was authorized for foreigners. It is much better than when it was first launched and the music, with some of Kôichi Sugiyama's best compositions, is now crystal clear, fluid and shows no signs of slowing. The game is playable with a very high-speed connection, although visually it remains hideous, a bit like a badly compressed *YouTube* video. The characters are often illegible on my little 3DS, but it is only for a few minutes, to "clear things up." When I first logged on, my avatar was inundated with 33,334 experience points, having been borrowed for a battle so many times. Instant level up. I sorted through the multiple messages that had piled up at the post offices, checked the few objects that I had put up for auction and picked up a little wad of cash too, the famous salary that was paid weekly.

---

61. There were some cases of gambling on the dice game, but this was soon modified. Today, even in Yûji Horii's beloved casino, the environment is safe and controlled.
62. Fans of the musical game *Ôendan*, published by Nintendo, about a group of Japanese supporters will understand exactly what this was.

THE LEGEND OF DRAGON QUEST

I was a little concerned about the tiny plot of land I had purchased early on at an extortionate price, near 1664th street in Glen, home of the Orcs. It was just land, because I had never bothered to build anything on it. I just wanted a little place just for me. My neighbor had literally built a manor house, and I managed to sneak inside. There was a governess dressed as a "maid," an ever-popular figure in Japanese imagery. I sat there for a few seconds, before fleeing, not wanting to go too far. I was always afraid that this construction, not being sufficiently visited, would end up being taken over by a "competent authority," like a state annexation.

I have often thought that there was something rather pathetic about going back to an abandoned **MMORPG**: you don't remember if you're strong enough, you lose your bearings. What is the next quest[63]? Does the equipment need updating? A few years after my first exploration, all I knew was that I was in a capital city, and that "Madhands" were rising up from the ground in the nearby desert. In fact, going back to *Ten* scares me even more now that I realize the time that must be spent there. Playing an **MMORPG** also means having the illusion of living a great adventure that will almost certainly leave nothing behind.

---

63. *Dragon Quest X* is quite good in this respect since it literally takes the player by the hand. Whole "summary of the previous chapter" pages are updated according to your progress, telling you where you are in the story. The *DQX* website also has a sort of interactive FAQ page, with all you need to catch up and stamps to fill up a grid. It is a very transparent system if you want to catch up, whether you are a beginner or intermediary player.

THE LEGEND OF DRAGON QUEST

Chapter VII — Dragon Quest XI: Echoes of an elusive age

"Adults were once legends for kids, Look, now it's the parents who are scared."

MC Solaar, *Les temps changent*.

CHAPTER VII — DRAGON QUEST XI: ECHOES OF AN ELUSIVE AGE

Eleven, saved from the waters

For once, let's start with the story, because it is important in this episode. One day, a sixteen-year-old kid discovers that he is a "chosen one," complete with magic powers and a mark that appears on his hand[1]. To keep things simple, we'll call him "Eleven[2]." As a baby, he was fished out of a wicker basket floating on a river by an old man. This introduction scene is actually a very faithful reproduction of the origins of Son Gokû, hero of *Dragon Ball*, when he arrives on Earth. The setting is the same, he who becomes the adoptive father of the hero holds the baby he has just rescued up to the heavens. This could also be interpreted as a reference to *The Lion King*, and the classic of all classics, Moses, saved from the waters. Luckily, the biblical metaphor stops here, and the game goes back to being a completely traditional RPG.

However, as soon as *DraQue XI* begins, it is clear that the traditional codes have been abandoned. The hero embodies this disruption in the saga's traditions. Eleven is not quite the usual protagonist, a young, inarticulate boy, traveling from city to city to solve the problems of the local populations. He is quite the opposite in fact, since he must start by saving his own neck. The Japanese subtitle of the game gives some indication of the nature of the adventure: *Sugisarishi toki o motomete*, i.e. "in search of lost time[3]."

Eleven appears to the descendant of a royal family that disappeared in mysterious circumstances. As soon as news of his return spreads through the kingdom, he is locked away by the reigning monarch. The mark on his hand shows that he is a hero, but the sovereign sees him as a child of the devil, said to be a sign of Armageddon, according to prophecy. The reason for this persecution is only revealed much later. The break from the traditional pattern of *Dragon Quest* is crystallized in the hero: the fate of a protagonist has never yet been as closely tied to the plot, and vice versa.

It is certainly the best *Dragon Quest* prologue in years. We are light-years away from the previous chapters: *DQVII* and its total decompression with a three-hour trek

---

1. The hero of the manga *Dai no Daibôken* also has a mark on his hand (on his forehead initially), in his case, the emblem of the dragon.
2. There is a tradition of the publisher giving the episode number as the hero's name on advertising documents. It is also a good way of differentiating them.
3. More precisely, Proust's work is entitled *Ushinawareta toki o motomete*, but the reference here is obvious. In the USA, the official subtitle, *Echoes of an Elusive Age*, is much less Proustian.

THE LEGEND OF DRAGON QUEST

before the first battle[4], *Dragon Quest VIII* announcing a chase at the speed of a cart. In *DQXI*, each companion has his own narrative arc, forming ties with the hero. It is a subtle difference, but the story is constructed in a similar manner to that of *Final Fantasy VI*. A choral tale, in which Toriyama's artistry makes a significant contribution to the attachment felt for this group of heroes. While Eleven's sleek hair may not inspire much, Row, the old monk and master of martial arts in the great *Dragon Ball* tradition, stands out immediately, and who could ignore the cheeky Camus?

He immediately became the heart-throb of *dôjinshi*[5] fans. This was a great surprise because, for the first time in years, the heroes drawn by Toriyama were popular not only for their designs but also for their characters. Early on in the adventure, I thought that the priestess Veronica, an adult trapped in a child's body, would become the kind of icon that only Japan can create and revere. But I saw too many works of fan-art of the handsome Camus giving massages to another male character, Sylvia, not to be stupefied by this enthusiasm.

Believe it or not, the *Dragon Quest* characters were, once again, truly memorable. For the first time, these characters became internet memes[6]. Firstly Camus, the famous hooded thief encountered during an incarceration, became the star of *yaoi*[7] productions. Martina, the team's sexy fighter[8], for whom a simple bug, i.e. an improbable and endless rod protruding from her head, also became a much repeated event. Akira Toriyama had succeeded: the characters of this episode were the most striking ones in years. Not since *DQV* and Bianca had a creation left such a mark on the *DraQue* public. Even the unbearable Sylvia managed to become popular.

THREE GAME PROPOSITIONS

The real challenge facing the Square Enix teams was to release three separate versions of *DQXI* on the same day: one for **PS4** and two others, for a single **3DS** cartridge. A conceptual extravagance that required players to make a choice.

In its **PS4** version, *DraQue* is an example of modernity, as *DQVIII* had been for PlayStation 2. It is obviously the "most beautiful" or at least the highest quality version, if game quality can be measured by the number of textures and polygons

---

4. This time was much shorter in the 3DS remake.
5. Comic fanzine whose content is often homoerotic, in this case parodying the story's male characters in a sexual fanfiction.
6. Image, video, or gif used and misused on the Internet. Note that the characters of *Final Fantasy* have been far more frequently the subject of such baseline jokes and mimicries since the 1990s, simply because the *FF* protagonists had always been promoted more than those of *DraQue*.
7. Literary genre (also called Boy's Love), like *shônen* or *shôjo*, whose stories are limited to male homosexual love stories. Although initially created for a primarily female readership, and by female mangakas, the audience today is much larger.
8. This is the expression used by Yûji Horii to describe his intentions to Toriyama, who then interprets them.

CHAPTER VII — DRAGON QUEST XI:
ECHOES OF AN ELUSIVE AGE

used. It was developed by Orca[9] and ended up being better highlighted by the TV offers. The home console version adopts a fully scaled representation, giving the novel impression of an open world, the style adopted to some extent by the eighth episode. This is obviously an illusion: although there is more space to explore, the level design is still largely based on partitioned areas and tunnels. There is, however, a simple explanation for this choice. The open world concept had been particularly in vogue for some years in the video game industry and, in spite of the many particularities of its market, Japan was no exception in this case. PS4[10] was the machine best suited to the promise of vast plains and deep dungeons, while guaranteeing good sales figures in 2017. However, the scale of the world remained a problem. The distances, which were often long, thus extended the length of the game. The slightest action took much longer than a traditional, more direct and more powerful RPG. So, for those who were afraid of wasting time, Square Enix and Yûji Horii concocted a 3DS version that worked incredibly well, more in line with the efficiency and comfort of a *Dragon Quest*.

The 3DS game, developed by Toylogic, actually contains two visions of the adventure: the first is in 3D, very similar to the style of *DQIX*. The second is all in old-fashioned 2D. Or at least, it aims to be, but the result is not quite up to Super Famicom standards. It could even pass as a demake of *DQXI*. Technically speaking, the 2D rendering is similar to the smartphone episodes, with a finesse that could be positioned between the rusticity of *DQV* and the glitter of *VI*. Obviously, as a veteran player, I still have a certain fondness for games that use 2D in 2017. The best years of pixel art are now behind us but independent producers continue to design worlds made up of tiny squares.

This change of perspective, from 2D to 3D, has consequences and thus eliminates some of the additions to the new episode. For examples, mounts are no use in a flat game. The same is true of the jump, an action inherited from *Dragon Quest X*, which is completely unnecessary in a world seen from above. Producing the game in 2D thus has a direct effect on how the adventure plays out. Unlike the skirmishes on PS4, 2D battles become random, like in the good old days of *DraQue* on the 8 and 16 bit consoles, just as they should be for an "old school" version.

This dichotomy between the two possibilities of the 3DS game makes you dizzy. So brilliant that it is actually quite intimidating. For the first two hours, the two screens of Nintendo's portable console show exactly the same adventure, shown in 3D and in 2D, in perfect synchrony. It is truly impressive, but when the time comes to make a choice, you can't help feeling disappointed. Luckily, the choice is not final and you can always switch from one representation to another by entering a church or stopping near a campfire. Square Enix obviously could not develop an entire RPG with two such different visions proposed simultaneously. For the introduction alone, it is

---

9. A studio that had already contributed to the development of *Dragon Quest X*.
10. Even the PS4 version had its delays.

easy to imagine the complexities of making sure the two screens are perfectly synchronized. A single action, like walking through a house or lifting a jar and breaking it to collect its contents, represents a sizable technical challenge, because no matter what the avatar does, it has to do it at the same speed in both 2D and 3D; imagine the meticulous attention required for that on the scale of an adventure that lasts around sixty hours. Just impossible. Being able to play anywhere, particularly in summer, is a significant advantage and having completed my adventure in the sun by the sea, I realized that I had made the choice most suited to my situation. I simply found the portable version, which was identical to the PS4 game, down to the nearest comma of dialog, more attractive. Even in polygons, it has the graphic direction of *DQIX*[11], i.e. somewhat squat, rather cute and colorful characters with large hands. My favorite detail in these characters is the heroes' pudgy fingers. An insignificant feature, but one that reflects the meticulous adaptation of Akira Toriyama's drawings.

Square Enix also pulled off another feat: bringing out the two games, i.e. three versions, for two consoles, on the same day. Everyone thought that *Dragon Quest XI* would be released for the thirtieth anniversary of the saga, i.e. in May 2016, but the game was not published until July 2017 in Japan. This delay was also due to the development of multiple other projects. They may have missed the anniversary date but it was still a masterstroke. Even the legendary Masahiro Sakurai had never managed to complete two *Smash Bros*[12] versions for the same day.

July 29, 2017, *DraQue XI* reached the shelves in Japan and, unsurprisingly, met with great success. More than two million copies sold in two days: the third best start for the series. The total results for the two versions[13] reached three million copies sold within a week, an exceptional performance bearing in mind the current sluggishness of the video games market in Japan. An impressive collectors' edition[14] was brought out for the occasion: a large box decorated with a sword, containing two fake spell books. These contain the two PS4 and 3DS games, side by side. Yûji Horii can be proud of having achieved a kind of *status quo* between the two rival manufacturers for a few days.

---

11. *DQIX* and *XI*, in the 3DS version of the latter, use a style called Super Deformed: a typically Japanese graphic representation with a slightly different scale for the body, which is smaller, and for the head, which is therefore larger.
12. *Smash Bros. for 3DS* came out several months before the Wii U version.
13. The publisher kept quiet about the Switch version, although it had already been announced. This iteration remained firmly fixed in everyone's minds, and it comes up in every single interview granted by Yûji Horii. But the mystery remains. The master continues to reply: "We're thinking about it."
14. Reserved for the publisher's website and certain stores such as Lawson which, as they had been doing for years, continued to put everything into *Dragon Quest*, to the extent that an entire shop of the kombini chain in Akihabara was decorated with Slimes, selling different kinds of merchandise from the saga.

CHAPTER VII — DRAGON QUEST XI:
ECHOES OF AN ELUSIVE AGE

Best of Dragon Quest

Generosity. This is the first adjective that comes to mind to describe *Dragon Quest XI*. At a time when other games were being divided into the series format, episode eleven is in complete opposition to this fragmented approach. It is a sort of a chunk of an adventure, presented to the player as a block with no DLC, no additional payable content. *DQXI* was, like its gameplay, completely old-school. Aside from the options included at its launch, the game marked the return to a more traditional offer: solo RPG. It had been almost ten years since *DraQue* had not used this simple form. This episode was also important to Yûji Horii and it had to be memorable. It was no coincidence that it came out in two formats at the same time: a first for a canonic episode. There was a good reason. For the thirtieth anniversary, probably for the last game involving all of the saga's founders, Horii chose to produce the same game three times with three different representations. Each representation corresponds to a specific era of the saga. 2D for its origins, 3D SD for the period of portable consoles and remakes and, finally, the contemporary PlayStation 4 version, testifying to the current state of the industry. This action was an unambiguous way of proving that the *Dragon Quest* saga had never changed. In spite of time, in spite of fashion, it had not altered but was still just as loved. It was a way for Horii to show that his work had remained intact; his creative style was still the same, even on a pixel scale.

Dragon Quest XI emanates a sort of surprising determination, the famous *Seikimatsu*[15]. It was the episode to end it all. The end of a cycle. The end of an era. The end of a generation. *DQXI* is probably the episode that marks the end of this bronze age. Even more likely, *Dragon Quest XI* is the last adventure produced by the saga's sacred trinity. Yûji Horii, at sixty-three, an age when most people are considering retirement, is still active. He has often said that his main motivation for *DQXI* was simply to make another episode. Kôichi Sugiyama, an impressive eighty-six, is equally motivated, and will probably continue until his dying breath. A slight loss of inspiration is perceptible, however: the last episode of the saga draws on a lot of its previous music and, with the exception of a few great tunes, *DQXI* is a medley of his career. Akira Toriyama, sixty-two, lacks enthusiasm. The mangaka made enough money from *D_{r.} Slump*, but continued his *Dragon Ball* series for its fans beyond breaking point. He is now tired and thus gives the impression of continuing his role in *DraQue* out of loyalty, for the work of his friend, or at the very least, out of a sense of duty.

The time capsule

With *DQXI*, Yûji Horii speaks of his work, his heritage, in its entirety. Eleven is one of the saga's most traditional inarticulate protagonists, however as the adventure

---

15. The famous sensation of the end of an era, mentioned in the introduction to this book.

THE LEGEND OF DRAGON QUEST

progresses, we get the impression that another generation of heroes came before. So this empty shell has a past? In the application, it seems as if Horii brought together the first three *DraQue* episodes into a single adventure[16]. This means that the construction of the Eleven character is akin to that of the heroes of Roto in every way. The creator's intention becomes so obvious that you begin to wonder if the hero of the first trilogy will not turn up, bang in the middle of *DQXI*. The reason for the link to *Dragon Quest III* for this last stand is simple: there is, once again, a question of nostalgia. Although it may look like a contemporary game, *DraQue XI* is like a time capsule: the game is like a sort of vintage café whose jukebox only contains ancient records. Absolutely everything in this latest episode is a cliché, a bit like a *best of* of the pages of a *Shônen Jump* magazine. And, like all good mangas of its kind[17], the baddies become good, there is a martial arts tournament and an initiatory quest.

HUMOR FROM ANOTHER ERA

The nostalgia in *Dragon Quest* is conveyed in different manners, notably via humor. Typically Japanese humor, relatively frivolous, and heavily tinted with the passing years. This unique humor, in both video games and mangas, is generally present in the same old clichés. Those of *shônen* tales obviously being the most popular: i.e. the famous bunny girls—sexily-clad young ladies with rabbit ears, straight out of Hugh Hefner[18]'s PlayBoy mansion—but also, and most of all, the "puff puffs"[19]. This "custom" started like a schoolboy prank—a young lady asks a man to close his eyes, then the screen goes dark, allowing the player/reader's imagination to take over. The joke has evolved since. The black screen has been replaced by a nasty old man or a strapping muscle-man, adorned with an executioner's mask[20], yet another of the strange obsessions of the Horii/Toriyama duo. In *DQXI*, a number of young ladies offer a "puff puff" moment, but different scenarios follow and, surprise surprise, one of the girls even pushes the hero into the void. The game is peppered with surreal moments of this kind. For example, a wise old man who had disappeared is recognized,

---

16. The idea of embodying several generations of heroes over several games is a tradition in J-RPG, started by *Dragon Quest III*, and it is an aspect that I am particularly fond of, probably for its Alexandre Dumas and Robert Merle style. Others have tried the same, with interesting results. For example: *Estopolis Denki 1* and *2*, better known as *Lufia 1* and *2* in the West. *Tales of Destiny 1* and *2* too, not forgetting *Shining Force*, which continued the stories of its characters in *Shining Force Gaiden 1* and 2 on Game Gear, later reissued on Mega CD.
17. "For young boys" is the literal meaning of the word *shônen*.
18. Founder of the magazine of the same name, see Chapter 8.
19. Described earlier in this book. This is the onomatopoeia corresponding to the action of rubbing your face between the breasts of a woman, generally for sexual pleasure.
20. The executioner's mask is a recurrent motif in Toriyama's work, which contains several versions: Gyûmaô's mask at the very beginning of *Dragon Ball*, Trunks and Son Goten both wear one for their participation at the grand martial arts tournament. Since *DQII*, masks are found systematically on funny NPCs throughout the series. Among fans, such characters are nicknamed *arakure*, a moniker used in *DQVII* when the tragicomic character appears in the player's village. *Jûjin* (prisoner) is another name that often comes up. Some *arakure* are more memorable than others. In fact, one of the most notable ones in *DQXI* wears a pink mask and works on Sylvia's boat. In *DQX*, you can even dress completely in *arakure*. Try putting あらくれ into a *Google* image search if you want a laugh.

CHAPTER VII — DRAGON QUEST XI:
ECHOES OF AN ELUSIVE AGE

in spite of his altered appearance, when he drops a men's magazine. As you probably are aware, senior characters are often implicated in this type of joke. Remember a certain Master Roshi? This unique brand of humor certainly contributes to the overriding sense of nostalgia that emanates from *DQXI*. These ancient jokes that have remained unchanged for thirty years are a true caricature of a golden age of Japanese pop culture from the 1980s. The problem, because there actually is one in this latest chapter of *DQ*, arises when they cease to be inoffensive. In this case, the perverted old grandpa caricature has become a homosexual character. Watch out, Sylvia is about to come on stage.

Sylvia, the distasteful character

The word "stage" is not chosen by accident because Sylvia is a character from the entertainment world. Long, slicked back hair, piercing eyes, Sylvia looks down on anyone who dares to address him. He wears what looks like a clown outfit, to match his showman status. Aside from his extravagant clothing, this character's particularity lies in his manner of speaking. He refers to himself using a female pronoun. In Japan, he is what is known as *Oneekei danshi*[21], or more trivially, *Okama*, the cliché version of the gay Japanese smartass. In the world of Japanese animation and video games, he represents glamor and extravagance.

To give you an example that actually occurs during the adventure, his panache reaches a climax while crossing an entire region aboard a carriage, adorned with a sort of pink peacock get-up, surrounded by his boys, cabaret dancers prancing around, putting on a show of their own. No, you're not dreaming. Sylvia is not even a secondary character, but one of the playable heroes, particularly powerful and extremely useful in combat; all his techniques give rise to wacky scenes[22]. The situations are generally caricatured, reminiscent of the *La Cage aux Folles*[23] film.

I doubt that Horii and Toriyama are homophobic, or even that they were consciously trying to convey a negative image of homosexuals. They are just two elderly men who are no longer quite up-to-date on the issue and who did not even consider the LGBT implications. They were simply reproducing, in the simplest manner possible, the same old jokes of a bygone age. Horii probably sees no harm in the outrageous dramatization of Sylvia, seeing it as harmless humor, as inoffensive as "bunny girls"

---

21. Literally a "man who acts like a sister."
22. I particularly recommend the Sexy Beam attack to give you an idea of the full extent of Sylvia's extravagance.
23. Édouard Molinaro's film, based on the play by Jean Poiret, starring Michel Serrault and Ugo Tognazzi, made its mark towards the end of the 1970s. This colorful, highly caricatured homosexual couple was for a very long time the only vision many French people had of the gay community. Even today, the debate continues over its influence, whether positive or negative. Some felt that the caricature was too much, but the movie does depict a stable, loving gay couple that raised a son who had been abandoned by his mother. France's image of homosexuals in *La Cage aux Folles* can therefore be compared with this Japanese representation of Sylvia.

and "puff puff". Society in Japan changes more slowly than it does in the West with respect to such issues of importance and *DraQue* has remained firmly rooted in the past.

The problem in *Dragon Quest XI*, as with any other game or movie sold abroad, is localizing it for foreign countries. As a general rule, Japanese creators do not produce their worlds with a global vision. They could not care less about how their creations will be viewed by the rest of the world. They are often quite astonished when Westerners appreciate their work. It is therefore important to recognize this naivety[24]. *Dragon Quest* is a name that is known and loved throughout the world, and conceiving the last chapter without bearing this in mind, ignoring it, was therefore problematic. Once the game was complete, how could it be localized properly without altering the nature of the initial production?

This is the ideal moment to praise the work of the translation teams, which, from Nintendo and Square Enix to Pokémon Company, often work wonders with the incongruous ideas of the Japanese creators. I have observed, seeing all my friends who became translators and working in the industry, that it is an extremely liberal sector. The people working in it are very cultured. There are plenty of women and homosexuals who we can easily imagine being uncomfortable with these clichés from another era.

Sylvia's caricature is extremely insensitive and proved complicated in terms of localization. Localization work generally tends to include certain modifications, such as name changes. Sylvia was an obvious candidate for a number of modifications[25]. Struggling translators glossed over his exclusively feminine phrasing to make it less carnivalesque and stigmatizing. However, there was nothing they could do about the technical aspects. Anything related to a character's adornments or gestures is difficult to alter *post-factum*. It is probably just as well that the Japanese version was not just dubbed[26].

These adaptations betray some of the author's initial intentions[27], but Sylvia could be made less grotesque, insulting even, to a Westerner. Even though Japanese developers have their own specific way of creating, I sometimes wonder if it would not be better for everyone if certain attitudes changed. The global impact of *Dragon Quest* was obviously no longer in doubt.

---

24. The naivety lies in the application because the story actually gives a very good reason for the excessive behavior of this character. We learn this later in the game when Sylvia finds his father, who is deeply homophobic.
25. Including the name: Sylvio would stand to reason.
26. Imagine the difficulties of a Western voice actor tasked with dubbing Sylvia. It may not be impossible, but it would definitely be complex. One *DQ* episode has already been dubbed for a Western version: *Dragon Quest VIII*.
27. Most translators often, and with good reason, cite the expression: "Traduttore, traditore," literally "translator, traitor."

CHAPTER VII — DRAGON QUEST XI: ECHOES OF AN ELUSIVE AGE

I realize that the desire to adapt the series for the Western world is a vain wish as long as *DraQue* continues to play on purely Japanese nostalgia. One of the most meaningful indications of this state of fact is the return of the famous *Fukkatsu no Jumon*, the resurrection code for *Dragon Quest I* and *II*. Better still, the old password works on *DQXI* with different results: starting the game with more equipment or a little further along. Starting your adventure at level ten makes little difference though, as the Holy Grail of this system is of course the famous *Dragon Quest I* episode that you collect free once the adventure is over[28]. Another huge nod to all the players over thirty. Unlike *Final Fantasy XV*, which displays "A *Final Fantasy* for fans and first-timers" whenever the game starts, *Dragon Quest* does not mention nostalgia, it embodies it. A kind of memento of the end of the Shôwa[29] era. The younger generation, those who were attracted by ads and discovered the series on smartphone or in manga form, may well be perplexed.

Dragon Quest Easy Type

DQXI is definitely turned towards the past. However, it bows to modernity in one particular matter: difficulty. A concession to attract a new generation of players. Genuine betrayal for the older players, because the adventure turns out to be very easy for a *DraQue*, to say the least. For the first time in the series, the energy of the team of heroes is refilled with each level-up. There are also a multitude of camps proposing saves and full regeneration. You can therefore complete the adventure without mishap or resistance and without encountering any passing difficulties. It is a shame because the careful dosing of the difficulty was another of the saga's chief assets.

The system remains unusually transparent, drawing on games from the great period of fifteen years previously. Inspired by *Final Fantasy X*, the abilities of each character can be customized using a sort of skill panel enabling point distribution—the famous sphere grid, which has since become a reference in RPG design. It initially appears a bit thin, but soon expands. Each character has its own abilities and specific weapons. In the end, all the heroes look like huge brutes, crushing the game's bosses, without even having to increase their level. Renkei, a sort of combo, this time inspired by *Final Fantasy XI*, offers a little variety and enables fighters' attacks to be linked, making up tidy little sequences, some of which can be hilarious. Finally, the Zone is a state achieved by the characters, a temporary aura that intensifies the warrior's abilities. These minor and not particularly original innovations make *DQXI* an RPG in which you can avoid all your enemies along the way, and even if you do encounter them, they offer little resistance.

28. We will come back to this in Chapter 10.
29. The Shôwa era (1926—1989) is the period of Emperor Hirohito, the longest to reign over the country. Nostalgia for the Shôwa era generally refers to the later years: reconstruction, cultural expansion, the advent of J-POP, video games, movies and hot summers spent collecting insects far from the city life.

THE LEGEND OF DRAGON QUEST

In this sense, even the forging action[30]—something that is relatively complex and precise in *Dragon Quest X*[31], for example—is more of a cinch, because you can always go back if you don't like the outcome. *DQXI* is therefore a walk in the park during which you can trample down the enemies and even the bosses. During the sixty-four hours it took me to reach the real end, I only lost one of my characters once. And even then it was because he was struck with an instant death spell. Achieving victory without risk makes you a spectator of the story. It is all the more annoying because this lack of challenge is coupled with redundancy in the goals and even unpleasant scenery. During the adventure, you have to come back to the same places several times over. This infernal backtracking means you have to cross the same continents methodologically three times. A rather unusual option for a *DraQue*. And yet, this way of artificially inflating the duration of the game is justified by the scenario thanks to a surprising twist, not a hint of which was leaked before the game's release—which is remarkable[32].

THE ULTIMATE WORLD (SPOILER ALERT)

The end of the world. This was a very popular theme in Japanese video games in 2016 and 2017. Month after month, countless games proposed their version of a destroyed, disembodied world, exempt of any human presence. At some point, *Final Fantasy XV*, *Zelda: Breath of the Wild*, *Nier Automata*, and even, to some extent, *The Last Guardian*, all look like an urbex[33] expedition in dusty ruins. *Dragon Quest XI* did not escape this trend. In this episode, the hero and his allies fail in their efforts to save the world. The true baddie then appears and the world falls into chaos[34]. The second part of the adventure therefore consists in the hero putting his team back

---

30. Forging is a somewhat arduous task in *DQX* because it requires a certain dexterity and multiple attempts. You have to adjust the gage to the required point with a series of hammer strikes. The difficulty lies in the fact that you have to take into account the temperature of the metal being struck and your energy, which is often not sufficient. If you fail, you lose all your material, which can represent a fortune. The *DQXI* forge is a no-brainer compared to the MMORPG version, in spite of being based on the same system.
31. These are not the only flaws in *Dragon Quest X*. As well as the jump, the hero has an autorun function that makes the hero run automatically, a typically MMORPG idea, allowing the team to run while you use the keyboard to do something else.
32. Obviously, what I am about to write may spoil the surprise, and that is not my intention, which is why I am warning you.
Spoiler alert
The biggest surprise of *Dragon Quest XI* is that the baddie wins. The sacred tree that we are supposed to protect is destroyed. The antagonist takes over the world, wreaks havoc throughout, disbands the hero's team, while the hero, thought to be dead, drowns at the bottom of the ocean. The second part of the adventure then consists in reforming the team by visiting each village and castle, and obtaining a return match from the new ruler of the world. There is even a third part that requires you to go back to the same places again to change the course of time. This backtracking is particularly exhausting, you can take my word for it.
33. Short for "urban exploration," which is another of my favorite activities, both in games and in real life.
34. In the game, this change of paradigm is particularly badly represented. The environments are similar, but the enemies have become stronger. It is difficult to imagine that the evil ruler is now in control of the planet. The population appears to be unaffected, slightly depressed perhaps, as if hungover after a disappointing election night.

CHAPTER VII — DRAGON QUEST XI: ECHOES OF AN ELUSIVE AGE

together. The real initiatory and redemptive journey only commences here, when the protagonist actually becomes a hero. The characters' arcs become very interesting, and Sylvia, incidentally, fills out his dramatic role. The truly dedicated and those who want the download code for *DQI*, still have to complete the "end game", the second part of the game, which is necessary to see the "real end". And for once, this second part of the adventure develops in a surprisingly disappointing manner. Yûji Horii had got us used to magnificent end games, like the confrontation with God in *Dragon Quest VII* or *DQVIII*, which delves into the detail of the protagonist's origins. In the eleventh episode, it is a matter of time travel. Once the last boss has been slain, the hero learns that there is another threat and that he must go back in time to correct certain events to find it. Horii loves plots involving time but this one is completely absurd: the hero spends his time resolving the concerns of his companions. He helps them to solve their problems directly, without allowing them the opportunity of rising up and succeeding by themselves. He becomes a sort of oracle with an answer for everything. The space-time continuum that he re-defines renders all his companions unnecessary, not to mention the player's investment, which loses all meaning. What good did all our hours of play do? It is one New Game + too many: hard to swallow, lazy, and *DQXI* could have done without it. It must, however, be completed to obtain the download code for *Dragon Quest I* on 3DS and PS4.

Dragon Quest XI is therefore a game that certainly brings happiness to those that try it. It is a typical J-RPG in all its destabilizing simplicity. It is also a good episode to start with, being complete and very representative of the essence of the saga. Its emotional sequences are effective, even when it comes to explaining Sylvia's origins, which is no mean feat. *Dragon Quest XI* is an imperfect but fascinating episode. Years later, people will think back fondly to the summer of 2017.

Produced by a group of old pals, aimed at a large population overly occupied by their smartphones and less inclined to play video games, *Dragon Quest XI* actually turns out to be prophetic. Yûji Horii's game has had its revolution, in the true sense of the word, i.e. a rotation around itself to return to its point of origin. Both modern and backward-looking, ambitious and decadent, it is a joyful and sometimes irritating game. Writer Philip Roth ponders the question of how much time can be spent recollecting the best moments of our younger years. As if the best thing about old age was simply the nostalgia of our favorite childhood memories.

THE LEGEND OF DRAGON QUEST

CHAPTER VIII — DRAGON QUEST AND ITS SPIN-OFFS

"Sacred cows make the best hamburger."

Mark Twain

CHAPTER VIII — DRAGON QUEST AND ITS SPIN-OFFS

There was a major turning point in the life of the *Dragon Quest* saga: the series became so huge and so important to its fans that it had to be extended beyond the canonic episodes. This point is easily identified: just after *Dragon Quest III*, the episode that took the series out of the standard Japanese RPG category and turned it into a "dream machine." As the episodes became more lavish, due to Yûji Horii's desire for more substantial narrative arcs for his protagonists, *Dragon Quest* opened up to new styles. Yûji often worked with other people for the spin-offs, sticking to production and only going back to these projects for the final mandatory adjustments. The last months' efforts often mean the difference between an average adventure and a perfectly balanced gaming experience. However, there was no question of Horii twiddling his thumbs and satisfying himself with just signing on the dotted line. Quite the opposite in fact: the master became a draconian supervisor. Taichi Inuzuka, producer of the very first *Dragon Quest Monsters*, remembers seeing his entire script rejected by Horii, who was actually in hospital at the time. There was no messing about with his series.

THE GREAT ADVENTURES OF A DEBONAIR MERCHANT

Torneko no Daibôken, the first *Dragon Quest* spin-off, was released on Super Famicom in 1993, marking a major turning point in the development of the franchise. This game, which I have already mentioned, was the beginning of the "dream machine," the moment when the saga really took off. *Torneko no Daibôken*[1] was the first example of the spin-off concept, which was in its very early stages in the Japanese gaming industry. The player can embody a protagonist who is not the chosen one, i.e. the avatar baptized by the player, but his counterpart. Torneko is a merchant, an anti-hero brought into the limelight. He remains a strong, sincere character, whose determination reminds me of Samwell Tarly in *Game of Thrones*, a man who is perfectly aware of his limits, but prepared to do anything to save his family. The player's view point is slightly altered: he still controls the protagonist, who is a rather chubby and kind-hearted merchant instead of the usual brave and muscular hero. Reminder: the *Pokémon* series also used this process[2] for its *Mystery Dungeon* spin-offs, in which

---

1. In this original translation of *Dragon Warrior IV*, Torneko was called "Taloon."
2. The *Pokémon* series and its spin-offs, as you are probably aware, have a number of points in common with the *DraQue* saga and spin-offs.

THE LEGEND OF DRAGON QUEST

the player is not a trainer, but a Pokémon[3]. In *Dragon Quest*, this surprising set-up worked perfectly. The mustached, debonair merchant in *DQIV* devotes his life to looting, exploring infinite dungeons to feed his family. Nothing to do with saving the world. *Torneko no Daibôken* is also different in its incredible game mechanism, invented by Kôichi Nakamura, a designer who was at the peak of his career. The principle was simple and addictive[4]. Each of Torneko's actions moves the game forward in time, a bit like a game of chess. Nothing happens between the moves, with either the enemies or the environment. In this simulated real time, in which each of the character's movements or actions counts for one turn, the entire set of dungeons evolves and comes to life as the protagonist progresses. I have often delayed my exploration by waving my sword around pointlessly, for example, or going back and forth to collect energy, but the hunger factor that is part of the game soon steps in, limiting the character's movements. Each trip is unique, since everything is random.

The most surprising thing about Torneko is that he is the most recurrent character in the *DraQue* world, apart from the monsters, like Slime. His smile, hidden behind a bushy mustache, reappears game after game. He is the star of no fewer than three *Fushigi no Dungeon* games and makes multiple appearances in the canonic episodes. He can be glimpsed in *DQVI, VIII* and *IX*, almost as a nod of acknowledgement. He is also in *Dragon Quest Heroes II* and, of course, *Itadaki Street*. No-one ever seems to get tired of this kind chap, a sort of Obelix that finally started a family.

DRAGON QUEST MONSTERS, THE "POKÉMON-LIKE" FAKE

Dragon Quest Monsters is the longest spin-off series. And if Horii did not feel cheated by the colossal success of *Pokémon*, which is loosely based on the ideas of *DraQue V*, it was because he already had a similar concept in mind. From the early 1990s, Horii and his producer Yukinobu Chida had been looking at the possibility of making an RPG based on breeding and training[5], simply by observing their team members' interest in horse racing.

The *DraQue Monsters* protagonist is Terry, the taciturn warrior of *DQVI*, but this was not his initial destiny. He was supposed to be the hero in the sixth episode of the saga but was sidelined because of his slightly offbeat design. However, he was an ideal character for an adventure involving the capture of monsters to be bred like cattle. While the fights are strictly the same as those of the canonic episodes, the evolution system in *DQM* is quite different. Each monster exists in both male and female versions

---

3. To be precise, the player is actually a human who has become a Pokémon.
4. A game principle that then inspired Chunsoft with yet another spin-off of *Fushigi no Dungeon*, *Fûrai no Siren* (Shiren the Wanderer), the first episode of which came out in 1995.
5. According to Inuzuka, historic producer of *Dragon Quest Monsters*, cited in "Iwata asks" published by Nintendo.

CHAPTER VIII — DRAGON QUEST AND ITS SPIN-OFFS

and cross-breeding is particularly recommended to obtain a monster of a higher level. Inspired by the *Megami Tensei* series, which had already developed this concept, the breeding structure then became the well-known formula used in the *Pokémon* saga. However, the system turned out to be slightly dull when the first tournaments were organized. All the participants tended to use the same three super-powerful monsters instead of varying them according to the corresponding elements, like in the *Pokémon* games.

In 1999, *Dragon Quest Monsters*[6] was the first episode to be released in the West, at a time when the saga had disappeared from the shelves, no more than a memory for the fans of Toriyama and import game enthusiasts. *DraQue Monsters* has now been around for almost twenty years, and is set to continue, but at one point, Yûji Horii considered suspending this spin-off series when sales had begun to tail off in 2003, just when *DQM: Caravan Heart*[7] came out.

However, the success of Nintendo's new console brought a second wind to *DQM*, leading to Horii's decision to call it *DQM: Joker*, as if it was the last card to be played by this line of heirs. Subsequently, another four would be released[8].

The "satellite" games, the extravagant ones that stray a little, were used as experiments and field tests for new concepts. There was no need to come up with new franchises when *Dragon Quest* could do it all, even toys.

THE LEGEND OF THE SACRED SWORD

Kenshin Dragon Quest: Yomigaerishi Densetsu no Ken[9] is a game in which the player, holding a little bit of plastic in his hand, could mimic the gestures of a swordsman to do away with any monsters that he came up against in the dungeons and plains of Enix's saga. However, in spite of the rich colors, the path proved to be rather dull, due to the linear nature of the adventure. The path was in fact predetermined for the entire game and, with a few rare exceptions, all you had to do was to go straight on to roll out the plot. *Kenshin Dragon Quest: Yomigaerishi Densetsu no Ken* is obviously light-years away from being Yûji Horii's most personal game. In 2003, the newly merged Square and Enix released a plastic sword, a toy to be connected to the TV. This may seem like nothing today, but it is likely that Satoru Iwata, who was always fascinated by new

---

6. It was released in Europe in 1999 under the direction of Eidos Interactive and just a year later in the USA.
7. More than five hundred thousand copies were sold, which is not negligible in today's market. Released in 2003 on GBA, *Dragon Quest Monsters: Caravan Heart* was the last game published by Enix before the Square merger became operational two days later. Unlike the first *DQM* based on episode *VI*, *Caravan Heart* is based on the Kiefer character from *Dragon Quest VII*. This chapter was totally different from *DQM1* and *2*, having done away with the breeding system. In this game, the main goal is to win monster "hearts."
8. *DQM: Joker*, *DQM: Joker 2*, a re-issue with a few additions, *DQM: Joker 2 Professional* and the same for *DQM: Joker 3* and *Joker 3 Pro*.
9. *Swordmaster Dragon Quest: Resurrection of the Legendary Sword* only came out in Japan in September 2003 and did not require a console. It was a stand-alone, simply connected to the TV.

techniques, was influenced by this unusual accessory when he created the Wiimote, the Wii's famous controller[10]. Another pioneering aspect of the *Dragon Quest* saga. This game can even be described as dually visionary because *Kenshin DQ* also returns to the basics of the first *DraQue* scenario: a kind of retrogame well in advance of its time.

It was a logical move for Square Enix to reuse this approach to the RPG as a toy with *Dragon Quest Swords: Kamen no Jôô to Kagami no Tô*[11], released on Wii in 2007 in Japan and the following year in the rest of the world. In this spin-off, the Wiimote replaced the toy sword. Unsurprisingly, the game is extremely limited and linear, since all you do is move along a corridor, gesticulating when confronted. The fights are also falsely random, since the enemies always appear in roughly the same places. The adventure, which lasts around ten hours, was much too short for a canonic *DQ*, and just long enough to prevent you from getting a sprained wrist. *DQ Swords* is highly representative of the productions of its era since the use of the Wiimote was more or less mandatory. You point the sensor at the TV to aim at your enemies, sweeping across the screen horizontally, vertically or diagonally, thrusting or slashing. It's fun, but this highly repetitive system soon gets boring. You can almost picture the Square Enix teams wondering how to fit this remote control into a traditional RPG. Like all games of its period, *DQ Swords* has aged very badly and, as far as I am concerned, the idea of digging out batteries for the Wiimote soon douses any vague desire to try it again. Luckily, Yûji Horii had preserved some of the RPG aspects of the saga, i.e. heroes whose level increased, experience points and a few bosses. A significant bonus was that the digitized voices of the protagonists came like a cool breeze to freshen up this somewhat off-putting adventure. Unlike *Kenshin DQ*, which explored the heritage of the series, this game had an original story written by Yûji Horii. With the exception of Kôichi Sugiyama, who found new talents to assist with the composition work, the Holy Trinity worked together, putting all its energy into this project that appears to be one of the most infantile.

SLIME'S OWN GAMES

The *Slime MoriMori*[12] series is another example of a diversification attempt, quite clearly supervised by Yûji Horii. For fans, it is a delicious adventure whose gameplay is focused on action, structured around the series' slimy mascot. The three episodes

---

10. This opened the way for what was called "motion gaming" where the controller was moved around in front of the screen to mime various actions, such as holding a fishing rod or a torch or swinging a sword, as was the case here.
11. *Dragon Quest Swords: The Masked Queen and the Tower of Mirrors* is the spiritual sequel to *Kenshin Dragon Quest*.
12. *Slime MoriMori* is adapted from a manga published in *V Jump*, *Slime Bôkenki*, in which the little blob has hilarious adventures alongside the most *kawaii* monsters of the series. It is a rare example of an "unpretentious little project" for young children, that ended up becoming a major commercial triumph. Note that the main character of *Go! Go! Ackman*, another series invented by Akira Toriyama for the same magazine, went on to become the hero of a handful of video games. In this comic series, the protagonist, Ackman, is a little demon who comes up against mischievous angels. The similarity to Trunks from *Dragon Ball* helped to boost the popularity of this license, which remains anecdotal in the career of its creator.

CHAPTER VIII — DRAGON QUEST AND ITS SPIN-OFFS

came out on Nintendo's portable consoles[13], a mobile format that was ideal for these games. They were actually great companions for my sleepless hours, particularly the second one, in which you control giant robots that fight duels against one another, like *kaiju*. At the time, I loved this refreshing version, totally different from a traditional *Dragon Quest* and playing on the modern references of Japanese pop culture—something that was not permitted by the doxa of the series. In the third opus, there is even an evil copy of the Statue of Liberty and a demonic matriochka, with an underlying treasure hunt and tales of pirates. *Slime MoriMori* is a bundle of joy and happiness, parody and grotesque humor, the likes of which are not permitted in the canonic *DraQue* episodes.

THE WHEEL OF FORTUNE

Itadaki Street[14] is a board game involving the purchase of properties to be able to charge rivals that land on them due to the roll of the dice: an obvious copy of *Monopoly*. *ItaSuto*, as it is known to its fans, was, above all, a pioneering game in the industry, being released years before *Mario Party*. It is not directly related to *DraQue* but certain connections formed over time. Yûji Horii worked on this project with his old ASCII comrades, with whom he published two of his first adventure games, and an old college buddy, Seisuke Ôkawa. His caricature style and second-degree humor were perfect for the project and his role as character designer. It is also amusing to note that Japan's two most memorable board games were also invented by two college friends. Horii and his long-time partner Akira Sakuma[15] never lost touch and *Momotarô Detetsu* and *ItaSuto* were also kept up for several years on Famicom. The series is currently on its fourteenth edition[16], and Square Enix has no intention of stopping there.

It is understandable if you have never played *Itadaki Street*, since it was only localized for Wii and DS. Incidentally, this turned out to be a version combining the worlds of *Mario* and *Dragon Quest*, thus creating a board game based on the various well-known characters of the two franchises. Although the goal was to design for a larger population, *Itadaki Street* is considered to be quite difficult. Even the testers who were supposed to review it were often defeated by the artificial intelligence, even in the Super Famicom episode. Personally, my solo victories can be counted on the fingers of one hand. Yûji Horii developed the levels backwards, starting with

---

13. On Game Boy Advance (*Slime MoriMori Dragon Quest: Shōgeki no Shippo Dan* in 2003), DS (*Slime MoriMori Dragon Quest 2* in 2005) and 3DS (*Slime MoriMori Dragon Quest 3: The Great Pirate Ship and Tales* in 2011) respectively, the *Slime MoriMori* games were developed by Tose, a company working in the shadows, but which has contributed to more than one thousand games since the 1980s. A true ghost developer, i.e. a subcontractor that sometimes saves projects that get off to a bad start.
14. Called *Fortune Street* for its American version.
15. See the first chapter for Yûji Horii's college memories.
16. Published by Enix since 1994, only too happy to have this lucrative little business in its hands.

the most difficult, and finishing with the easiest. The only problem was that no-one could do it: all the testers were crushed by the formidable AI and very unfavorable odds with the dice. Horii therefore came up with a tutorial board, but that was also too difficult. He then produced an even easier initiation level. *ItaSuto* is so hard that it is best played against friends, rather than confronting the computer's implacable artificial intelligence.

Itadaki Street, this parodied mecca of capitalism, has become a meeting point for worlds that were never intended to cross paths. It was an opportunity for the *Dragon Quest* and *Final Fantasy* sagas to finally come together on PlayStation 2 and PSP. *ItaSuto* was selected again in 2017 to become the thirtieth anniversary game for the two series on PS4 and PS Vita. Heaven for fans, the old characters of *DraQue* came to life in little 3D bodies, all dubbed by young actors. Bianca from *DQV*, Hassan from *DQVI* and Maribelle from *DQVII* against Sephiroth, Cloud and Kefka from various *FF* episodes. The fantasies of countless players became reality, but only on the squares of a board game.

DRAGON QUEST IN THE ARCADES

In Japan, if a license is used in an amusement arcade, it is a sure sign of its popularity. To ensure exposure to as wide a population as possible, Square Enix surfed the wave of a trend: arcade games based on a playing card system. However, the company was not interested in smoky rooms filled with *Street Fighter* fans[17]. No, the *Dragon Quest: Monster Battle Road*[18] games were placed in department stores, shopping malls and even train stations in 2007. They could also be found in stores alongside *gachapons*, Japanese vending machines that distributed a little figurine in exchange for a few quarters.

Playability obviously had to be ultra-simple to suit the target public. The fights were generally held in a coliseum and the player's team was formed at random or using cards from his collection, to be scanned by the arcade machine[19]. The machine thus only required two buttons and all you had to do was to continue steadily through the game, provided you had your best cards[20]. A replica sword in Roto's characteristic colors was seemingly embedded in the center of the machine, so children were sure

---

17. After the boom years of the Capcom, Namco, SEGA and SNK era, the arcade market dwindled away. Innovation enabled its survival, for example with cards containing IC chips, a bit like those now used for public transport passes. This meant players could have a certain rank, the game could be personalized, and, above all, it could be saved along with the statistics.
18. The title, as much as the system itself, comes from *Monster Battle Road* in *Dragon Quest VIII*, where a team was formed to fight in graded and ranked duels.
19. You could play without cards, but some of the fun was lost.
20. Young players could also take photos with their mobile phones or a Nintendo DSi application to generate a set of ready-to-use virtual cards, or to use them again later. *Battle Road Mobile* was released subsequently.

CHAPTER VIII — DRAGON QUEST AND ITS SPIN-OFFS

to spot it from afar. It was a high-quality machine, which was normal since it was the fruit of a collaboration between Square Enix and Taito[21], the publisher and specialist manufacturer of arcade games. These games generated huge profits, but required little production time because *Battle Road* reused much of the *DraQue VIII* world. Other bosses and characters were added with various iterations and updates. Billions of yen poured into the coffers of Square Enix thanks to a simple license spin-off. Its success continued, with the latest version of *Battle Road, II Legend*, in 2010. A Wii version was made with an optional joystick to reproduce the arcade game control[22], i.e. a large sword set in stone, like an *anime*-flavored Excalibur.

For its anniversary in 2016, Square Enix released *Dragon Quest: Monster Battle Scanner*, whose machine had a dragon-shaped joystick to read the QR codes and bar codes on the cards. The game obviously attracted players' collector instincts: one game and a free card for one hundred yen meant a captive and enthusiastic audience.

THE MONSTER PARADE

"Yes, level up!" cried Kanpei, showing me his current *Dragon Quest: Monster Parade* session on his smartphone. Kanpei is the kid in the family with whom I had eaten lunch, by chance, while hiking in the southwestern part of Japan. "Open Garden" was indicated on this cute house, which had resisted the last earthquake that shook the region of Kumamoto on April 14, 2016. After multiple shopping expeditions in Tokyo, *gaijins* tend to forget what a friendly and hospitable place Japan is outside the mega-city. So there I was, in a garden with a real Japanese family and eight-year-old Kanpei, who was giving me a lecture on his very own *Dragon Quest*. His little fingers danced over his smartphone, which was way more powerful than mine.

In *Dokodemo Dragon Quest Monster Parade*[23], the young Kanpei was guiding a caravan while managing a little group of monsters parading in front. Other nastier creatures were waiting in ambush. You had to make it through two enemy attacks to get to the next step. The fights were fully automated, but you could affect their outcome by hitting the enemies. Kanpei had been playing this almost-free game for so long that he hardly even needed to look at the screen, guided by the sound effects alone. At the end of certain sessions, the game proposes new beasts for capture, but Kanpei did not care, as he already had plenty. He looked invincible.

---

21. Square Enix started buying up Taito, the company behind *Space Invaders* and *Bubble Bobble*, as of 2005. Today, after a multitude of status changes and mergers, it is simply called Taito Corporation.
22. Expensive and impractical controllers are something of a tradition for Square Enix, which often used an episode release to propose one in the shape of a Slime.
23. Released in September 2014, only in Japan, on PC and mobile platforms.

THE LEGEND OF DRAGON QUEST

The "walking RPG"[24] system is not new and this category of games remains very popular in Japan. They can almost be considered as reverse tower defense[25] games, because you control the attacking camp. It is a simple concept that any license can use, as any skin can be adapted. Its most popular contemporary is *Super Robot Taisen X-Omega*[26]. There is absolutely no fun in seeing your characters go up a level automatically.

It is both fascinating and terrifying to see just how much Japanese video games have changed since the advent of smartphones. Like all games of its kind, *Dragon Quest Monster Parade* is completely free. This is a fairly obvious con that soon requires players to pay up. As my grandfather used to say: "There is little other than birdsong in this world that's free." And he was quite right. The business model of *Monster Parade* is therefore based solely on additional purchases made by the player and not the actual downloading of the game.

However, the number of game downloads is exhibited by the publisher like a trophy. It is even amusing to observe that the more Square Enix communicates its results, the better the product performs.

There is always a catch with this type of free game. In *Dragon Quest Parade*, it is an additional currency, crystals, used to buy the adventure's most precious assets. These fictional objects are obtained by paying real yen in the real world. There is supposed to be a warning and limitations on possible transactions by young players and it is therefore theoretically impossible for a minor to empty his or her parents' back account. However, a number of catastrophic situations have been reported[27]. If the product is well-designed, addiction will do the rest, like in a casino, and the consequences can be dramatic. *Dragon Quest Monster Parade* surfed the wave of *Complete Gacha* games, often abbreviated in Japanese to *CompuGacha*. *Gacha* comes from the *gachapon* concept, a direct reference to the vending machines that distribute a capsule, generally containing a little figurine, in exchange for between one hundred and five hundred yen[28]. *CompuGacha* therefore sums up the business model of these so-called *Freemium* games, which are advertised as being free but which ultimately reward those who pay. It is a particularly lucrative method for publishers. In games like *DraQue*, this consists in encouraging the player to buy crystals to be wagered in a lottery-style system. This is the only way of getting the best monsters, characters, weapons and cards, depending on the game. Another trick is to add a limited number of very rare prizes during a special promotion. Even if only five percent of all those

---

24. Not be confused with walking simulators, which are popular now.
25. Real-time strategy game where you defend your positions against successive enemy attacks.
26. This one is not in the least bit original, being based mainly on the concept developed by SEGA's *Chain Chronicle*, one of the publisher's biggest mobile successes.
27. Some Japanese addicts have spent several million yen.
28. In principle, you do not know what you will win, although some stores have become specialized, selling all the figurines of a collection in sets or even individually.

CHAPTER VIII — DRAGON QUEST AND ITS SPIN-OFFS

who download the game actually pay, the amounts involved are still not to be sneezed at. And the mobile market pushes the vice even further.

Some Japanese MVNOs[29] signed partnership agreements with the publishers of *Gacha* games, granting exclusive use of certain characters or weapons. The only way for players to obtain the rarest objects and outfits was then to sign a contract with the MVNO.

Having studied all the mechanisms involved in *Dragon Quest* products, quite frankly, Square Enix comes out relatively unscathed. The obligation to buy in order to progress more quickly is not too obvious in *Monster Parade*, *Hoshi no Dragon Quest* or *DQM Super Light* to mention only the most recent. It is almost as if they had returned to the rule of *DraQue X*, "Game design should not result in dependency," the principle proclaimed by Jin Fujisawa at CEDEC 2013[30]. In fact, *Dragon Quest* products for smartphones arrived slightly after the trend, when the business had already been partially regulated by the Shôhishachô[31]. Numerous complaints were filed in 2012 concerning these micro-transactions. *CompuGacha*, which literally consists in forcing the player to indulge in double lotteries to obtain ultra-rare prizes, has been more or less banned. However, some publishers still manage to get around the new legislation and the offer is so diverse that it is difficult to monitor the changes in this ultra-accessible casino.

Please note that I use the casino image on purpose. Amusement arcades are recurrent in all the episodes and have been since the third *Dragon Quest*. Yûji Horii and Kôichi Sugiyama are both keen casino players. They made them important meeting places in the saga, filled with slot machines, poker tables and bunny girls[32] with jazzy music in the background, a slightly dated representation of bygone days. The series' obsession with bunny girls, present right up until 2017, is part of it. Gambling and board games are a true passion for old Yûji Horii[33], to the point that he has invested heavily in the sector.

---

29. An MVNO (Mobile Virtual Network Operator) is an operator that does not own the telephone lines, but rents them from network owners and sells them on in the form of plans under its own brand.
30. Computer Entertainment Developers Conference, see Chapter 6.
31. Consumer affairs agency
32. Initially imposed by *Playboy* magazine, bunny girls have been an important part of Japanese nightlife since the 1970s. Proto-cosplay, they became the incarnation of the attractive, sexily-clad assistant who is *kawaii* at the same time, thanks to the rabbit ears. The best-known Japanese bunny girl in the West is probably Bulma from the manga *Dragon Ball*, when she had to wear this famous costume. The fixation with this avatar of sexism from the *Hustler* years (*Hustler* is a monthly American porn magazine) was continued in *Dragon Quest*, since Horii was clearly keen on this style. In time, it became "*Asobinin*," a real job in the third episode, and could be adopted by either a male or a female character.
33. And for Kôichi Sugiyama, who is also a keen collector of board games.

THE LEGEND OF DRAGON QUEST

THE DRAGON QUEST OF STARS

Back home in Kumamoto, Kanpei continues to play on his smartphone. The way in which the little boy plays *Dragon Quest* is radically different from the way of his parents, who sit cross-legged just a few centimeters from the TV. Times have truly changed: ways of playing, games, publishers. Although the Square Enix teams and Yûji Horii went to great lengths to propose a story that bore some similarity and continuity with the other episodes of the *DraQue* saga, mobile games are systematically based on the addictive mechanism created. Through these products, the series became dematerialized with an eclectic offer that is actually quite different from what it once was, in terms of both content and form. These downloadable games are an integral part of the publishers' strategies in the Japan of the smartphone generation. One product that holds almost all records in all categories is *Puzzle & Dragons*, a combination of a puzzle game and an RPG. This is the game that really made the *gacha* a fundamental strategy. Little development is required for this type of game and the investment is mostly in communication, in the form of TV adverts broadcast during prime time.

The target is the general public in the broadest sense of the word. All Japanese publishers dream of reproducing this phenomenon and publishing the next *PazuDora*[34].

I remember Yûji Horii's face when I asked him what game he liked to play. With a wide smile and quite proud to be giving me a scoop for the portrait I was writing about him then for *Gamekult*, he answered *Candy Crush*. It was 2016. Although *Dragon Quest Monster Parade* was not quite as successful as the latter or *PazuDora*, it was still a hit. At the time, an honorable performance on smartphone was the equivalent of the success of a traditional console game, which was much more expensive, and therefore risky, to produce. This observation led to an anonymous person causing alarm among a number of the saga's fans when *DQXI* was released. Would the next canonic episode be vampirized by a smartphone game, like *Hoshi no Dragon Quest*[35]? Such concern was understandable because the latter is literally the perfect form of a *DraQue* adapted to the smartphone format.

Dragon Quest is very good at adapting to its public and the *Hoshi no Dragon Quest* episode is a perfect example. It even has a certain audacity that a traditional episode would not have dared. For example, the exploration of outer space and other planets are possibilities that fall way beyond the usual specification for a *DraQue*. The product is more like *Monster Parade*[36] in its wandering and the highly automated confrontations,

---
34. The nickname for *Puzzle & Dragons*.
35. "*Dragon Quest of the stars*," released on October 15, 2015 on smartphone, remained blocked outside Japan until one day in 2017, when it finally appeared in the stores with no explanation or even any promotion.
36. The most amusing innovation was probably the possibility of shaking the phone to recruit nearby adventurers. You could also export your character's model to print it in 3D, but sadly, I never had the opportunity to do this.

CHAPTER VIII — DRAGON QUEST AND ITS SPIN-OFFS

but this time, the heroes are human. The clever fights also include typical RPG elements in real time. From the themes to the gameplay, these minor details make *Hoshi* the episode that is most similar to a traditional *Final Fantasy*. It offered a glimpse of the direction in which *Dragon Quest* was headed, a trend continued in *DQX* not surprisingly, and which went beyond the framework of the online world.

In *HoshiDraQue*, if you pay, you not only get access to a lottery that proposes much better weapons, but you can also continue to play when your endurance gage is empty[37]. This is one of the classic limits of smartphone offers: if you spend a few yen, you can play non-stop, without taking a break. The adventure is divided into chapters, each one taking place on an entire continent. The adventure is like *Dragon Quest IX* which moves in a straight line. I never made it to the end because it really is very long and mainly, like all smartphone products, because it demands particular dedication and organization. It requires a constant 4G connection too of course, which is quite common in Japan, even in the public transport networks.

The problem with all these products is the degree of difficulty. Mobile *DraQue* games are no exception, whereas the strength of Yûji Horii's games is their perfect balance. Smartphone games have to be accessible to all the new users attracted by the multitude of adverts. Once grabbed, new players' interest must be maintained. Square Enix, like the other publishers, used events to do this: limited duration dungeons, a special tombola or, best of all, a collaboration. This is a partnership with another license or company, a visibility exchange whose terms are obviously deliberately opaque. The king of such operations is, once again, *PazuDora*. *Dragon Quest* had the advantage of an incredible history, enabling the creation of events based on its own past. What better way to rekindle interest than by proposing the charismatic monsters of previous episodes? In one *Hoshi no Dragon Quest* operation, the whole of Japan got together to vanquish Zoma, one of the *Dragon Quest III* bosses. The characters were represented as in a strategy game by Koei, with pointed helmets like Nobunaga Oda[38] and Ieyasu Tokugawa[39].

HEROES AND ACTION

Stripped of its narrative obligations, *Dragon Quest* became a mine of adaptation potential. For more than a decade, Musou games, or *Dynasty Warrior*-like games as

---

37. As with most mobile experiences, game time is limited. Players must wait before restarting the game. In *HoshiDraQue*, this limit is represented by an endurance gauge.
38. Nobunaga Oda, a *daimyô* from the Sengoku era, was one of the country's three unifiers. The company Koei, now called Koei Tecmo, has since used his image and legend. He has starred in dozens of war games, such as *Nobunaga no Yabô* (*Nobunaga's Ambition*) and in numerous *Musô*-type games, which combine action with a certain idea of Japanese history.
39. The figures of the conquering sovereigns of the Sengoku era are an inexhaustible source of inspiration for video games, even the most unusual, *Pokémon Conquest*, featuring Nobunaga together with Pokémons.

THE LEGEND OF DRAGON QUEST

they are known in the West, proliferated. *Hokuto no Ken*[40], the *Gundam* saga and *The Legend of Zelda* all used the Musou formula. One day, *Dragon Quest* decided to do the same. I have written so many articles in my life on Musou that I should be fed up with them. They are, after all, more or less the same, i.e. a mass action game in which the enemies, hordes of soldiers, group together to be vanquished by a hero with a single swing of a lance, sword or ax. Obviously this is something of a caricature, but I love this genre, and the pleasure of playing is almost hypnotic. Some describe it as "guilty pleasure," but I always found that Musou games are far more than just that. In a way, this style of game filled the gap left by *Final Fight* or *Double Dragon*, arcade classics that became extinct sometime around the end of the 1990s. Square Enix attempted the conversion of its leading license with *Dragon Quest Heroes*[41]. As was to be expected, the exercise was highly successful. The game offers an astute mix of new protagonists and heroes from episodes *IV, V, VI, VII* and *VIII*. For the first time, some of them were given voices. Amazingly[42], Yûji Horii and the game's producers, who I met during a *Heroes* promotional tour, deny any similarity to Koei Tecmo's initial offering. This spin-off product is actually a sort of action game with an RPG-like system that is not dissimilar to Falcom's *Ys* series[43]. The originality, at least for the first *Heroes*[44], was that it used the famous Tower Defense mechanism, the same as that used in *Monster Parade* and *Hoshi no Dragon Quest*. The bodies of the monsters, whose spirits are gathered in the form of large stones, are used to block the various new enemies that rain down upon us like a spring shower. It was a truly brilliant way of doing the same thing differently.

"EXPLOITATION GAME"

Dragon Quest Monsters, Joker, Heroes, Monster Parade, the arcade versions and other mobile games are all spin-offs. Some stand out more than others, having earned varying degrees of success and cutting loose from the original saga. *Torneko no Daibôken*, the first of these spin-offs, is a typically Japanese example of the spin-off becoming a sub-franchise in its own name[45]. Copying an existing concept, adapting it by changing a few of its characteristics and selling it differently is commonplace in Japan. Sub-genres

---

40. *Fist of the Northstar.*
41. Released in 2015, the first chapter was subtitled *Yami Ryū to Sekaiju no Shiro* (*The World Tree's Woe and the Blight Below*). The second opus, published between 2016 and 2017 on the different platforms, was called *Futago no Ô to Yogen no Owari* (*Twin Kings and the Prophecy's End*).
42. It is very common, if not systematic, for Japanese creators to deny any borrowing in the games. No, *Minecraft* did not inspire *Dragon Quest Builders*; no, *Shin Sangoku Musou* did not inspire *Dragon Quest Heroes*; no, *Hearthstone* did not inspire *Dragon Quest Rivals*... But we will come back to this.
43. Falcom's *Ys* series was, for many years, the only alternative to *Zelda* in the field of what was then generally referred to as action-RPG in France. The first episodes were widely available in the West on SEGA Master System or on CD-Rom for the NES console. The series is therefore very dear to its fans.
44. *Dragon Quest Heroes II* was released on May 27, 2017, the exact date of the thirtieth anniversary, being something of a quickly produced sequel because there was nothing else on hand for the celebration. It is a classic sequel: a longer, more complicated game, with more similarities to the RPG genre, but it is also more laborious.
45. Nintendo is particularly known for this type of spin-off with *Dr. Mario, Mario Golf, Mario Tennis, Mario Kart*, etc.

CHAPTER VIII — DRAGON QUEST AND ITS SPIN-OFFS

often come into being and grow to the extent that they become cult. *Jidai-geki*, samurai films, have thus become a real institution, whether in the form of Kurosawa's epic sagas or exploitation feature films, like the *Lone Wolf & Cub* series. Similarly, and under the impulse of a few key works such as *Tetsujin 28-gô* and *Mazinger Z*, the robot *anime* sub-category has become a noble genre, with several families and numerous series of its own[46].

The series copy one another, inspire each other, develop mutually and sometimes find an original way of existing. However, their creators are often behind trends that inspire whole series of very similar games. Although Kôichi Nakamura, creator of *Torneko no Daibôken*, acted as Squaresoft's advisor for the development of *Chocobo's Mysterious Dungeon*[47], this did not last long. A number of copies were produced. The team behind the first *Mystery Dungeon*, who I met by chance during a promotion campaign, expressed their frustration with the "fakes," which they held to be at least partly responsible for the public's waning interest. This issue is more than a simple industrial problem: it is just difficult to protect good ideas, and even Square Enix knew this. The *Dragon Quest Rivals* project came into being because of *Hearthstone*. *Rivals* is a game that is extremely similar to the Blizzard hit, but solely based on *DraQue* monsters.

REBUILDING DRAGON QUEST

The problems facing "borrowed" concepts vary quite considerably depending on the projects. I remember my first contact with *Dragon Quest Builders* at Tokyo Game Show 2015. The demonstrator handed me the controller and, seeing that I was a *gaijin*, asked if I was familiar with *Minecraft*. I answered: "No problem, I know it well." However, during the promotion campaign, which lasted for more than five months, the word *Minecraft* was never mentioned. The name of Mojang's game was never cited in any advert. *Minecraft* is a real phenomenon in Japan, which is perhaps even more surprising than elsewhere in the world. It was this game that kept Sony's PS Vita alive during its darkest hours. It also holds the original record for the best-selling dematerialized third-party game[48] on Wii U; a Microsoft product to boot[49]. And it is not over yet, because *Minecraft* is pursuing its insolent career on Nintendo Switch. Its universal nature means it leaves its mark. It has also been incorporated into the national culture, even in *sentaï* series. In *Dôbutsu Sentai Zyuôger*, the brave heroes control a robot that is no more than a modeled assembly of animals, like in

---

46. Don't get me started on what could be the subject of a whole new book. From *Grendizer* to *Evangelion*, *Gundam*, *Transformers*, *Gurren Lagann* and *Macross*, Japanese robotology is an absolutely fascinating topic and deserves the attention merited by its importance.
47. A dungeon RPG in which the player is a Chocobo.
48. A game developed by a studio that is not part of the console manufacturer's firm, in this case Nintendo.
49. One of the best-sellers on Wii U and PS Vita is thus a Microsoft product, a comical situation to say the least.

THE LEGEND OF DRAGON QUEST

Minecraft. The *Dragon Quest Builders* team was well aware of the importance of the best construction video game ever, but carried on regardless.

My first *Minecraft* sessions were particularly intoxicating. The kind you remember forever: a whole universe at hand, to be shaped however I wanted, allowing my imagination to run free. *Dragon Quest Builders* did not disappoint me, although it does take the protagonist and player by the hand. From the beginning, you have to rebuild what looks like a small village, with an inn, a store, etc. You have plans to help you and they must be followed to the letter. The first thing to do is to find components to build the various structures. It is obviously not as rich as *Minecraft*—it is impossible to transform a little farm into an industrial facility raising battery chickens—but the creations are conform to the *Dragon Quest* spirit.

Kazuya Ninou was in the wings, directing. The game designer was particularly well reputed for taking and transforming existing concepts. Before his participation in the *Final Fantasy XIV* redesign, he had developed a solid reputation with the creation of *Sekaiju no Meikyû*[50] for Atlus. *Dragon Quest Builders* was his version of *Minecraft*, although this was not admitted, and it turned out to be completely adapted.

The adaptation of the *DraQue* world as cubes to be put together, broken and rebuilt was primarily a theoretical experience. The current trend was demaking, i.e. turning 3D volumes into 2D flats[51], but this proposed the opposite. The pixels of the first episode were put into three dimensions. It was an intermediary graphic representation in the video game's history. It was brilliant in every way: an incredible but modest achievement for Square Enix. The game did not call for creativity but acuity, a bit like following LEGO instructions rather than attempting to create something from our own imagination. *Dragon Quest Builders* is like a huge box of LEGO with the instructions that we always wanted for *Minecraft*.

The other stroke of genius was the narrative. The adventure begins the moment the first *Dragon Quest* hero gives up. In the original 1986 game, if Roto's descendant accepts Dragonlord's pact, becoming an ally of the evil king, the game comes to an end. And this is where *Builders* begins. Unlike its pastel-colored appearance, the world turns out to be dark, with no light, no hope. It is a parallel to the *Dragon Quest I* world, a scary, post-apocalypse world that must be rebuilt. Piece by piece.

With this simple product that bears every resemblance to a clone, the publisher developed a new channel and designed a unique franchise, like *Dragon Quest Monsters* had been. Square Enix thus offered a glimpse of the most interesting possibilities of its heritage. Yûji Horii, the faithful General Director, raises important

---

50. Known as *Etrian Odyssey* in the West.
51. See chapter 7.

CHAPTER VIII — DRAGON QUEST AND ITS SPIN-OFFS

questions concerning the heritage of his own creation in these latest non-canonic productions. A glimpse of post-Horii. What will remain of *Dragon Quest* when all is already *Dragon Quest*?

THE LEGEND OF DRAGON QUEST

Chapter IX — Music, harmony and dissonance

"If someone starts a speech with a concession, beware of what is to come. In cauda Venenum."

Umberto Eco,
Turning Back the Clock.

CHAPTER IX — MUSIC, HARMONY AND DISSONANCE

It starts like every, or nearly every, other *DraQue*. The music, remember? Hunting horns, like an orchestra getting ready to play the main theme of its piece. The official fanfare of the series rings out when you press "Start". However, what comes next is not quite the same as the canonic *Dragon Quest* episodes. This is no traditional RPG, but a musical RPG. Four heroes marching through a plain, then entering a dungeon to ultimately confront a boss at the end of the excursion. Something in the formula has changed. This game is *Theatrhythm Dragon Quest*. Instead of pressing a button to validate fight commands in windows of variable austerity, you sound out the rhythm. Actually, to be precise, you have to press the button at the exact moment when a note comes into a little circle on the screen, certain proof that you are in time with the beat. *Theatrhythm Dragon Quest* is one of the few games based on almost all of the "official" composer's works for a series.

Japan has a long tradition of these so-called rhythm games, which come in a multitude of different forms. A realistic piano keyboard, fake record turntable DJ-style, plastic drum kit, guitar or even a traditional Japanese drum, anything can be used to keep in time (with varying degrees of success) with the rhythm imposed by the music notes that appear on the screen. In *Theatrhythm Dragon Quest*, the 3DS pen offers a mix between a bass drum pedal and the baton of an orchestra conductor. If you stop your rhythm, the music stops instantly.

Towards the end of the 1990s, the popularity of this type of game was mainly upheld by Konami with its range of *Bemani*, named after its emblematic game, *Beatmania*, and whose other well-known successes include *Pop'n Music* and *Dance Dance Revolution*[1]. A more recent trend consists in taking a character or a world from a popular video game to be able to use already familiar soundtracks to attract an initial public of fans[2]. One such example is the *Persona* series, with *Dancing All Night*. Proposing a musical game based on *DraQue* was therefore not as outlandish as it may first appear.

---

1. Other examples include *Para Para Paradise*, *GuitarFreaks* and *DrumMania*, a drum game, all designed to be played with a plastic accessory. *Guitar Hero* simply copied Konami's method to conquer the Western market, which had previously remained immune to the *Bemani* craze.
2. Japanese developers also proposed new licenses based on their musical concepts. *PaRappa The Rapper* by Masaya Matsuura for Sony, and Tetsuya Mizuguchi's *Space Channel 5* for SEGA are two notable examples from the PlayStation and Dreamcast generations, a flourishing era for the Japanese industry.

THE LEGEND OF DRAGON QUEST

A CAREER-SPANNING GAME

Theatrhythm Dragon Quest was one of the few *Dragon Quest* projects for which Akira Toriyama had absolutely nothing to do. The star here was not even Yûji Horii, but the third member of the saga's trinity, Kôichi Sugiyama. He is one of the few composers to have his own game, which includes almost all the elements of his major work. His greatest hits, his most emblematic tunes... they are all part of it.

Theatrhythm Dragon Quest was not, strictly speaking, an original project. The foundations already existed in the form of a musical game released for the twenty-fifth anniversary of *Final Fantasy*. The name is rather bizarre, but that is hardly surprising: *Final Fantasy*'s Tetsuya Nomura, artist and mentor, and something of a guru too[3], brought this original concept to life, choosing an unpronounceable name, as he was wont to do. It didn't stop his products from selling. Two episodes of *Theatrhythm* came out based on Square Enix's other major world, achieving a certain success. For the publishers, aside from the packaging costs, this type of product was relatively inexpensive to produce, because all the music already existed and the copyrights had been negotiated some time previously. Furthermore, the publisher was smart: it was a way of maximizing profits by turning well-known tunes that fans wanted to hear into new downloadable, payable content. The *Dragon Quest* version did not even stoop to the lowly ranks of the DLC strategy, since all additional content was free. Such good intentions are an indicator of the series' popularity.

As a fan of the genre, I played the tuneful challenges of *Theatrhythm Final Fantasy* enthusiastically time and time again. The system was fun and easy enough, the characters were modeled like puppets and, in the *Dragon Quest* version, they were as cute to watch as their *FF* counterparts, which made the whole experience all the more pleasant.

No rhythm games are particularly difficult, which suits me perfectly, since personally, if I find that such games are beyond my ability after a few attempts, I inevitably feel that I am wasting my time. I get the impression that I would be better off spending my time learning an actual musical instrument, rather than bashing out complicated tunes with a tiny stylus on a games console.

For the first time though, under similar conditions and on the same system, *Dragon Quest* was beaten by *Final Fantasy*. There are various explanations for this, the main factors being the players' lassitude and, most of all, the lack of surprise.

Less marketing, an outdated medium[4], or simply the fact that people were becoming less interested in rhythm games are other possible reasons. Perhaps the truth is a combination of all these. However, I believe there is a fundamental musical reason.

---

3. At least for the period between *Final Fantasy VII* and *XV* when Tetsuya Nomura became the company's strongman, an artist who was able to build very diverse projects on the sole basis of his name. In other words, he was bankable, to use the movie industry term.
4. So many people had 3DSs back then, but their popularity was extremely seasonal, depending on the releases of major successful licenses, such as *Dragon Quest*, *Monster Hunter* and *Pokémon*.

CHAPTER IX — MUSIC, HARMONY AND DISSONANCE

"But aren't all the pieces a bit the same?" was my first comment upon hearing the announcement of this *Dragon Quest* release. What hope for musical diversity in a game that is so completely submerged in Sugiyama's work?

"SIMILAR" TUNES

The difference between the musical worlds of *Final Fantasy* and *Dragon Quest* lies in the propensity for variety. With *FF*, we are delighted to rediscover the fire of each episode, with its distinctive personality and exciting moments. Uematsu changed styles several times with the different iterations, sometimes even being assisted by other composers, or leaning more towards rock or electro. Each tune thus defines and represents the adventure for which it was created and the whole experience of the episode. *DraQue* music is based more on the overall atmosphere than on the specific evocation of an episode. The best test, in my opinion, is to switch the music. Imagine the opening theme of *DQX*, the battle melodies of *III*, the dungeon tunes of *V* and the caravan jingle in *IV* in a single game. Well that is exactly what Square Enix was doing with its "minor" projects. *Hoshi no Dragon Quest*[5], released on iOS, used a potpourri of music from the canonic episodes. To be precise, those pieces that I just mentioned. As if Sugiyama intended them to be interchangeable.

Legend has it that the emblematic opening theme was composed in just five minutes. Kôichi confirms the legend, but likes to add that it actually took him fifty-four years and five minutes! Fifty-four years for his age when he composed his best-known, world-famous melody.

Fifty-four years' experience that enabled him to come up with this emblematic piece. Fifty-four years, and an entire career behind him. I have cited a number of his compositions from the animation world, but I think I must mention *Densetsu Kyojin Ideon* once again. This *mechas* series, unlike any other, imagined by Yoshiyuki Tomino, caused a great stir among the generation of Japanese viewers who discovered it on TV. As I mentioned before, the creator of *Mobile Suit Gundam* exercised no restraint in eliminating characters to whom viewers had become attached in his famous series. A true massacre, concealed by the lively, colorful drawings of the early 80s. To accompany the annihilation, Kôichi Sugiyama composed joyful melodies, somewhere between the orchestral, disco and pop sounds of the era. A total contrast with the cosmic catastrophe that he was illustrating musically. Apart from *Dragon Quest*, this is my favorite of Sugiyama's works. But the composer's mark goes further still.

Between the end of the 1950s and the 1980s, he composed more than two thousand tunes for TV and radio adverts. Another detail helped the artist to establish himself: in Japan, at the start of each advert, the author of each piece is generally cited at the bottom of the screen. This was another reason for Sugiyama's decision to write his

---

5. A smartphone project, which was certainly not minor in terms of income—see the chapter on *Dragon Quest* spin-offs.

THE LEGEND OF DRAGON QUEST

name in hiraganas rather than the kanjis chosen for him by his parents[6]. He is more than a recognized talent, being known throughout his country, like John Williams is elsewhere in the world, but his international fame is limited to the success of *Dragon Quest*.

AN OLD MAN AND HIS MUSIC

Kôichi Sugiyama, born on April 11, 1931, is officially the oldest video game composer. He had already been there and done that when he began his work on *Dragon Quest*. At the age of three, he was playing his first scales and at fifteen, produced his first composition. Four years later, he wrote his first ballet for children. He is prolific, and a look at his resume today suggests the kind of urgent need to create in any form whatsoever that is specific to those who survived the war. The young Kôichi, and this is important to fully understand the man, obviously experienced the war and years of hardship while he was at elementary school in Nagoya, where he lived throughout the Second World War. This may not be obvious in his work but you can sense it in the man, who is extremely talkative and quick to move from one combat to the next.

"There is no experience to be gained from running away, either in life or in games," as he likes to say[7].

I have already mentioned that he is a composer of "firsts." He wrote not only the first orchestral recording but also the first ballet based on a video game. Let's not forget that this pioneer literally pushed video game music to become a culture of its own, which also helped it to become legitimate as such. The first symphonic concerts that he organized were not just about his own recognition; he has always promoted his colleagues, such as Kôji Kondô and Nobuo Uematsu, acting as a true patriarch of the genre that he helped to develop. Thus, when he directs the Orchestral Game Concert, his own creation, most of the concert is devoted to his colleagues' compositions, before the show closes with a theme from *Final Fantasy* or *Chrono Trigger*[8].

A MULTITUDE OF INFLUENCES

He often cites Beethoven, Bach and Debussy when asked about his idols and influences. However, and I may not be alone in this, I have mainly found similarities with Serguëï Prokofiev's airs, and particularly *Peter and the Wolf*. In fact, his influences are multiple, because as well as those cited above, we should also mention Handel, probably a little Mahler and the late baroque years of King Louis XIV of France. Here, I

---

6. Kôichi Sugiyama explains that he writes his name in hiraganas because the characters chosen by his parents are too complicated.
7. Interview in *Yomiuri Online*, 2015.
8. Five series of concerts with different orchestras, a rare opportunity to hear live versions of the music from *Sim City*, *Secret of Mana* or *Kirby*, arranged by Kôichi Sugiyama himself.

CHAPTER IX — MUSIC, HARMONY AND DISSONANCE

am thinking in particular of a French composer of Italian origin, Jean-Baptiste Lully, whose ballet music bears an obvious similarity to the castle theme of *Dragon Quest*. The resemblance is so evident that I can sometimes almost hear Lully beating time to one of his minuets[9] with a huge conductor's staff, as he once did[10]. If it is perhaps the most memorable image for me, it is also because the first thing you have to do in a *Dragon Quest* is to ask for an audience with the local king.

Each of Kôichi Sugiyama's compositions is evocative of something, be it a place or circumstance. For the first *Dragon Quest* in 1986, there were only eight different pieces of music, one for each place. It was the first time that an RPG adopted this kind of musical structure, which went on to become the norm. There are so few that you can recall them all from memory: the opening, Radatome castle, the plain, the city, the battles, the caves, King Dragon and the finale. The gentle chant that accompanies a stroll through the plain thus gives way to a faster beat for a battle. Then a confrontation with a boss later on stirs feelings of urgency[11]. This might seem obvious today, but back in 1986, it was all new.

In the early years, Kôichi Sugiyama's work was particularly limited by the technical constraints of the consoles. He remembered[12] what Kôichi Nakamura used to repeat: "We don't have room. And we don't have time." The young coding genius, to whom we owe the first five episodes of *Dragon Quest*, was well aware that music was still a poor relation in the world of video games during the cartridge years, when memory space was limited. Then, you had to fight to add another tune, to make room for another little sound, because the Famicom could only produce three sounds at a time. Sugiyama played his tunes and simplified them for Nakamura to accomplish his miracles. The goal was that each synthetic modulation more or less represented an instrument. Although it was obvious for the percussion instruments, a better ear was needed to identify the trumpets, piano and violin… The five sound channels were all devoted to this operation, with charming results. It was all down to electronic sounds, a little imagination and a Famicom pushed to its limits.

When the Super Famicom came out, it had five to eight sound channels and, unlike the previous model, they were all able to manage samples, which made synthetic instruments possible along with all the little miracles of this generation of games[13]. Assisted by its specific sound processor, Kôichi Nakamura and his team worked wonders with Sugiyama's compositions.

---

9. The ever-baroque Sugiyama composed his own minuets for *Dragon Quest*.
10. An activity that proved fatal to this superintendent of royal music, because he accidentally stabbed his toe with his heavy staff, causing gangrene which ultimately spread to his brain.
11. It is important to distinguish the music of the final boss from the themes of the intermediary bosses, which only appear with *Dragon Quest V*. The intermediary boss themes from the other episodes have been added with the various remakes.
12. In the book *Kôichi Sugiyama Works, Yûsha Sugiyan Lv 85* on his career.
13. In my view, the Super Famicom period was the climax of this era, between chiptune and true orchestration. From Yûzô Koshiro to Falcom's JDK Band, Nobuo Uematsu, Kaori Nakabai and Kôji Kondô, the composers then seemed to be more concerned with producing a good tune than sophisticated orchestration.

THE LEGEND OF DRAGON QUEST

In spite of the technical limits that have since disappeared, the composer managed to give *Dragon Quest* an atmosphere inspired by the classic European repertoire. I have already discussed the Overture and the baroque style of the castle music but time and technique enabled him to add more details and to broaden his influences. *DQV*, for example, has a short clarinet solo. The bar's official tune, introduced by *DraQue IX*, is a sort of polka, based on Sugiyama's concept of an old-school European pub where patrons come to get drunk in a friendly, jolly atmosphere. Since I became aware of this, the image comes back to me every time I go in to change my team.

With *DraQue III*, Sugiyama composed specific tunes with different influences to suit the different atmospheres. The melodies for temples and churches were inspired by requiems, and organs were added when this became possible[14]. Whenever an event had to be emphasized, such as a vehicle taking off[15], he returned to the French baroque style. Jipang, the famous fictional version of Japan[16], had an all-Asian interpretation. Jazz was used for the first time in this episode to evoke the USA with a strong boogie-woogie flavor; jazz also became the basis for the casino's emblematic theme. Oriental music made an entrance to illustrate the visit of the pyramids.

For this episode, so important to the fans, he composed a total of eighteen pieces. The Super Famicom remake was an opportunity to add a further six.

Finally, with *Dragon Quest IV*, he opted for specific character themes. One was particularly memorable, the theme for Torneko, once again. The kindly merchant's adventures were enhanced with clever use of the double bass. Starting from this simple theme, Kôichi Sugiyama composed the entire soundtrack for *Torneko no Daibôken*, the series' first spin-off game[17]. Fate can be ironic, as this dungeon-RPG was created and developed by Kôichi Nakamura[18], who initially doubted the composer's ability to adapt to the requirements of a video game.

"It is really difficult to innovate when writing music for battles since the concept is always the same," admits Sugiyama. For a single adventure, he wrote four or five before deciding which one to use. He then tried to find a melody that players would not become bored with after thousands of battles. The first notes of battle music are generally dramatic. I like to push my heroes to the very limits of their abilities and have experienced thousands of random fights, but even for me, the first few notes always seem to announce the worst: a fight I could lose. Kôichi Sugiyama's magical touch was to add a slightly threatening percussion theme. A

---

14. Which he also did with the pieces he orchestrated again for the Super Famicom version.
15. In *Dragon Quest*, vehicles are often totally imaginary. While *IV* proposes a very traditional airship, *DQV* opts for a flying bed, inspired by *Little Nemo*, written by Windsor McCay. *DQVII* returns to the totally ordinary flying carpet or simply a rather strange stone that floats in the air. *IX* and *X* both employ trains.
16. See chapter 3.
17. See chapter 8.
18. See previous chapters.

CHAPTER IX — MUSIC, HARMONY AND DISSONANCE

strike of a hi-hat, a snare drum and the player was ready to fight. Sugiyama knew just how to galvanize a gamer, because of course he was one. And a very good one at that.

Sugiyan[19] was a dedicated pioneer of video gaming from the early 1980s. More generally, he had gaming in his blood because from a very early age he played mah-jong, backgammon and mostly Monopoly, whose different versions he collected. He even has the very first edition ever marketed in the USA as well as all its Japanese versions. He also knows plenty about video games. As we have already discovered, he became known to Enix thanks to a survey card intended for players[20]. He loves war games and is the kind of player who raises all his *Dragon Quest* characters to their maximum level in every single version. His efficient tone changes probably come from his excellent knowledge of RPG, and the idea of a challenge that he knew he had to transpose.

THE BEST OF SUGIYAMA

It is interesting to see that, in its generally orchestrated version, his music has become rich and flourishing. He now plays around with instruments and synthetic possibilities to add more character to his music. There are harp and piano sounds and, of course, the inevitable brass instruments that appear to be a trademark of Western-style heroic fantasy, which remains largely based on European baroque.

If I had to pick just one record, it would probably be the *Dragon Quest X* music, his most accomplished and richest work. There is an art to composing music that you do not get fed up with after four hundred hours spent playing the game.

This soundtrack includes my favorite version of the fanfare and an inevitable battle theme. Midway between homage, perfection of his art and variety in situations, the forty-two pieces[21] of *DraQue X* sum up the scope of the artist's expertise, his relatively simple and sometimes bewitching harmonies, so brilliant that they were often reused in episode *XI*. *Ten* is also the only episode of the series for which use of an orchestra was a foregone conclusion for Sugiyama, from the very beginning.

"THE MORE THINGS CHANGE, THE MORE THEY STAY THE SAME"

This brings us back to the oft-raised issue of the "same thing" syndrome. There is a certain truth to such claims, because both visually and musically, *Dragon Quest* never moved away from the purely *shônen* style, recalling the spring day in 1986

---

19. His gamertag.
20. See chapter 2.
21. Not counting a few pieces from versions *2.0*, *3.0* and *4.0*.

when the series took the Famicom by storm. It was precisely that nostalgic feeling that Yûji Horii and Kôichi Sugiyama were after. When *Dragon Quest* returned to the West after a decade-long absence, a certain number of critics reported an "old-fashioned" soundtrack, to be polite. This caused a certain reaction, which became so important that *Dragon Quest VIII* was modified with an orchestral version of the OST for the *gaijin*. Synthetic arrangements were set aside for real instruments[22]. This major change caused uproar among fans: for the first time, the "superior" version was not the Japanese one. Music orchestration varied quite widely from one version to another. Unlike the Japanese versions which benefited from the symphonic recordings, the western 3DS versions of *Dragon Quest VII* and *VIII* were deprived of the sounds of the Tokyo Metropolitan Symphonic Orchestra. The MIDI soundtracks of the 3DS cartridges came directly from smartphone conversions, a solution chosen for cost reasons. For each orchestra session, there were several dozen musicians to be paid, not forgetting the production costs[23].

I would like to describe one last facet of Sugiyama's music: its repetitive nature, which has been the topic of some mockery. The ability to reuse their own music is traditional among movie and video game composers and it is easy to find common points between an artist's different works; this applies to Sugiyama as well as to other well-known composers, such as Joe Hisaishi. It is impossible not to recognize the battle theme from *Dragon Quest IV* in the soundtrack of *Jigoku no Mushi*, a Tatsuo Yamada film released in 1979. Similarly, *DraQue* can be identified in *Ideon*. Sugiyama's music is easily recognizable with its whims and mannerisms. The franchise's most recent productions readily glean nuggets from his repertoire, as if trying not to ask too much of an old man[24]. This raises the question of the master's successor, which will soon become a fundamental issue for future iterations: will Sugiyama's tunes survive in future games? It is also possible to consider all the elements of his work as a huge heroic fantasy database, from which Square Enix will be able to pick and choose.

The direct consequence of the imprint left by the last episodes, added to the memories of *Dragon Quest Heroes* and mobile games, is that we no longer know where the pieces came from. They are all familiar, undeniably "*DraQue*," but we have probably heard them to the point of saturation. Personally, I have always accepted these tunes, both familiar and novel, as an essential part of the *Dragon Quest* experience. For thousands of Japanese players, Sugiyama's melodies are like a comforter. This also means that the music fully corresponds to the emotion, a fundamental aspect of video games, and all the more so for an RPG.

---

22. A number of other modifications were also made to *Dragon Quest VIII* for its Western release. Real character descriptions, icons for objects and other such details make *DraQue* less frugal, but were not in the original version. Although the music was majestically orchestrated, the sound effects were modified to make them less kitsch, and some were even removed from the game.
23. It is interesting to note that Square Enix often repeated that *Dragon Quest VII* 3DS, which was never intended to leave Japan, actually owes its release to letters from French fans, which was the largest community of fans outside Japan, proportionally speaking. The enthusiasm must have been contagious because who could forget the ecstatic Yûji Horii announcing *Dragon Quest VIII* 3DS on the stage of the Japan Expo in 2016.
24. See chapter 6.

CHAPTER IX — MUSIC, HARMONY AND DISSONANCE

A REACTIONARY ARTIST

Since I presented a detailed portrait of Yûji Horii, I should also reveal the darker side of Sugiyama, worlds away from the image of the friendly, smiling grandpop portrayed by official photos. He is involved in a number of major topics and I can just imagine the trouble Square Enix has gone to try and control his various mediatized outings. Kôichi Sugiyama is obviously a nationalist. Surprisingly, he does not criticize America because it is Japan, above all, that drives him. In one of his recent declarations[25], he castigated his country which he believed to be in the grip of a civil war between pro- and anti-Japanese. He blamed the media, claiming they present a negative image of the national anthem and love of the flag, values associated with the nation's conservative right wing. He also stated that, again, in his opinion, the Internet and its spirit of freedom would fortunately enable the free expression of patriotic opinions. Here is a brief presentation of his ideology. At the dawn of his eighty-sixth year, ready to hand over to the "young" generation, the composer left the board of *Hôsôhôjunshu o motomeru shichôshanokai*, of which he is one of the founding members, on March 28, 2017. Often shortened to *Shichôsha no kai*, this is a surveillance group which aims to improve media programs and, more specifically, their ethical standpoint.

This was no trial run, for seven years earlier Sugiyama had already helped to create Media Patrol Japan, a group that has since been disbanded but whose objectives were exactly the same. *Shichôsha no kai* is a lobbying association born from a surge of nationalism that spread through the country at the time, largely due to the Japanese legal reforms concerning the Japan Self-Defense Forces. After the end of the Second World War, Japan was not permitted to participate in any military activity outside its own territory, but in 2015, which coincided with the creation of *Shichôsha no kai*, it became possible for Japanese forces to assist an allied country in difficulty, provided the goal was self-defense. This reform was broadly supported by the associations close to *Shichôsha no kai*, whose goal was actually to ensure "fair" treatment of certain social and moral values in the media[26]. In fact, it was an active form of lobbying which, under the guise of aiming to get the media to focus on these social values, was more like a nationalist propaganda tool. In particular, they used surveys, opinion polls and public complaints[27] against the media as action levers. Its creed was to scrutinize anti-patriotism.

It would be easy to catalog all these Japanese lobbyists of the extreme right as "dogged nationalists," but this neglects the complexity of the Japanese political system.

---

25. In a 2012 editorial published in the *Shûkan Post*.
26. As is the case in many other countries, defiance against the media in Japan is currently at a level never previously attained. This feeling is enhanced by social networks, completely liberated from any censorship and more or less anonymous, such as *Twitter*, for example, and has intensified notably since the Fukushima nuclear plant incident.
27. For example, they raised the alarm and passed on complaints about Kamé Sennin's inappropriate behavior (Master Roshi in English) towards young girls in the *Dragon Ball* anime.

My sociology professor, Kazuhiko Yatabe[28], taught me about Japanese reactionary ideology, one day revealing a whole range of extremely controversial Japanese literature and manga, starting with Yoshinori Kobayashi's saga, *Shin Gômanism Sengen Supesharu Sensô Ron*. It was obviously not the kind of book recommended by manga fans, who prefer to describe the diversity of the media with stories about swimming, cooking or even cycling, for example. Reactionary manga exists and, what's more, it enjoys great success. *Sensô Ron* is literally an instruction manual for accessible, patriotic, Japanese revisionism, written by a friend of Kôichi Sugiyama. It gives an idea of the efficiency of Japanese negationist rhetoric. Kobayashi delves into every intellectual divergence and every potential inaccuracy to support an ultra-nationalist theory and a geopolitical doctrine. Page after page, he denies the existence of comfort women and the Nanking massacre[29]. I would like to offer a brief reminder of these two crimes perpetrated by the Imperial Japanese Navy and Army. The first is a euphemism, also called *ian-fu*, for the massive sex slave organization set up in Asia by Japan, particularly during the Second World War. The number of victims identified depends on the countries concerned, but the Korean Central Agency has put forward the figure of two hundred thousand for Korean women alone, and the Chinese are even more alarmist, with estimates of at least four hundred thousand victims, counting all nationalities.

The Nanking massacre was an abject war crime. Hundreds of thousands of civilians and war prisoners were assassinated, tortured and raped by soldiers of the Imperial Japanese Army during a six week period in 1937. Again, there has much bitter debate about the actual number of victims. The verdict of the Nanking war crimes tribunal in 1947 gave the figure of three hundred thousand victims, recalling that the Imperial Army burned the corpses to destroy as much evidence as possible. I have included these historic facts in a book intended to celebrate a joyous video game because Kôichi Sugiyama is an ardent negationist and a notorious revisionist.

If he had been satisfied with just composing a few pieces of music to support his political friends to the right of the right wing, which he did occasionally, that might have been acceptable (even a good opportunity for a joke or two), and supporting such political activities financially is within his rights, but it is important to point out that negationism is an extremely insidious doctrine that is even punishable by imprisonment in certain countries, such as Germany. In this particular case, it made relations between China, South Korea and Japan very difficult for many years.

Revisionism aims to reduce the significance of a crime by diminishing its amplitude, casting doubt upon witnesses and generally denigrating the victims. Denying crimes or pain is a bit like a second death. It is an abject posture, always for ideological and political purposes, cloaking itself in the "truth," but ultimately serving nationalistic impulses.

---

28. Professor and senior lecturer of sociology at Paris Diderot. As well as the multiple books to which he contributed, he wrote the Japanese pages of the weekly *Courrier International* newspaper for many years.
29. Another of Kobayashi's causes is the school textbook reform. His goal was to return to other points, such as the Marco Polo bridge incident, which Japan used as a pretext for sending military forces into China in 1937, marking the start of the Second Sino-Japanese War.

CHAPTER IX — MUSIC, HARMONY AND DISSONANCE

The greatest feat of Kôichi Sugiyama and his partisans was the purchase of a full-page advert in The Washington Post in 2007. Entitled *The Facts*, this article, whose first signatory was Sugiyama[30], was the work of his Committee for Historical Facts. A full page to denounce the "slander" supposedly suffered by Japan and its soldiers[31]. A page denying the very existence of comfort women, one of Japan's many war crimes. Manipulating details, rounding down statistics, rejecting definitions, claiming that no women were ever victims of "sexual slavery" at that time. Ideas that Sugiyama hammers home during his "political" interviews. The purpose of this operation was to criticize US House of Representatives Resolution 121, ratified on July 30, 2007, calling upon the Japanese government to apologize to the comfort women and to include their story in the Japanese school curriculum. After the vote, Sugiyama rejoiced in the fact that only a handful of representatives were present for the vote. The composer, initiator of the project, concluded that their advert had been successful.

The power of these negationist groups serves as a fundamental reminder that if you are engaged in the judicial system, you must be absolutely irreproachable. Sugiyama and his allies make the most of the tiniest areas of gray left by time and historians. The slightest imprecision serves to hone their arguments. In fact, when it was revealed that Seiji Yoshida's text, on which Resolution 121 was largely based, was in fact fictitious, all those committed to getting Japan to acknowledge its responsibility were discredited. In *Sensô Ron*, Yoshinori Kobayashi used photographs employed by his opponents, montages that he denounced. He attained his objective: he discredited his opponents, putting all those fighting to remember Nanking in a difficult position.

A STREAMLINED OFFICIAL PORTRAIT

The portrait of Kôichi Sugiyama would not be complete without all these details. There is plenty of evidence of his fully assumed activism on the Internet, as he has given a number of interviews in which he develops his ideology. The official version, however, skips over this. There is not a single word on his public standpoints in the official book on his career, which was published for the thirtieth anniversary of *Dragon Quest*. His smiling face is surrounded by stars of music and video games, alongside a man disguised as a space lobster, one of the *Ultraman* baddies, or next to Shigeru Miyamoto and Kôji Kondo. His worst admissions are that he does no sport, and that he eats and smokes after each composition.

On the subject of Sugiyama's follies, I would really have preferred to mention his "smokers' group," intended to promote the cultural aspects of tobacco, yet another association he presides. It is almost laughable, this dedication to protecting the rights of nicotine consumers, but in his rejection of "anti-smoking hysteria," he does not

---

30. In truth, *The Washington Post* was probably the only newspaper that accepted to publish this page of propaganda, unlike *The New York Times* and others.
31. Widely broadcast thereafter via the Internet.

THE LEGEND OF DRAGON QUEST

merely denounce "anti-smoker fascism," like his comrades. His association also calls into question the official figures, casting doubt on public health measures and even the notion of passive smoking. When expressing his concerns about health obsessions, "imported from the US like a fashion trend," he says that the country "which first had Christ as its God, then had money, and now health care has come into fashion." It is hard not to see such words as the reactionary obsessions of an old man. Trying to appreciate an artist's work while ignoring his opinions and even his actions is not always easy. There is no method. So, from time to time, I listen to *Love Song Sagashite*, a piece composed between the first two episodes of *DraQue*. It was one of the marketing events of the series, a partnership between a record producer and a video game publisher, dating back to January 1987. At the time, Anna Makino was a fourteen year old idol from Okinawa. She went on to lead the Super Monkey's group, another member of which was the future star Namie Amuro. *Love Song Sagashite* was her first hit. A live version is available on *YouTube*, in a video where she is dancing to this gentle melody written by Kôichi Sugiyama. This song, now mostly forgotten in spite of its 33rd place in Oricon[32], became the anthem of *Dragon Quest II*. It is played from the start of the game, in an obviously synthesized version, if you enter the good old *Fukkatsu no Jûmon*, the legendary save password. It became the tune of purists, cited as a reference for connoisseurs in the menus of *Dragon Quest Battle Road Victory* and *DraQue & Final Fantasy in Itadaki Street Special*. The last time I heard it was for the installation menu of *DraQue X* on Wii. I love this song, which I have had playing every morning while writing this book.

Dragon Quest memories remain engraved in my mind, and this is partly thanks to its music. Music forever associated with hours of random battles crammed into a tiny window. With its churches ringing out organ melodies even though you have just woken up having lost half your money and found all your companions in coffins. That is what I choose to retain of Kôichi Sugiyama. Not the image of an openly reactionary, misguided composer, but an old man whose art addresses winks and nudges to his listeners, reminding them of their youth. After all, *Dragon Quest* is a mischievous and nostalgic heroic fantasy world.

---

32. Oricon is the organization that publishes the lists of best-selling records in Japan every day, week, month and year.

THE LEGEND OF DRAGON QUEST

Chapter X — Dragon Quest, heritage

"Old age cannot be cured, it must be prepared."

Pablo Picasso

CHAPTER X — DRAGON QUEST, HERITAGE

LET'S GO to the end, the very end. The end of *Dragon Quest XI*. You cannot measure heritage until the very end. Armed with my telephone, here I am, shooting the game's conclusion in burst mode. No, I'm not feeling nostalgic about a long adventure that is finally over. I'm doing it because I was told that something special would happen, at lightning, blink-and-you-miss-it speed. After slaying the final boss and watching the closing credits scroll up the screen, a rather unusual sequence appears: a nostalgic montage of all the *Dragon Quest* versions released to date. Screenshots from the games, tunes, a headline for each episode... Produced like a promotional trailer, the video is truly astonishing and you almost expect to see a release date and price displayed.

As part of a documentary, this discreet invitation to fans would not bother me. However, I actually find this look back from the final moment of the latest episode somewhat unpleasant. *Dragon Quest* has no need to emphasize its nostalgic fabric: the name itself is evocative of nostalgia, the whole series embodies nostalgia. Such an emblematic saga should not have to list the great times spent with its players over the past three decades. There is clearly a parallel to be drawn here with *Final Fantasy XV*, another emblematic RPG, released eight months before *DQXI*. After ten years in the making, Square Enix's somewhat sheepish announcement during the opening sequence of its long-awaited game: "A *Final Fantasy* for fans and first-timers." As if it was ever going to be anything else! There is a palpable form of concern among the developers responsible for these old licenses. Franchises obviously suffering in a constantly changing market. We are witnessing the end of an era, bathed in the famous feeling of *Seikimatsu*[1]. This closing sequence of *DQXI* is a perfect illustration.

Just a few days after *DraQue XI* came out, a rumor began to spread: the first episode of the saga would be given away "free" once you had completed the entire adventure. The inverted commas refer not only to this "rumor" but also to the penny-pinching reputation of the publisher. Square Enix has always been seen as miserly in all matters related to *Dragon Quest*. For example, the series was left out of the NES Classic Mini. At the end of 2016, Nintendo released a nugget of video game history: a miniature reproduction of the Nintendo Entertainment System, containing thirty legendary games from the past. Emblematic names such as *The Legend of Zelda* and *Final Fantasy* were in it and these games were available for both Western and Japanese versions of the machine. It was a huge success, selling more than two million copies[2]. But

---

1. A feeling of melancholy, already described in the introduction to this book.
2. 2.4 million machines sold between 2016 and 2017.

THE LEGEND OF DRAGON QUEST

there was not a single episode of *Dragon Quest* in this little capsule of memories. The same was true for the Super NES Mini. The reason was simple: from the publisher's viewpoint, why accept lower royalties by including its games in a compilation, when unit sales of *Dragon Quest* were still doing very well in multiple formats? The latest major compilation containing *DraQue I, II and III* for Wii, released for the saga's twenty-fifth anniversary, sold more than four hundred thousand copies[3]. However, most of the offer is now available on smartphone, for around eighteen dollars. This is an unusually high price bearing in mind that the predominant economic model for mobile phones is the Freemium model[4], but it does not appear to prevent relatively high sales. This explains why Square Enix refused to include *Dragon Quest* episodes in the NES and the Super NES Mini.

But let's get back to the closing sequence of *DQXI*. If I persisted, it was because I wanted the much-vaunted gift from Square Enix: the first *Dragon Quest*. To get it, you had to use the famous resurrection code[5] *Fukkatsu no Jumon*, used in *DQI* when the cartridges still had no save batteries. For all those who don't have a photographic memory, this password can be seen in a dialog box when the post-credit video in *DQXI* illustrates the saga's original episode. The window is only displayed for the player to make out the code for a very short time, which is why I was armed with my telephone to photograph the screen. There is no way of knowing who first found this out, but the news spread like wildfire across the Internet. The password alone was not enough though, you had to complete *DQXI* entirely[6] to enable *DQI* to be downloaded on PS4 or on 3DS. There was also a time limit on the offer, which was only valid for a year.

And that was not all, because seeing the enthusiasm generated, Square Enix was not only giving away the first episode of the series, but added the second and third chapters to its magnanimous offer. Although, you had to pay for the second and third chapters, because obviously generosity has its limits. This was announced at the *Dragon Quest* Natsu Matsuri[7] 2017. An ideal opportunity for the team to unveil the sales figures for *DQXI*. Surrounded by his producers, all dressed in kimonos, Yûji Horii was jubilant, because the last episode had exceeded all forecasts, selling more than three million copies of its two versions. He concluded the event with the triumphant declaration that the Nintendo 3DS would now be the only console for

---

3. Square Enix had not expected to sell as many and the beautiful anniversary box currently trades at twice its original price, which was only four thousand four hundred yen, i.e. forty dollars. For this price, you also got a one-hundred-and-thirty-page edition of the *Famicom Shinken* magazine.
4. To which *Dragon Quest* made a significant contribution, with several major products that were available at the same time: *Dragon Quest Monster Parade*, *Hoshi no Dragon Quest* and *DraQue Monsters Super Light*, before *DQ Rivals* was released. See chapter 8.
5. See chapter 3. The *Dragon Quest I* and *II* "save code" on Famicom.
6. Here, I am talking about the real end, once you have completed the two narrative arcs, the first of which ends with "To be continued." Only one download per player.
7. "The *Dragon Quest* summer festival," an event broadcast online, during which Horii and his team review *Dragon Quest* news.

CHAPTER X — DRAGON QUEST, HERITAGE

which all the canonic episodes of the series could be obtained, without exception[8]. At this precise moment, the union between Nintendo and *Dragon Quest* appeared to be indestructible.

As we have already observed, Square Enix can hardly be described as a generous publisher. So what was this offer all about? Why "give away" *Dragon Quest I*? In fact, there was a very good reason behind the gift. It was a message, a legacy you might say, an inheritance for players.

THE STRATEGY OF NOSTALGIA

Video games evolve constantly, but always in parallel with technology, the two being indissociable. As time passes, the classics of an era fade away, like old photos left out in the sun. However, the quality of *Dragon Quest* games is such that its aura remains fixed in the minds of players. This expertise and genius are widely recognized throughout the industry as well as among the public. The slightest mention of the name *DraQue* stirs up fond memories for the saga's loyal fans and every episode has its own particular fragrance and flavor for each generation of players. This is all the more so for the Japanese who were lucky enough to grow up with the series. For them, *Dragon Quest* is more than a profitable video game franchise, but little treasures, concentrated memories of past times. Square Enix was well aware of this and made the most of it, releasing remakes regularly over more than twenty years, from the time of the Super Famicom, to be precise. Producing large numbers of remakes and remastered versions of past successes was not commonplace during this period.

In order to exist, *Dragon Quest* had to be passed on from one generation of players to the next, ensuring that the license spanned across all ages, finding a new target audience each time[9]. In fact, promoting the heritage of *Dragon Quest* was a priority for Horii from a very early stage, an approach that ultimately became etched in the saga's DNA. For the creators of *DQ*, the players' attention must not be allowed to waver between the canonic episodes. So, to fill the gaps, up-to-date versions of past classics regularly invaded the shelves. Games that inevitably attracted nostalgic gamers, while introducing younger players to the earlier episodes of the saga. Players in their thirties delved back into their first *DraQue* adventures, while waiting for the next one to come out. The virtuous circle of constant nostalgia. The *Pokémon* series has also implemented this strategy with great success, applying it brilliantly and even more regularly than Square Enix did for *DQ*.

---

8. This minor miracle was possible thanks to the compatibility of the DS remakes of *DQIV*, *V* and *VI*. Along with *Dragon Quest IX*, released in 2009, the DS version of *Dragon Quest X*, the only MMORPG available on the portable console, and *DQXI*, of course, you could get the entire series at the same time on a single system. In a way, Nintendo's little portable system, which was already more than six years old when *DraQue XI* came out, became the ultimate *Dragon Quest* machine.
9. This was perfectly understood by the famous *Dragon Quest XI* advert, mentioned in the introduction.

THE LEGEND OF DRAGON QUEST

Memory is maintained by consistency and frequency. Not surprisingly, the first *Dragon Quest* is the episode available for the most platforms[10]. Since its beginnings on MSX, then Super Famicom, Wii and not forgetting Game Boy, the descendant of Roto has traveled through so many formats that it is difficult to identify its true origins. Its visual appearance changed slightly with the consoles. The *DQI* version that came with *DQXI* drew on a smartphone iteration released four years previously. This explains its rather unusual appearance: a 2D grain that we are not used to seeing on either 3DS or PS4, due to the much better resolution of today's miniature screens. The mobile version of *DQI* represents the final form of a thirty-year-old game. The adventure is essentially the same, but it has changed to adapt to the market and players' new habits. Now, no matter where you are, the *Dragon Quest* world, the same one as in 1986, is at your fingertips.

A closed loop. *Dragon Quest XI* could not have had a better ending. The last episode offers an interesting backward step, with an adventure in a past and present saga. Roto isn't mentioned, but you can tell that Horii and his team thought about including him. Should they refer to the first trilogy, the one that made *DraQue* the cultural institution that it is today? Apparently not, but as we have already seen in this book, the question of nostalgia is treated differently in *DQXI*. The look in the rear-view mirror, nostalgia, is a central issue in the saga's evolution. From its early editions, whose distribution was limited but achieved great success, to its current status as a legend, *Dragon Quest* is a franchise that has always remained the same. As its popularity grew, an amusing anecdote illustrates this dichotomy. On April 1, 2012, without warning, *Google* announced *Google Maps 8-bit*, a Famicom cartridge that enabled users to connect to the Internet. In a hilarious video[11], the technology giant presented its innovation. The video shows three members of a Japanese family, sitting on the living room tatami. The father inserts the *Google Maps 8-bit* cartridge into the Famicom and a pixelated version of a world map appears on the TV screen. We could almost be there. Certain details are just so accurate, like the sound effects or the need to blow into the cartridge to get it to work—something that all Megadrive, NES and SNES players have all done at least once. The music of the menu is the *Dragon Quest* theme and the family moves around the world using the Zoom teleportation spell. It was an April fool's prank, but a delightfully successful one. And, as the fake *Google* ad explains, you can go monster hunting on this retro map. Certain landmarks are thus inhabited by monsters well known to players; you might find a Golem guarding the Square Enix offices in Shinjuku. The company took the prank even further, putting a *Quest* button on its *Google Maps* website, transforming the real world into an 8-bit version pixelated map.

---

10. MSX, NES, SNES, Game Boy Color, Game Boy Advance, Nintendo DS, Nintendo 3DS, Wii, Wii U, mobile phones, PlayStation, PlayStation 2, PlayStation 3 and PlayStation 4.
11. https://www.youtube.com/watch?v=rznYifPHxDg&feature=youtu.be

CHAPTER X — DRAGON QUEST, HERITAGE

A PATRIMONIAL MASTERPIECE

The scene takes place in a narrow, typically Japanese house in 1986. Reiji Watanabe, a young student, is trying to study, without much success. His father calls him. He wants to ask him a few questions about the *Dragon Quest* game that has just come out. Reiji, although angry about being interrupted, goes downstairs to his father. The exams are looming, and it is not easy for him to concentrate, living above the family's amusement arcade. "Look, Reiji, a Metal Slime!" cries the father. "Ah! Oh! It's gone." The young man has had enough, and walks out, slamming the door behind him. Suddenly, one of the arcade clients approaches, without introducing himself. It is Yûji Horii, who explains to the father: "Metal Slime is actually a very shy monster. That's why it leaves as soon as it appears." Horii then runs off, making the same characteristic noise as the monster, a sound that an entire country associates with running away.

This scene comes from an episode of the *No Con Kid*[12] series. The situation may seem trivial but it is a perfect illustration of the creator's popularity: Yûji Horii had become a highly respected figure of Japanese heritage. His smile and good humor pop up quite naturally in documentaries, master classes and a variety of family TV shows. The influence of his work was felt throughout the nation and his aura had spread well beyond the world of video games: *Dragon Quest* was a national phenomenon. As well as all the merchandising, references to the work abounded: on TV, in mangas and in popular language. *Dragon Quest* was everywhere.

The influence of *Dragon Quest* proved so important that an entire series was directly based on Horii's work. *Yûsha Yoshihiko to Maô no shiro*[13] contains very faithful copies of the major components of *DraQue V*, including the monsters and certain elements of language and clichés specific to video games. Even the cape and hood of the sitcom's hero are identical to those of the main character in *DQV*. This hero, called Yoshihiko, sets out to find a miraculous herb with the power to save his village, condemned by a strange illness. The adventure inevitably takes him to the confines of a castle inhabited by an evil king. Yoshihiko is not alone in his quest to save widows and orphans, like in *Dragon Quest*, but assisted by a troop of adventurers. However, the brigade is less effective and charismatic than in the game. To help the brave Yoshihiko, there is a slightly ridiculous and pathetic Buddha, a girl who wants to kill the hero over a misunderstanding, a shabby magician and a wily knight. It is a heroic fantasy sitcom that imitates RPGs: one hilarious scene shows the team, parading one after another, exploring a house, breaking all the pots they come across and opening all the cupboards. When they talk to the woman in the kitchen, she repeats the same

---

12. *No Con Kid* for *No Continue Kid: Bokura no Game Shi*, was a live series by TV Tokyo, which broadcast twelve episodes in 2013. Created and written by Dai Satô, screenwriter of dialogs for anime series such as *Ghost in the Shell: Stand Alone Complex* and *Cowboy Bebop*, it attempted an extremely meta approach to the nostalgia of Japanese video games in the 1980s and 90s. Other famous game designers also made cameo appearances, including Katsuhiro Harada, producer of *Tekken*, and Masanobu Endô, creator of *Xevious*.
13. Literally, "The Hero Yoshihiko and the Demon King's Castle."

THE LEGEND OF DRAGON QUEST

words over and over, like any self-respecting minor NPC. The mimicry even includes the sound effects, which really do sound as if they came from *Dragon Quest*. Series 2 and 3 of *Yûsha Yoshihiko to Maô no shiro* also deserve a mention: like the games, they present a new generation of heroes—their descendants—who must now battle evil.

Yûsha Yoshihiko to Maô no shiro had little in terms of production resources, the monsters were made of pasteboard, the special effects unimpressive and the acting unconvincing. The series is a parody, recycling the codes known to an entire generation in a style of its own. The program was broadcast on TV Tokyo, and in spite of the presence of a talking Slime, remained a pure parody. There was no official content in it and Square Enix received no royalties of any kind. If I had to place it on the humor scale, it would be somewhere alongside *Monty Python*, with characters that totally believe in what they are doing but with a taste for ridiculous pranks in the tradition of Japanese *manzai*[14].

Two other series were released with different themes[15], but always with the spirit of *Dragon Quest V*[16].

A PUBLISHING PHENOMENON

Another way to observe the social phenomenon of *Dragon Quest* is to go to a bookshop, not to the books about video games[17], but the section on personal development. Next to the guides on how to become a good leader thanks to *Gundam*, are books based on Horii's work. One of them explains how to manage a business in reference to *DraQue*. Another invites readers, in English, to "reprogram their lives" with *Dragon Quest*[18]. Written by a former Enix employee, which is how the author introduces himself, the work aims to restore readers' motivation through the prism of RPGs, and *DQ* in particular.

However, the most obvious imprint of *Dragon Quest* in paper format remains manga. A manga in a Japanese book store caught my eye one day. As a fan of J-RPG, there is nothing surprising about that, given the clever play on words in its title: *Final ReQuest*.

---

14. The traditional stage form of the Japanese comedy duo style for which Takeshi Kitano is known.
15. *Yûsha Yoshihiko to Akuryô no kagi*: *The Hero Yoshihiko and the Key of the Evil Spirit*, and *Yûsha Yoshihiko to Michibikareshi Shichinin*: *The Hero Yoshihiko and the Seven Chosen Ones*.
16. More surprisingly, Square Enix then launched into Japanese drama, with *Final Fantasy XIV: Dad of light*, except that in this case, it was a mise en abîme in which a father and son bond through the game that brings them back together: *FFXIV*. This was an adaptation of an amateur novel published on a blog and adapted quite officially by Square Enix, even including game sequences.
17. The golden age of *Dragon Quest* guide books lasted until the advent of the Internet, when entire solution websites and "wiki" pages proliferated. At the time, Enix was selling them in pairs for a single series, one on the story and the other on the fights and monsters. Nowadays, to boost book sales that are flailing under the effects of online competition, Square Enix tries to include free gifts and goodies with the games. Smartphone games and *Dragon Quest X* are particularly good platforms for these marketing actions.
18. "Reprogram your life to the *Dragon-Quest*."

CHAPTER X — DRAGON QUEST, HERITAGE

The rather unusual cover portrayed harsh colors and pixelated characters. On the *obi*, the advertising band wrapped around books to make them stand out on the shelves, a sentence signed by Yûji Horii: "Game designer of the *Dragon Quest* series." In a tagline standing out in a box that looks like a *DraQue* dialog window, Horii explains his preferred choice in his characteristic style: "This is it, I've found it. This manga is nostalgic but new at the same time."

The graphic novel by Ichirô Kusaka is an exact copy of the visual identity of an RPG. The first few pages are illustrated like the old instruction manuals hidden in Famicom game boxes. The artistic style then quickly changes to pixel art, with squared, voluntarily simplified drawings and dialogs encased in windows. Unlike most mangas, this is a color production and it is both innovative and magnificent. It is easy to understand why Yûji Horii likes it so much with its efforts to tell a story using only limited resources.

There have been many *Dragon Quest* mangas and Yûji Horii actually participated in the production of several of them. Although often cited as "supervisor," his actual role remains vague. Did he help to write the stories? Did he just validate the ideas proposed? Was it more a question of him making suggestions on how to proceed? No-one really knows. The manga adaptations of *Dragon Quest VI* and *VII* simply copy the game process, thus presenting him as the original author. However, this format has its limits. After fourteen volumes, publication of the *Dragon Quest VII* graphic novel was suspended for years. You wonder how its publisher, Gangan Comics, found the strength to adapt such a long adventure[19]. The answer is simple: it didn't.

Of all the works in which Yûji Horii was involved, *Dai no Daibôken*[20] was probably the most important. Published by Shûeisha following the agreement enabling Akira Toriyama's participation, its authors Riku Sanjô and Kôji Inada showed great ingenuity in including as many elements as possible of the world created by Horii. There are references to the first episodes of the saga and to its immense bestiary and spells. The manga was so popular[21] that Horii even asked to use a few ideas in his next games[22]. The irony of a manga adapting the concepts and routines of an RPG is that the thirty-seven volumes of adventure published over seven years[23] only represent around ten weeks in the game history, barely eighty-five days during which the heroes grow and become legends. At the time of its publication, I was reading this *shônen* with at least as much enthusiasm as for *Dragon Ball*. What is truly good in *Dai no Daibôken*, is how the adventure is presented through the prism of RPG. The heroes

---

19. *Dragon Quest VII* has always been known as the longest episode, representing at least a hundred hours' play.
20. See note 7 in the first chapter.
21. There were three medium-length films of *Dai no Daibôken*, incorrectly described as OAVs, released during Toei Anime Fairs. These are typically Japanese events in which three films for children are proposed in a single showing, generally during the school holidays. The famous *Dragon Ball Z* OAVs come out for such events.
22. Here, I am referring to spells such as GigaSlash, borrowed from the manga for use in the video games.
23. Published in Japan between 1989 and 1996.

THE LEGEND OF DRAGON QUEST

gain levels, change equipment, learn spells and confront increasingly powerful bosses. Actually, good RPG is perhaps, deep down, a good *shônen*[24].

The first *Dragon Quest* trilogy has also been adapted as a manga, by Fujiwara Kamui. It is a strange mixture of the artistic pretensions of independent writers and the *shônen*[25] writing tradition. The twenty-one tomes of *Emblem of Roto*[26] come between the scenarios of *DraQue I* and *III*. It was the first time that an author other than Horii touched the heritage of the saga's creator with the master's consent. *Dragon Quest* has become a component of modern Japanese culture and will always exist in one form or another. Its creators have had a truly unique influence on artists, gaming fans and of course the general public.

---

24. Which is also why *Final Fantasy IV* is my favorite episode. It is the most *shônen* of all the *FF*s. The heroes sacrifice themselves, the baddies eventually turn good, and happy feelings abound.
25. The choice of Kamui Fujiwara may come as a surprise. In fact, he was selected in 1991 by Enix and Gangan Comics, which belonged to Square Enix, because his style was different from that of Akira Toriyama.
26. By the same author as the manga *Dragon Quest VII*, *Roto no Monshô* also enjoyed a level of media attention usually reserved for an RPG episode. A medium-length animated film adaptation released in Japanese cinemas in 1996 during the GW Anime Festival.

THE LEGEND OF DRAGON QUEST

Conclusion

"There are two ways through life. The way of Nature and the way of Grace. You have to choose which one you'll follow."

Mme O'Brien, *The Tree of Life*.

CONCLUSION

From Every Angle

July 15, 2017: a few days before the release of *Dragon Quest XI*, Yûji Horii went back to the city of his birth, Sumoto, on Awaji Island. In spite of the numerous typhoons that year, the weather was fabulous. Next to the city's port, between the library and a small museum, there is a statue. Yûji Horii poses beside it before a crowd of photographers, for its inauguration. Gleaming bronze, it sparkles in the sun, like an ancient relic. A sword rises up from a granite stone, to the left, a shield bears the name and emblem of Roto and to the right of the weapon, there is a Slime, radiant as ever. Horii's smile is wide; his joy is palpable as he stands beside the memorial that he is still alive to see. And he should indeed be proud: it is the first monument in history to a video game creator. *Dragon Quest* is at its peak: recognized, immortalized in a statue, idolized by fans. *Dragon Quest* is going down in history. *Dragon Quest* is now thirty years old.

The memorial in Sumoto is as symbolic as the objects represented: the sword to ward off evil, the shield protecting against catastrophes and blows of fate, and the Slime[1] embodying luck and mischief. The name of the saga is spelled out in gold letters on the pedestal: *Dragon Quest*. Just below it, *Soshite densetsu he*, "The Seeds of Salvation," the subtitle of the third and most popular episode, the one that made the series a legend. The inscription is completed by "Life is a role-playing game." Yûji Horii, visibly amused, announces: "You can pray to whoever you want." The founder of *DraQue* is not just here to inaugurate the monument, he is also the host of a huge event. After Tokyo and Osaka, his childhood city is temporarily hosting the commemorative *Dragon Quest* anniversary exhibition. What's more, treasure hunt lovers can take part in a stamp rally around the city. The landmarks of Yûji Horii's life have become stages where kids can get a stamp on a map of the city. Of course, Square Enix is sponsoring the whole event and Sumoto has been sketched as a *DraQue* village.

Back to 2016. Yûji Horii is wearing a khaki shirt, as if about to go to war. He is posing in an armchair with a large folder in his hands. This scene is from a documentary broadcast for the thirtieth anniversary of his saga. After watching it several times, I noticed a detail that some may find trivial, but which is actually very representative. Yûji Horii is one of the few employees to wear a badge around his

---

1. As well as being the first video game monument, it is also interesting to note that the little bronze Slime is also the only monument paying tribute to Akira Toriyama.

neck. He is the creator of *Dragon Quest*, the actual founder of Japanese-style RPG, but when he enters the Square Enix premises, he does so as a stranger, showing his badge. You might have thought they rolled out a red carpet, but no. When it comes to working, no-one blinks an eye. As close to his teams as ever, Yûji Horii looks on, plays and, above all, verifies. It has become his leitmotiv since he began carving out the masterpiece of his life. He is an extraordinarily conscientious man. The documentary shows him checking *Dragon Quest XI*. Another day, he turns up at a meeting playing *Pokémon Go*. His colleagues wait for him to finish capturing his creature before getting down to work. Yûji Horii still wants to create and to surprise his fans. The portrait depicted in the documentary is a very faithful one: hard-working, committed, dreamy-eyed and oh so charismatic. My impression of him from our interviews is exactly that shown in this commemorative video: hidden behind his glasses, Yûji Horii never stops thinking about his work.

Hidden is a word that also sums up another of the three founders of the series: Akira Toriyama. "He is truly a good person" is how Akio Iyoku, editor in chief of *V Jump*, described the legendary artist when he first began. Thirty years later, the aura of mystery around him remains opaque. Again in *V Jump*, Iyoku offers a behind-the-scenes look at his work, which, in this case, consists in introducing Toriyama and the development team for *Dragon Quest XI*. An apparently simple request is on the agenda: for the next part of the story, the new *DQXI* hero has to wear a hood. Toriyama replies by email that he could of course make the modification, "but" he would then have to alter the position of the sword and therefore the belts. He also indicates that he is not overly keen and that he would prefer to leave him as he is. If you are accustomed to discussions with Japanese companies and organizations, you will recognize the language of a typical refusal in this country. No-one is going to get Toriyama to do anything that he doesn't want to do!

To understand Akira Toriyama's mindset in 2017, you only have to listen to his public declarations. Here is his last message, in full, from the documentary released by NHK for the saga's anniversary.

CONCLUSION

Hello, this is Akira Toriyama.

I'm terribly sorry that I can't appear in person, because public exposure is no good for me.

It was very easy to convince me to take on the job of character designer for *Dragon Quest*. "What the heck is a role-playing game?", I thought. That was the sort of time it was. Really, if I had known that it would still be going on after 30 years, I don't think I would have taken the job! Honestly, if I had known how long it would last, I would have politely declined. I'm not good at doing the same thing over and over again.

Designing characters for *DraQue* is fun but difficult work. Nowadays, there are a lot of people working on the series, and all of the ones responsible for designing characters are good and serious people, so I don't have to do as many designs. I'm personally not terribly interested in designing wholesome characters, so I don't have many variations to offer. Also, because the series is a fantasy, there is a certain established time period and setting that you can't remove for your design work. Every time we return to that period, it gets harder and harder, and it becomes a situation where we have to use every trick in the book. To have such a highly specific design setting limits your artistic options, and since I like to create fanciful designs every once in a while, I created tons of designs that were rejected, back in the old days, but I got to paint countless small-fry monsters which is what I love to do, and sometimes I get nostalgic for that. But don't worry. I've undertaken this work with the full principle of my being, and so this time with *Dragon Quest XI*, I'm also endeavoring to design with all of my might.

It will be a little while still before it's ready to be released into the world, but please look forward to it.[2]

Akira Toriyama

---

2. Message translated by Paul Chapman for *Crunchyroll*:
http://www.crunchyroll.com/anime-news/2016/12/30-1/akira-toriyama-dishes-on-designing-characters-for-dragon-quest

THE LEGEND OF DRAGON QUEST

It doesn't take a psychologist to realize that Toriyama has had enough of *Dragon Quest*. He is already one of, if not the richest artist in Japan[3]. He does not need more money and his boredom is related to the series itself. He is tired of drawing the same characters, the same monsters, the same worlds. Toriyama is quite simply exhausted. *Dragon Quest* has become the telephone that rings every two or three years reminding him that it is time to get back to work. But he no longer needs to.

More surprisingly, the past few years have been very rich for the mangaka. He who only drew small projects, limiting himself to one-shots, seems to have found his taste for work again. Or at least, he is gradually resuming control over his key work. In 2013, he was involved in the scenario of the *Dragon Ball Z: Kami to Kami*[4] film. Two years later, he was even more implicated in another feature film, *DBZ, Fukkatsu no 'F'*[5] resulting in the TV series: *Dragon Ball Super*. In spite of these projects, Toriyama has always shied away from the eye of media, and his rare appearances are enough to drive his fans wild.

Unlike Toriyama, Kôichi Sugiyama still seems just as happy adapting his jingles for the different episodes of the saga. For the thirtieth anniversary of *Dragon Quest*, he published a book of testimonials called: *Sugiyan level 85*[6]. In it, Sugiyama gives the impression of being more relaxed than Toriyama, brimming over with the joys of life, not caring that he is once again composing the same variations of work over and over. The anniversary documentary shows how solitary his work actually is. First, we see him composing, with a pencil, music score and his piano. Then, he meets the producer in his studio to make sure that the tone of his arrangements is right for the game scenes, working with actual images[7]. In fact, on that day, the result of the *DraQue XI* fair is perfect. The producer even allows a little joke: "We don't even have to send that one for Mr. Horii to listen to!" It just goes to show how comfortable he is with the composer's work and his faith in the result. And with good reason, because over the past thirty years, Sugiyama has composed more than four hundred pieces.

When you witness such determination in creating adventures, the obvious question arises: How long will they carry on? Until *Dragon Quest XII*?

If the golden age of *Dragon Quest* was the Nintendo period and the silver age the PlayStation era, then the bronze age, symbolizing communication and intercommunication, is the current period. Which means only one milestone, one perspective for the series remains: the modern era. When the era will move on without its original authors. What will happen when Yûji Horii decides to hang up his gloves, when

---

3. Depending on the year, his activities, the popularity of *Dragon Ball* and of course the other mangas in vogue, Toriyama is one of Japan's best-paid artists.
4. *Dragon Ball Z: Battle of Gods*.
5. *Dragon Ball Z: Resurrection 'F'*.
6. 85 for Kôichi Sugiyama's age.
7. Sugiyama is provided with a little information on the scenario and a single image for his composition work. He has to do the rest.

CONCLUSION

Sugiyama stops his symphonic concerts and Toriyama finally gets fed up with work in general? What will remain of *Dragon Quest* once its founders have gone?

The advantage *Dragon Quest* has over its competitors, such as *Final Fantasy*, is that Yûji Horii has absolute power over his work. There is no committee telling him what to do[8]. He has been the king of his castle for thirty years already. One day, the saga will have to do without this happy trio, these three artists with their unique destinies. The modern age of *DraQue* will begin when they jump ship. The series will continue for sure, not only because of the financial implications, although that will obviously be a major argument, but most importantly, for the cultural bond. One day, like each of us, *Dragon Quest* will have to learn to live without its parents.

Each chapter of the saga has become a classic in its own way. The initial foundations were revised year after year to make it attractive to new audiences. Like the major fictitious characters of the 20th century, such as Mickey Mouse, Batman and James Bond, the series will be continued for future generations. Stirring the imaginations of adventurers with little regard for fashion. That is probably the greatest power of this incredible nostalgia-creating machine, a bit like the productions of the Ghibli movie studio. The saga is so effective and so reassuring that it melts away our reason and blurs our lucidity. This feeling, somewhere between the memories of a time when we did not yet exist and the impression of a time when we will no longer exist, is fundamental in a country like Japan. On an island where everything is regularly destroyed and rebuilt again, *DraQue* has become a strong, simple link that communicates with everything else.

---

8. Unlike *Dragon Quest*, the *Final Fantasy* saga is overseen by the *Final Fantasy* committee. We know nothing about this highly secretive group, which is only mentioned once in *V Jump*, during a joint interview with the producers of the three leading Japanese RPG series: Hideo Baba (*Tales of*), Yôsuke Saitô (*Dragon Quest*) and Shinji Hashimoto (*Final Fantasy*). Hashimoto, being teased by Saitô, reveals the existence of a committee composed of illustrious team members of recent *Final Fantasy* releases, such as Naoki Yoshida, Hajime Tabata, Motomu Toriyama, and Yoshinori Kitase, to name but a few. The committee aims to preserve the quality of the *Final Fantasy* series.

BIBLIOGRAPHY

BOOKS

Dragon Quest I.II Official Guide Book, Enix, 1994.
ISBN 978-4870257412

Dragon Quest 25th Anniversary Book, Shûeisha, 2011.
ISBN 978-4087796056

Dragon Quest 25th Anniversary Bôken no Rekishishô, Square Enix, 2011.
ISBN 978-4757534070

Dragon Quest 25th Anniversary Monsters Daizukan, Square Enix, 2011.
ISBN 978-4757535831

Dragon Quest X: Online Daibôiken World Guide, Shûeisha, 2012.
ISBN 978-4087796377

Dragon Quest Museum, catalog, 2016.

Fujiwara Kamui, *Dragon Quest Saga: Emblem of Roto*, Volumes 1 to 21, Ki-oon, Japanese publishing division of GanGan Comics.

Horii Yûji, *Dragon Quest 30th Anniversary Dragon Quest Meigenshû "Shindeshimautoha nanigotoda!"*, Square, Enix, 2016.
ISBN 978-4-7575-5045-2

Ishinomori Shôtarô and Takizawa Hiroyuki, *Dragon Quest no michi*, Enix, 1990.
ISBN 978-4900527263

Junzo, *Jinsei DraQueka Manual*, Wani Books, 2015.
ISBN 978-4847093395

Jump Comics Perfect Book 1: Dragon Quest: Daï no Daibôken, Shûeisha, 1995.
ISBN 978-4088588810

Kohler Chris, *Power-Up: How Japanese Video Games gave the World an Extra Life*, Dover, 2004-2016.
ISBN 978-0486801490

Kusaka Ichirô, *Final ReQuest 1*, Kôdansha, 2015.
ISBN 978-4063765489

THE LEGEND OF DRAGON QUEST

Riku Sanjô and Kôji Inada, *Dragon Quest: The Great Adventure of Dai*, 37 volumes, Japanese editions by Shûeisha.

Sugiyama Kôichi, *Works Yûsha Sugiyan LV85*, Square Enix, 2016.
ISBN 978-4-7575-5046-9

Susumu Yamaguchi, *DraQue ga dekireba eigyô ga wakaru*, Doyoukan, 2012.
ISBN 978-4496049279

Szczepaniak John, *The Untold History of Japanese Game Developers Volume 1*, self-published, 2014.
ISBN 978-099296007

Szczepaniak John, *The Untold History of Japanese Game Developers Volume 2*, self-published, 2015.
ISBN 978-1518655319

Toriyama Akira, *Dragon Quest Illustrations*, Shûeisha, 2016.
ISBN 978-4-0879-2508-1

ONLINE ARTICLES AND WEBSITES

"Horii Yûji Interview", *Waseda Weekly*, Special Issue, 3/8/2016.
https://www.waseda.jp/inst/weekly/features/specialissue-draque1/
https://www.waseda.jp/inst/weekly/features/specialissue-draque2/

Barder Ollie, "Kazuhiko Torishima on shaping the success of Dragon Ball and the origins of Dragon Quest", *Forbes*, 2015.
https://www.forbes.com/sites/olliebarder/2016/10/15/kazuhiko-torishima-on-shaping-the-success-of-dragon-ball-and-the-origins-of-dragon-quest/#6a3c842125e5

DraQue no Horii Yûji san, Sumotoshi ni furusato nôzei, 2008.
http://web.archive.org/web/20081211072323/http://www.kobe-np.co.jp/news/shakai/0001510007.shtml

Andreyev Daniel, "Cahier *Dragon Quest* : pourquoi ça marche ?" [online], *Gamekult*, 2016.
https://www.gamekult.com/actualite/cahier-dragon-quest-pourquoi-ca-marche-163745.html

Andreyev Daniel, "Cahier *Dragon Quest* : Yûji Horii, la légende continue" [online], *Gamekult*, 2016.
https://www.gamekult.com/actualite/cahier-dragon-quest-yuji-horii-la-legende-continue-150301.html

BIBLIOGRAPHY

ANDREYEV Daniel, "Cahier *Dragon Quest* : Days of Future Past" [online], *Gamekult*, 2016.
https://www.gamekult.com/actualite/cahier-dragon-quest-days-of-future-past-164171.html

"Sakuma Akira x Masuda Shôji" [online], *Denfaminicogamer*, 2016.
http://news.denfaminicogamer.jp/projectbook/momotetsu/2
http://news.denfaminicogamer.jp/projectbook/momotetsu/3

ROSEN Daniel, "Thou hast Played a game! — a history of olde english in localizations" [online], *Built to Play*, 2014.
http://builttoplay.ca/features/2014/5/20/ye-olde-videoed-game-translations-a-history-of-olde-english-in-localizations

"Chunsoft Nakamura Kôichi Interview", *Itmedia*, 2006.
http://www.itmedia.co.jp/games/articles/0607/26/news062.html

"Horii Yûji x Kazuo Koike" [online], *4Gamer*, 2009.
http://www.4gamer.net/games/072/G007233/20091107003/

"*DraQue* no Horii Yûji, Kaihatsu Stop shita Maboroshi no Sakuhin gekihaku" [online], *Walker+*, 2016.
https://news.walkerplus.com/article/76628/

"Aratamete Horii Yûji toiu paradigm Shift ni tsuite" [online], *Automaton*, 2016.
http://jp.automaton.am/articles/columnjp/dragon-quest-30th-anniversary/

Blog by Akira Sakuma, December 2004.

"Sekai ga Alefgard ni natta "Google map 8 bit" kôkai", *Weekly ASCII*, 2012.
http://weekly.ascii.jp/elem/000/000/082/82360/

Shachô ga kiku, "*Dragon Quest IX* : Hoshizora no mamoribito", *Nintendo*, 2009.
https://www.nintendo.co.jp/ds/interview/ydqj/vol1/index.html

Video interview: "*DQIX*: Sentinels of the Starry Skies — Iwata asks : The History of *Dragon Quest*", *YouTube*, 2010.
https://youtu.be/WsqTZU2OX5U

Shachô ga kiku "*Dragon Quest Monsters* Terry no Wonderland 3D", *Nintendo*, 2012.
https://www.nintendo.co.jp/3ds/interview/creators/vol17/index.html

Shachô ga kiku "*Dragon Quest X*", *Nintendo*, 2012.
https://www.nintendo.co.jp/wii/interview/s4mj/vol1/index.html

Shachô ga kiku *Dragon Quest VII 3DS*, *Nintendo*, 2015.
https://www.nintendo.co.jp/3ds/interview/creators/vol24/index.html

Mitaku Ryô, *"DraQue Uminooya"*, *Sankei West*, 2015.
http://www.sankei.com/west/news/150408/wst1504080004-n1.html

"*Portopia Renzoku Satsujin Jiken* no butai o meguru" [online], *Gaimuman*, 2005.
http://www.itmedia.co.jp/games/articles/0509/06/news029.html

Dragon Quest X Mezameshi Bôkensha no Hiroba, official website.
http://hiroba.dqx.jp/sc/

Dragon Quest X Mezameshi Bôkensha no Hiroba, Kokuseichôsa, 2016.
http://hiroba.dqx.jp/sc/topics/detail/1ee3dfcd8a0645a25a35977997223d22/

Dragon Quest IX jôhô blog.
http://blog.square-enix.com/dqix/

Dragon Quest X, official Chinese website.
http://dq.sdo.com/web1/index.html

Sugiyama Kôichi Kyô no Nihon ha "Nihongun vs Hannichigun no naisenjôtai", *News Post Seven*, 2012.
http://www.news-postseven.com/archives/20120925_144970.html

AienkaTsûshin, tobacco lovers' association, official website
http://aienka.jp/

"*Dragon Quest X* 100 Manpon Toppatsu shitakotomo arakani", *Famitsû*, 2014
https://www.famitsu.com/news/201403/27050617.html

Garratt Patrick, "Mr *Dragon Quest* : The Cursed King", *Eurogamer*, 2006.
http://www.eurogamer.net/articles/i_dragonquestviii_ps2

"Square, Enix and Namco reveal first Tie-up details" [online], *IGN*, 2001.
http://www.ign.com/articles/2001/06/18/square-enix-and-namco-reveal-first-tie-up-details

"*Dragon Quest IX* no Yûmei Player, "Masayuki" Interview Kanzenban o otodoke!" [online], *Famitsû*, 2009.
https://www.famitsu.com/game/news/1229530_1124.html

BIBLIOGRAPHY

Tairiku CEDEC 2013, "Nihonjin no tame no MMORPG no kaihatsu" [online], *4Gamer*, 2013.
http://www.4gamer.net/games/139/G013996/20130822039/

Taitai, "MMORPG no omoshirosatte nanda ?" [online], *4Gamer*, 2014.
http://www.4gamer.net/games/139/G013991/20140307079/

Game Memo, "*Dragon Quest*, 30shûnen no kinenhi ga Awajishima ni tôjô" [online], *ga-m.com*, 2017.
http://ga-m.com/n/dragon-quest-30th-kinenhi-awajisima/

Tenchô no tsubuyaki nikki, "Dragon Quest Museum Selections Awajishima ittekita !" [online], 2017.
http://www.call-t.co.jp/blog/mt/archives/entry/017975.html

Videos

"*DraQue* o tsukuta Otoko Horii Yûji Special", *Game Center CX: S13* N°106, (7/10/2010, FujiTV)

Dragon Quest 30th Soshite AtatanaDensetsu he, NHK, 2016.

NoCon Kid - Bokura no GameShi N°4 (25/10/2013, TV Tokyo)

Yûsha Yoshihiko, TV, 45 episodes, DVD, Tôhô.
Series 1: "Maô no shiro", 2011.
Series 2: "Akuryô no kagi", 2012.
Series 3: "Michibikareshi 7nin" 2016.

"Yûji Horii V-Jump '97 Q&A Session" [video online], *YouTube*, 1997.
https://youtu.be/kYHoOgJ5S6U

"Yûji Horii Interview in e-Jump on PlayStation" [video online], *YouTube*, 2000.
https://youtu.be/ZvLp0uRpYwM

"Message from Dragon Quest creator, Yûji Horii" [video online], *YouTube*, 2014.
https://youtu.be/JyalwRFro2g

"Shigesato Itoi x Kôichi Sugiyama" [video online], *YouTube*, 1987
https://youtu.be/Pm1kQJR_zhE

"Interview with Yûji Horii" (Dragon Quest III era) [video online], *YouTube*, 1988.
https://youtu.be/dPFXeFgbSSs

THE LEGEND OF DRAGON QUEST

"*Dragon Quest VI* Kaihatsu Interview" [video online], *YouTube*, 1995?
https://youtu.be/p-CCpK5AlbE
https://youtu.be/pcvdNDgn4Xg

"FNN Date Line" [video online], *YouTube*, 1988.
https://youtu.be/ogGfhFbLXAY
https://youtu.be/UKy1V0OsojY

Dragon Quest III release [video online], *YouTube*, 1988.
https://youtu.be/AQI0IPb1HeY
https://youtu.be/J_6Im4WE39k

"Nakamura Kôichi Interview, *Pasocon Sunday*" [video online], *YouTube*, 1988.
https://youtu.be/3GQgHVYx7IM

"Game Wave 20seiki Game Gyôkaishi 80 Nendaihen" [video online], *YouTube*, 2002.
https://youtu.be/wmeMxnUOQZY

"Dragon Quest CM mix(1-8)" [video online], *YouTube*, 1986-2004.
https://youtu.be/g8jw_eXTvPU

"Google Maps 8-bit for NES" [video online], *YouTube*, 2012.
https://youtu.be/rznYifPHxDg

"*Tetsuko's Room*, Akira Toriyama interview" [video online], *YouTube*, 1983.
https://youtu.be/4JOnoZXtIN8

"Sugiyama Kôichi san no kimi ga yo" [video online], *YouTube*, 2011.
https://youtu.be/0DC0xcBCeuI

"Soft na Otokotachi no Hard na Game" [video online], *YouTube*, 1995.
https://youtu.be/6ZgWS1CKpOA

MAKINO Anna, "Love song sagashite" [video online], *YouTube*, 1987.
https://youtu.be/kZ2t-DXVv_w

"*Chrono Trigger* announcement ceremony" [video online], *YouTube*, 1994.
https://youtu.be/7IGPTckkPoM

"Hokkaidô Rensasatsujin Okhotsk ni Kiyu, the towel" [video online], *YouTube*
https://youtu.be/1YbebFj_ass

BIBLIOGRAPHY

"*Dragon Quest XI* Tokubetsu Web Eizô Ano Koro, Bokura ha Yûsha datta" [video online], *YouTube*, 2017.
https://youtu.be/fPR1oWqp4-Y

After Bit, #18, "*Dragon Quest*: L'odyssée du Roi Maudit - Les musiques de *Dragon Quest*" [video online], *YouTube*, 2014.
https://youtu.be/OxV4lRowvrw

"*Dragon Quest* Natsu Matsuri 2017 Stage Live" [video online], *YouTube*, 2017.
https://youtu.be/iH-vyWcjhs4

"*Dragon Quest X* TV CM Bôkenshatachi no kiseki Tokubetsuhen" [video online], *YouTube*, 2017.
https://youtu.be/RAAw3rsOxrQ

"*Dragon Quest X* Bôkenshatachi no kiseki Episode 1" [video online], *YouTube*, 2017.
https://youtu.be/igl-TKt9-q4

"*Dragon Quest X* Bôkenshatachi no kiseki Episode 2" [video online], *YouTube*, 2017.
https://youtu.be/uR_jCpmOfX0

MISCELLANEOUS ARTICLES

SUGIYAMA Kôichi, "Paid advertisement concerning Comfort Women run in the *Washington Post*" [online], 2007.

http://www.sdh-fact.com/essay-article/273/

https://fr.scribd.com/document/115984903/Paid-Advertisement-concerning-Comfort-Women-Run-in-the-Washington-Post-Facts-Are-Our-Only-Weapon#

Text available in original form online or reproduced here: http://sakuramochi-jp.blogspot.fr/2011/10/he-facts-purpose-of-this-paid-public_01.html
Warning from the author: text presenting revolutionist theories on the Nanking massacre and comfort women.

"Signatories to the June 14th *Washington Post* The Facts" advertisement [online], 2007.
http://www.jiaponline.org/documents/Jun14AdALLSignatoriesLIST.pdf

MAVRIK, "Tortue Géniale : son éthique remise en cause au Japon" [online], *Hitek*, 2017.
http://hitek.fr/actualite/dragon-ball-tortue-geniale-ethique_13252

THE LEGEND OF
DRAGON QUEST

Author's Acknowledgments

AUTHOR'S ACKNOWLEDGMENTS

— Amandine, for her patience and keen eyes.

— Puyo and Greg, my *Gaijin Dash* buddies.

— To Ahmed and Fabien.

— To the whale eater in Asakusabashi station (thanks for the *Taipien Kumamon* too).

— My *After Hate* and *Super Ciné Battle* podcast companions, Benjamin François and Stéphane Bouley. Ready for more adventures?

— My aunt, who has always protected me during difficult times.

— To Mehdi and Nicolas.

— Thanks to all those who enabled me to meet Yûji Horii on various occasions.

— Thanks to all the readers and listeners who have been following me for years, and who appreciate my work. It means so much to me.

— Thanks to my parents, forever with me.

— Thanks to Akira Toriyama, Kôichi Sugiyama and obviously Yûji Horii.

❀ ALSO AVAILABLE FROM THIRD ÉDITIONS:

- *Zelda. The History of a Legendary Saga – Volume 1*
- *Zelda. The History of a Legendary Saga – Volume 2: Breath of the Wild*
- *Metal Gear Solid. Hideo Kojima's Magnum Opus*
- *The Legend of Final Fantasy VI*
- *The Legend of Final Fantasy VII*
- *The Legend of Final Fantasy VIII*
- *Dark Souls. Beyond the Grave – Volume 1*
- *Dark Souls. Beyond the Grave – Volume 2*
- *The Works of Fumito Ueda. A Different Perspective on Video Games*
- *The Strange Works of Taro Yoko. From Drakengard to NieR: Automata*
- *Fallout. A Tale of Mutation*
- *BioShock. From Rapture to Columbia*